R for Data Science

Learn and explore the fundamentals of data science with R

Dan Toomey

PUBLISHING

BIRMINGHAM - MUMBAI

R for Data Science

First published: December 2014

Production reference: 1201214

Published by Packt Publishing Ltd.
Livery Place
35 Livery Street
Birmingham B3 2PB, UK.

ISBN 978-1-78439-086-0

www.packtpub.com

Credits

Author
Dan Toomey

Reviewers
Amar Gondaliya

Mohammad Rafi

Tengfei Yin

Commissioning Editor
Akram Hussain

Acquisition Editor
Subho Gupta

Content Development Editor
Sumeet Sawant

Technical Editors
Vijin Boricha

Madhuri Das

Parag Topre

Copy Editors
Roshni Banerjee

Sarang Chari

Project Coordinator
Aboli Ambardekar

Proofreaders
Jenny Blake

Ameesha Green

Sandra Hopper

Indexer
Mariammal Chettiyar

Production Coordinator
Arvindkumar Gupta

Cover Work
Arvindkumar Gupta

About the Author

Dan Toomey has been developing applications for over 20 years. He has worked in a variety of industries and companies in different roles, from a sole contributor to VP and CTO. For the last 10 years or so, he has been working with companies in the eastern Massachusetts area.

Dan has been contracting under Dan Toomey Software Corporation as a contractor developer in the area.

About the Reviewers

Amar Gondaliya is data scientist at a leading healthcare organization. He is a Big Data and data mining enthusiast and a Pingax (`www.pingax.com`) consultant. He is focused on building predictive models using data mining techniques. He loves to play with Big Data technologies and provide Big Data solutions.

He has been working in the field of data science for more than 2 years. He is a contributor at Pingax and has written multiple posts on machine learning and its implementation in R. He is continuously working on new machine learning techniques and Big Data analytics.

Mohammad Rafi is a software engineer who loves data analytics, programming, and tinkering with anything he can get his hands on. He has worked on technologies such as R, Python, Hadoop, and JavaScript. He is an engineer by day and a hardcore gamer by night. As of writing this book, he is fanatical about his Raspberry Pi.

He has more than 6 years of very diversified professional experience, which includes app development, data processing, search expert, and web data analytics. He started with a web marketing company named Position2. Since then, he has worked with companies such as Hindustan Times, Google, and InMobi.

Tengfei Yin earned his Bachelor of Science degree in Biological Science and Biotechnology from Nankai University in China and completed his PhD in Molecular, Cellular, and Developmental Biology (MCDB) with focus on Computational Biology and Bioinformatics from Iowa State University. His research interests include information visualization, high-throughput biological data analysis, data mining, machine learning, and applied statistical genetics. He has developed and maintained several software packages in R and Bioconductor.

www.PacktPub.com

Support files, eBooks, discount offers, and more

For support files and downloads related to your book, please visit www.PacktPub.com.

Did you know that Packt offers eBook versions of every book published, with PDF and ePub files available? You can upgrade to the eBook version at www.PacktPub.com and as a print book customer, you are entitled to a discount on the eBook copy. Get in touch with us at service@packtpub.com for more details.

At www.PacktPub.com, you can also read a collection of free technical articles, sign up for a range of free newsletters and receive exclusive discounts and offers on Packt books and eBooks.

https://www2.packtpub.com/books/subscription/packtlib

Do you need instant solutions to your IT questions? PacktLib is Packt's online digital book library. Here, you can search, access, and read Packt's entire library of books.

Why subscribe?

- Fully searchable across every book published by Packt
- Copy and paste, print, and bookmark content
- On demand and accessible via a web browser

Free access for Packt account holders

If you have an account with Packt at www.PacktPub.com, you can use this to access PacktLib today and view 9 entirely free books. Simply use your login credentials for immediate access.

Table of Contents

Preface

R is a software package that provides a language and an environment for data manipulation and statistics calculation. The resulting statistics can be displayed graphically as well.

R has the following features:

- A lean syntax to perform operations on your data
- A set of tools to load and store data in a variety of formats, both local and over the Internet
- Consistent syntax for operating on datasets in memory
- A built-in and an open source collection of tools for data analysis
- Methods to generate on-the-fly graphics and store graphical representations to disk

What this book covers

Chapter 1, *Data Mining Patterns*, covers data mining in R. In this instance, we will look for patterns in a dataset. This chapter will explore examples of using cluster analysis using several tools. It also covers anomaly detection, and the use of association rules.

Chapter 2, *Data Mining Sequences*, explores methods in R that allow you to discover sequences in your data. There are several R packages available that help you to determine sequences and portray them graphically for further analysis.

Chapter 3, *Text Mining*, describes several methods of mining text in R. We will look at tools that allow you to manipulate and analyze the text or words in a source. We will also look into XML processing capabilities.

Chapter 4, Data Analysis – Regression Analysis, explores different ways of using regression analysis on your data. This chapter has methods to run simple and multivariate regression, along with subsequent displays.

Chapter 5, Data Analysis – Correlation, explores several correlation packages. The chapter analyzes data using basic correlation and covariance as well as Pearson, polychor, tetrachoric, heterogeneous, and partial correlation.

Chapter 6, Data Analysis – Clustering, explores a variety of references for cluster analysis. The chapter covers k-means, PAM, and a number of other clustering techniques. All of these techniques are available to an R programmer.

Chapter 7, Data Visualization – R Graphics, discusses a variety of methods of visualizing your data. We will look at the gamut of data from typical class displays to interaction with third-party tools and the use of geographic maps.

Chapter 8, Data Visualization – Plotting, discusses different methods of plotting your data in R. The chapter has examples of simple plots with standardized displays as well as customized displays that can be applied to plotting data.

Chapter 9, Data Visualization – 3D, acts as a guide to creating 3D displays of your data directly from R. We will also look at using 3D displays for larger datasets.

Chapter 10, Machine Learning in Action, discusses how to use R for machine learning. The chapter covers separating datasets into training and test data, developing a model from your training data, and testing your model against test data.

Chapter 11, Predicting Events with Machine Learning, uses time series datasets. The chapter covers converting your data into an R time series and then separating out the seasonal, trend, and irregular components. The goal is to model or predict future events.

Chapter 12, Supervised and Unsupervised Learning, explains the use of supervised and unsupervised learning to build your model. It covers several methods in supervised and unsupervised learning.

What you need for this book

For this book, you need R installed on your machine (or the machine you will be running scripts against). R is available for a number of platforms. This book is not constrained to particular versions of R at this time.

You need an interactive tool to develop R programs in order to use this book to its potential. The predominant tool is R Studio, a fully interactive, self-contained program available on several platforms, which allows you to enter R scripts, display data, and display graphical results. There is always the R command-line tool available with all installations of R.

Who this book is for

This book is written for data analysts who have a firm grip over advanced data analysis techniques. Some basic knowledge of the R language and some data science topics is also required. This book assumes that you have access to an R environment and are comfortable with the statistics involved.

Conventions

In this book, you will find a number of text styles that distinguish between different kinds of information. Here are some examples of these styles and an explanation of their meaning.

Code words in text, database table names, folder names, filenames, file extensions, pathnames, dummy URLs, user input, and Twitter handles are shown as follows: "We can include other contexts through the use of the kmeans directive."

A block of code is set as follows:

```
kmeans(x,
centers,
iter.max = 10,
nstart = 1,
algorithm = c("Hartigan-Wong",
                    "Lloyd",
                    "Forgy",
                    "MacQueen"),
trace=FALSE)
```

Any command-line input or output is written as follows:

```
seqdist(seqdata, method, refseq=NULL, norm=FALSE,
  indel=1, sm=NA, with.missing=FALSE, full.matrix=TRUE)
```

New terms and **important words** are shown in bold. Words that you see on the screen, for example, in menus or dialog boxes, appear in the text like this: "You can see the key concepts: **inflation**, **economic**, **conditions**, **employment**, and the FOMC."

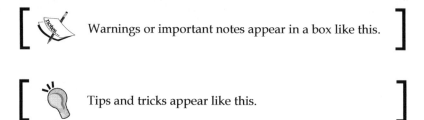

Warnings or important notes appear in a box like this.

Tips and tricks appear like this.

Reader feedback

Feedback from our readers is always welcome. Let us know what you think about this book—what you liked or disliked. Reader feedback is important for us as it helps us develop titles that you will really get the most out of.

To send us general feedback, simply e-mail feedback@packtpub.com, and mention the book's title in the subject of your message.

If there is a topic that you have expertise in and you are interested in either writing or contributing to a book, see our author guide at www.packtpub.com/authors.

Customer support

Now that you are the proud owner of a Packt book, we have a number of things to help you to get the most from your purchase.

Downloading the example code

You can download the example code files from your account at http://www.packtpub.com for all the Packt Publishing books you have purchased. If you purchased this book elsewhere, you can visit http://www.packtpub.com/support and register to have the files e-mailed directly to you.

Downloading the color images of this book

We also provide you with a PDF file that has color images of the screenshots/diagrams used in this book. The color images will help you better understand the changes in the output. You can download this file from: https://www.packtpub.com/sites/default/files/downloads/0860OS_ColoredImages.pdf.

Errata

Although we have taken every care to ensure the accuracy of our content, mistakes do happen. If you find a mistake in one of our books—maybe a mistake in the text or the code—we would be grateful if you could report this to us. By doing so, you can save other readers from frustration and help us improve subsequent versions of this book. If you find any errata, please report them by visiting http://www.packtpub.com/submit-errata, selecting your book, clicking on the **Errata Submission Form** link, and entering the details of your errata. Once your errata are verified, your submission will be accepted and the errata will be uploaded to our website or added to any list of existing errata under the Errata section of that title.

To view the previously submitted errata, go to https://www.packtpub.com/books/content/support and enter the name of the book in the search field. The required information will appear under the **Errata** section.

Piracy

Piracy of copyrighted material on the Internet is an ongoing problem across all media. At Packt, we take the protection of our copyright and licenses very seriously. If you come across any illegal copies of our works in any form on the Internet, please provide us with the location address or website name immediately so that we can pursue a remedy.

Please contact us at copyright@packtpub.com with a link to the suspected pirated material.

We appreciate your help in protecting our authors and our ability to bring you valuable content.

Questions

If you have a problem with any aspect of this book, you can contact us at questions@packtpub.com, and we will do our best to address the problem.

1
Data Mining Patterns

A common use of data mining is to detect patterns or rules in data.

The points of interest are the non-obvious patterns that can only be detected using a large dataset. The detection of simpler patterns, such as market basket analysis for purchasing associations or timings, has been possible for some time. Our interest in R programming is in detecting unexpected associations that can lead to new opportunities.

Some patterns are sequential in nature, for example, predicting faults in systems based on past results that are, again, only obvious using large datasets. These will be explored in the next chapter.

This chapter discusses the use of R to discover patterns in datasets' various methods:

- **Cluster analysis**: This is the process of examining your data and establishing groups of data points that are similar. Cluster analysis can be performed using several algorithms. The different algorithms focus on using different attributes of the data distribution, such as distance between points, density, or statistical ranges.

- **Anomaly detection**: This is the process of looking at data that appears to be similar but shows differences or anomalies for certain attributes. Anomaly detection is used frequently in the field of law enforcement, fraud detection, and insurance claims.

- **Association rules**: These are a set of decisions that can be made from your data. Here, we are looking for concrete steps so that if we find one data point, we can use a rule to determine whether another data point will likely exist. Rules are frequently used in market basket approaches. In data mining, we are looking for deeper, non-obvious rules that are present in the data.

Cluster analysis

Cluster analysis can be performed using a variety of algorithms; some of them are listed in the following table:

Type of model	How the model works
Connectivity	This model computes distance between points and organizes the points based on closeness.
Partitioning	This model partitions the data into clusters and associates each data point to a cluster. Most predominant is k-means.
Distribution Models	This model uses a statistical distribution to determine the clusters.
Density	This model determines closeness of data points to arrive at dense areas of distribution. The common use of DBSCAN is for tight concentrations or OPTICS for more sparse distributions.

Within an algorithm, there are finer levels of granularity as well, including:

- **Hard or soft clustering**: It defines whether a data point can be part of more than one cluster.

- **Partitioning rules**: Are rules that determine how to assign data points to different partitions. These rules are as follows:
    - **Strict**: This rule will check whether partitions include data points that are not close
    - **Overlapping**: This rule will check whether partitions overlap in any way
    - **Hierarchical**: This rule checks whether the partitions are stratified

In R programming, we have clustering tools for:

- K-means clustering
- K-medoids clustering
- Hierarchical clustering
- Expectation-maximization
- Density estimation

K-means clustering

K-means clustering is a method of partitioning the dataset into *k* clusters. You need to predetermine the number of clusters you want to divide the dataset into. The k-means algorithm has the following steps:

1. Select *k* random rows (centroids) from your data (you have a predetermined number of clusters to use).
2. We are using Lloyd's algorithm (the default) to determine clusters.
3. Assign each data point according to its closeness to a centroid.
4. Recalculate each centroid as an average of all the points associated with it.
5. Reassign each data point as closest to a centroid.
6. Continue with steps 3 and 4 until data points are no longer assigned or you have looped some maximum number of times.

This is a heuristic algorithm, so it is a good idea to run the process several times. It will normally run quickly in R, as the work in each step is not difficult. The objective is to minimize the sum of squares by constant refining of the terms.

Predetermining the number of clusters may be problematic. Graphing the data (or its squares or the like) should present logical groupings for your data visually. You can determine group sizes by iterating through the steps to determine the cutoff for selection (we will use that later in this chapter). There are other R packages that will attempt to compute this as well. You should also verify the fit of the clusters selected upon completion.

Using an average (in step 3) shows that k-means does not work well with fairly sparse data or data with a larger number of outliers. Furthermore, there can be a problem if the cluster is not in a nice, linear shape. Graphical representation should prove whether your data fits this algorithm.

Usage

K-means clustering is performed in R programming with the kmeans function. The R programming usage of k-means clustering follows the convention given here (note that you can always determine the conventions for a function using the inline help function, for example, ?kmeans, to get this information):

```
kmeans(x,
centers,
iter.max = 10,
nstart = 1,
algorithm = c("Hartigan-Wong",
```

```
                              "Lloyd",
                              "Forgy",
                              "MacQueen"),
    trace=FALSE)
```

The various parameters are explained in the following table:

Parameter	Description
x	This is the data matrix to be analyzed
centers	This is the number of clusters
iter.max	This is the maximum number of iterations (unless reassignment stops)
nstart	This is the number of random sets to use
algorithm	This can be of one of the following types: Hartigan-Wong, Lloyd, Forgy, or MacQueen algorithms
trace	This gives the present trace information as the algorithm progresses

Calling the kmeans function returns a kmeans object with the following properties:

Property	Description
cluster	This contains the cluster assignments
centers	This contains the cluster centers
totss	This gives the total sum of squares
withinss	This is the vector of within sum of squares, per cluster
tot.withinss	This contains the total (sum of withinss)
betweenss	This contains the between-cluster sum of squares
size	This contains the number of data points in each cluster
iter	This contains the number of iterations performed
ault	This contains the expert diagnostic

Example

First, generate a hundred pairs of random numbers in a normal distribution and assign it to the matrix x as follows:

```
>x <- rbind(matrix(rnorm(100, sd = 0.3), ncol = 2),
                matrix(rnorm(100, mean = 1, sd = 0.3), ncol = 2))
```

We can display the values we generate as follows:

```
>x
                    [,1]            [,2]
```

```
[1,]    0.4679569701   -0.269074028
[2,]   -0.5030944919   -0.393382748
[3,]   -0.3645075552   -0.304474590

...

 [98,]   1.1121388866    0.975150551
 [99,]   1.1818402912    1.512040138
[100,]   1.7643166039    1.339428999
```

The the resultant kmeans object values can be determined and displayed (using 10 clusters) as follows:

```
> fit <- kmeans(x,10)
> fit
K-means clustering with 10 clusters of sizes 4, 12, 10, 7, 13, 16, 8,
13, 8, 9
Cluster means:
          [,1]          [,2]
1     0.59611989    0.77213527
2     1.09064550    1.02456563
3    -0.01095292    0.41255130
4     0.07613688   -0.48816360
5     1.04043914    0.78864770
6     0.04167769   -0.05023832
7     0.47920281   -0.05528244
8     1.03305030    1.28488358
9     1.47791031    0.90185427
10   -0.28881626   -0.26002816
Clustering vector:
   [1]   7 10 10  6   7  6  3  3  7 10  4  7  4  7  6  7  6  6  4  3 10
 4  3  6 10  6  6  3  6 10  3  6  4  3  6  3  6  6  6  7  3  4  6  7  6
10  4 10  3 10  5  2  9  2
  [55]  9  5  5  2  5  8  9  8  1  2  5  9  5  2  5  8  1  5  8  2  8
 8  5  5  8  1  1  5  8  9  9  8  5  2  5  8  2  2  9  2  8  2  8  2  8
 9
Within cluster sum of squares by cluster:
 [1] 0.09842712 0.23620192 0.47286373 0.30604945 0.21233870 0.47824982
0.36380678 0.58063931 0.67803464 0.28407093
 (between_SS / total_SS =   94.6 %)
Available components:
[1] "cluster"       "centers"       "totss"         "withinss"      "tot.
withinss" "betweenss"     "size"          "iter"          "ifault"
```

If we look at the results, we find some interesting data points:

- The Cluster means shows the breakdown of the means used for the cluster assignments.

- The Clustering vector shows which cluster each of the 100 numbers was assigned to.

- The Cluster sum of squares shows the totss value, as described in the output.

- The percentage value is the betweenss value divided as a percentage of the totss value. At 94.6 percent, we have a very good fit.

We chose an arbitrary cluster size of 10, but we should verify that this is a good number to use. If we were to run the kmeans function a number of times using a range of cluster sizes, we would end up with a graph that looks like the one in the following example.

For example, if we ran the following code and recorded the results, the output will be as follows:

```
results <- matrix(nrow=14, ncol=2, dimnames=list(2:15,c("clusters","s
umsquares")))
for(i in 2:15) {
   fit <- kmeans(x,i)
   results[i-1,1] <- i
   results[i-1,2] <- fit$totss
}
plot(results)
```

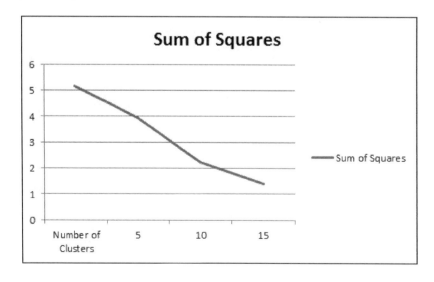

If the data were more distributed, there would be a clear demarcation about the maximum number of clusters, as further clustering will show no improvement in the sum of squares. However, since we used very smooth data for the test, the number of clusters could be allowed to increase.

Once your clusters have been determined, you should be able to gather a visual representation, as shown in the following plot:

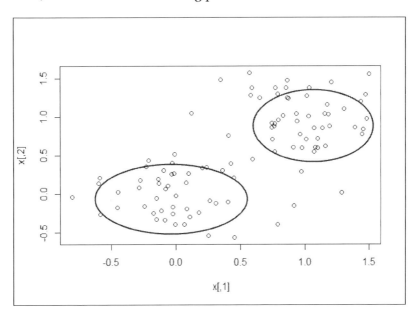

K-medoids clustering

K-medoids clustering is another method of determining the clusters in a dataset. A medoid is an entity of the dataset that represents the group to which it was inserted. K-means works with centroids, which are artificially created to represent a cluster. So, a medoid is actually part of the dataset. A centroid is a derived amount.

When partitioning around medoids, make sure that the following points are taken care of:

- Each entity is assigned to only one cluster
- Each entity is assigned to the medoid that defines its cluster
- Exactly *k* clusters are defined

The algorithm has two phases with several steps:

- **Build phase**: During the build phase, we come up with initial estimates for the clusters:

  1. Choose random *k* entities to become medoids (the *k* entities may be provided to the algorithm).

  2. Calculate the dissimilarity matrix (compute all the pairwise dissimilarities (distances) between observations in the dataset) so that we can find the distances.

  3. Assign every entity to the closest medoid.

- **Swap phase**: In the swap phase, we fine-tune our initial estimates given the rough clusters determined in the build phase:

  1. Search each cluster for the entity that lowers the average dissimilarity coefficient the most and therefore makes it the medoid for the cluster.

  2. If any medoid has changed, start from step 3 of the build phase again.

Usage

K-medoid clustering is calculated in R programming with the pam function:

```
pam(x, k, diss, metric, medoids, stand, cluster.only, do.swap,    keep.
diss, keep.data, trace.lev)
```

The various parameters of the pam function are explained in the following table:

Parameter	Description
x	This is the data matrix or dissimilarity matrix (based on the diss flag)
k	This is the number of clusters, where 0 is less than *k* which is less than the number of entities
diss	The values are as follows: • FALSE if x is a matrix • TRUE if x is a dissimilarity matrix
metric	This is a string metric to be used to calculate the dissimilarity matrix. It can be of the following types: • euclidean for Euclidean distance • manhattan for Manhattan distance
medoids	If the NULL value is assigned, it means a set of medoids is to be developed. Otherwise, it is a set of initial medoids.

Parameter	Description
stand	If x is the data matrix, then measurements in x will be standardized before computing the dissimilarity matrix.
cluster.only	If the value set is TRUE, then only clustering will be computed and returned.
do.swap	This contains a Boolean value to decide whether swap should occur.
keep.diss	This contains a Boolean value to decide whether dissimilarity should be kept in the result.
keep.data	This contains a Boolean value to decide whether data should be kept in the result.
trace.lev	This contains an integer trace level for diagnostics, where 0 means no trace information.

The results returned from the pam function can be displayed, which is rather difficult to interpret, or the results can be plotted, which is intuitively more understandable.

Example

Using a simple set of data with two (visually) clear clusters as follows, as stored in a file named medoids.csv:

Object	x	y
1	1	10
2	2	11
3	1	10
4	2	12
5	1	4
6	3	5
7	2	6
8	2	5
9	3	6

Let's use the pam function on the medoids.csv file as follows:

```
# load pam function
> library(cluster)

#load the table from a file
```

```
> x <- read.table("medoids.csv", header=TRUE, sep=",")

#execute the pam algorithm with the dataset created for the example
> result <- pam(x, 2, FALSE, "euclidean")
Looking at the result directly we get:
> result
Medoids:
      ID Object x   y
[1,]   2        2 2 11
[2,]   7        7 2  6
Clustering vector:
[1] 1 1 1 1 2 2 2 2 2
Objective function:
   build      swap
1.564722 1.564722
Available components:
 [1] "medoids"    "id.med"     "clustering" "objective"  "isolation"
 [6] "clusinfo"   "silinfo"    "diss"       "call"       "data"
```

Evaluating the results we can see:

- We specified the use of two medoids, and row 3 and 6 were chosen
- The rows were clustered as presented in the clustering vector (as expected, about half in the first medoid and the rest in the other medoid)
- The function did not change greatly from the build phase to the swap phase (looking at the Objective function values for build and swap of 1.56 versus 1.56)

Using a summary for a clearer picture, we see the following result:

```
> summary(result)
Medoids:
      ID Object x   y
[1,]   2        2 2 11
[2,]   7        7 2  6
Clustering vector:
[1] 1 1 1 1 2 2 2 2 2
Objective function:
   build      swap
1.564722 1.564722

Numerical information per cluster:
```

```
sizemax_dissav_diss diameter separation
[1,]     4 2.236068 1.425042 3.741657    5.744563
[2,]     5 3.000000 1.676466 4.898979    5.744563

Isolated clusters:
 L-clusters: character(0)
 L*-clusters: [1] 1 2

Silhouette plot information:
   cluster neighbor sil_width
2        1         2 0.7575089
3        1         2 0.6864544
1        1         2 0.6859661
4        1         2 0.6315196
8        2         1 0.7310922
7        2         1 0.6872724
6        2         1 0.6595811
9        2         1 0.6374808
5        2         1 0.5342637
Average silhouette width per cluster:
[1] 0.6903623 0.6499381
Average silhouette width of total data set:
[1] 0.6679044

36 dissimilarities, summarized :
   Min. 1st Qu.  Median    Mean 3rd Qu.    Max.
 1.4142  2.3961  6.2445  5.2746  7.3822  9.1652
Metric :  euclidean
Number of objects : 9

Available components:
 [1] "medoids"    "id.med"    "clustering" "objective" "isolation"
 [6] "clusinfo"   "silinfo"   "diss"       "call"      "data"
```

Downloading the example code

You can download the example code files from your account at http://www.packtpub.com for all the Packt Publishing books you have purchased. If you purchased this book elsewhere, you can visit http://www.packtpub.com/support and register to have the files e-mailed directly to you.

The summary presents more details on the medoids and how they were selected. However, note the dissimilarities as well.

Plotting the data, we can see the following output:

```
#plot a graphic showing the clusters and the medoids of each cluster
> plot(result$data, col = result$clustering)
```

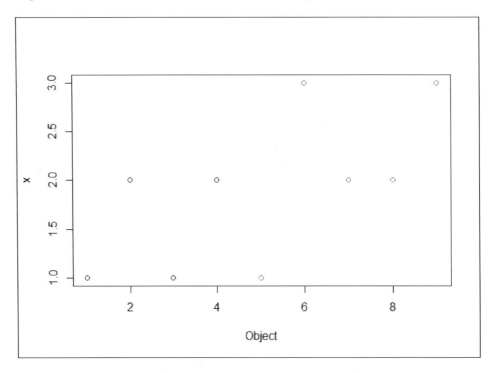

The resulting plot is as we expected it to be. It is good to see the data clearly broken into two medoids, both spatially and by color demarcation.

Hierarchical clustering

Hierarchical clustering is a method to ascertain clusters in a dataset that are in a hierarchy.

Using hierarchical clustering, we are attempting to create a hierarchy of clusters. There are two approaches of doing this:

- **Agglomerative (or bottom up)**: In this approach, each entity starts as its own cluster and pairs are merged as they move up the hierarchy
- **Divisive (or top down)**: In this approach, all entities are lumped into one cluster and are split as they are moved down the hierarchy

The resulting hierarchy is normally displayed using a tree/graph model of a dendogram.

Hierarchical clustering is performed in R programming with the `hclust` function.

Usage

The `hclust` function is called as follows:

```
hclust(d, method = "complete", members = NULL)
```

The various parameters of the `hclust` function are explained in the following table:

Parameter	Description
d	This is the matrix.
method	This is the agglomeration method to be used. This should be (a distinct abbreviation of) one of these methods: ward.D, ward.D2, single, complete, average (= UPGMA), mcquitty (= WPGMA), median (= WPGMC), or centroid (= UPGMC).
members	This could be NULL or d, the dissimilarity matrix.

Example

We start by generating some random data over a normal distribution using the following code:

```
> dat <- matrix(rnorm(100), nrow=10, ncol=10)

> dat
            [,1]       [,2]        [,3]        [,4]        [,5]
[,6]
 [1,]   1.4811953 -1.0882253 -0.47659922  0.22344983 -0.74227899
0.2835530
 [2,]  -0.6414931 -1.0103688 -0.55213606 -0.48812235  1.41763706
0.8337524
 [3,]   0.2638638  0.2535630 -0.53310519  2.27778665 -0.09526058
1.9579652
[4,]   -0.50307726 -0.3873578 -1.54407287 -0.1503834
Then, we calculate the hierarchical distribution for our data as
follows:
> hc <- hclust(dist(dat))
> hc
```

```
Call:
hclust(d = dist(dat))

Cluster method   : complete
Distance         : euclidean
Number of objects: 10
```

The resulting data object is very uninformative. We can display the hierarchical cluster using a dendogram, as follows:

```
>plot(hc)
```

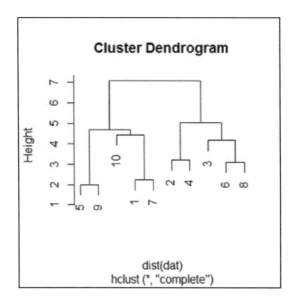

The dendogram has the expected shape. I find these diagrams somewhat unclear, but if you go over them in detail, the inference will be as follows:

- Reading the diagram in a top-down fashion, we see it has two distinct branches. The implication is that there are two groups that are distinctly different from one another. Within the two branches, we see **10** and **3** as distinctly different from the rest. Generally, it appears that we have determined there are an even group and an odd group, as expected.

- Reading the diagram bottom up, we see closeness and similarity over a number of elements. This would be expected from a simple random distribution.

Expectation-maximization

Expectation-maximization (EM) is the process of estimating the parameters in a statistical model.

For a given model, we have the following parameters:

- x: This is a set of observed data
- z: This is a set of missing values
- T: This is a set of unknown parameters that we should apply to our model to predict z

The steps to perform expectation-maximization are as follows:

1. Initialize the unknown parameters (T) to random values.
2. Compute the best missing values (z) using the new parameter values.
3. Use the best missing values (z), which were just computed, to determine a better estimate for the unknown parameters (T).
4. Iterate over steps 2 and 3 until we have a convergence.

This version of the algorithm produces hard parameter values (z). In practice, soft values may be of interest where probabilities are assigned to various values of the parameters (z). By hard values, I mean we are selecting specific z values. We could instead use soft values where z varies by some probability distribution.

We use EM in R programming with the `Mclust` function from the `mclust` library. The full description of `Mclust` is the normal mixture modeling fitted via EM algorithm for model-based clustering, classification, and density estimation, including Bayesian regularization.

Usage

The `Mclust` function is as follows:

```
Mclust(data, G = NULL, modelNames = NULL,
       prior = NULL, control = emControl(),
       initialization = NULL, warn = FALSE, ...)
```

The various parameters of the `Mclust` function are explained in the following table:

Parameter	Description
data	This contains the matrix.
G	This contains the vector of number of clusters to use to compute BIC. The default value is 1:9.
modelNames	This contains the vector of model names to use.
prior	This contains the optional conjugate prior for means.
control	This contains the list of control parameters for EM. The default value is List.
initialization	This contains NULL or a list of one or more of the following components: • hcPairs: This is used to merge pairs • subset: This is to be used during initialization • noise: This makes an initial guess at noise
warn	This contains which warnings are to be issued. Default is none.

List of model names

The `Mclust` function uses a model when trying to decide which items belong to a cluster. There are different model names for univariate, multivariate, and single component datasets. In each, the idea is to select a model that describes the data, for example, VII will be used for data that is spherically displaced with equal volume across each cluster.

Model	Type of dataset
Univariate mixture	
E	equal variance (one-dimensional)
V	variable variance (one-dimensional)
Multivariate mixture	
EII	spherical, equal volume
VII	spherical, unequal volume
EEI	diagonal, equal volume and shape
VEI	diagonal, varying volume, equal shape
EVI	diagonal, equal volume, varying shape
VVI	diagonal, varying volume and shape
EEE	ellipsoidal, equal volume, shape, and orientation
EEV	ellipsoidal, equal volume and equal shape

Model	Type of dataset
VEV	ellipsoidal, equal shape
VVV	ellipsoidal, varying volume, shape, and orientation
Single component	
X	univariate normal
XII	spherical multivariate normal
XXI	diagonal multivariate normal
XXX	ellipsoidal multivariate normal

Example

First, we must load the library that contains the `mclust` function (we may need to install it in the local environment) as follows:

```
> install.packages("mclust")
> library(mclust)
```

We will be using the `iris` data in this example, as shown here:

```
> data <- read.csv("http://archive.ics.uci.edu/ml/machine-learning-
databases/iris/iris.data")
```

Now, we can compute the best fit via EM (note capitalization of `Mclust`) as follows:

```
> fit <- Mclust(data)
```

We can display our results as follows:

```
> fit
'Mclust' model object:
 best model: ellipsoidal, equal shape (VEV) with 2 components

> summary(fit)
--------------------------------------------------
Gaussian finite mixture model fitted by EM algorithm
--------------------------------------------------

Mclust VEV (ellipsoidal, equal shape) model with 2 components:

 log.likelihood   n df      BIC       ICL
     -121.1459 149 37 -427.4378 -427.4385

Clustering table:
  1   2
 49 100
```

Simple display of the `fit` data object doesn't tell us very much, it shows just what was used to compute the density of the dataset.

The `summary` command presents more detailed information about the results, as listed here:

- `log.likelihood (-121)`: This is the log likelihood of the BIC value
- `n (149)`: This is the number of data points
- `df (37)`: This is the distribution
- `BIC (-427)`: This is the Bayesian information criteria; this is an optimal value
- `ICL (-427)`: Integrated Complete Data Likelihood—a classification version of the BIC. As we have the same value for ICL and BIC we classified the data points.

We can plot the results for a visual verification as follows:

```
> plot(fit)
```

You will notice that the `plot` command for EM produces the following four plots (as shown in the graph):

- The BIC values used for choosing the number of clusters
- A plot of the clustering
- A plot of the classification uncertainty
- The orbital plot of clusters

The following graph depicts the plot of density.

The first plot gives a depiction of the BIC ranges versus the number of components by different model names; in this case, we should probably not use **VEV**, for example:

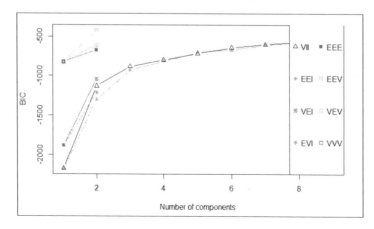

This second plot shows the comparison of using each of the components of the data feed against every other component of the data feed to determine the clustering that would result. The idea is to select the components that give you the best clustering of your data. This is one of those cases where your familiarity with the data is key to selecting the appropriate data points for clustering.

In this case, I think selecting **X5.1** and **X1.4** yield the tightest clusters, as shown in the following graph:

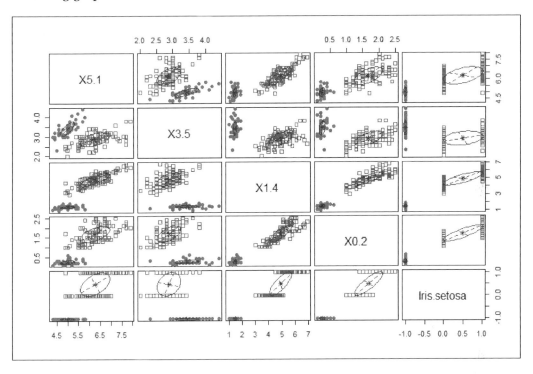

The third plot gives another iteration of the clustering affects of the different choices highlighting the *main* cluster by eliminating any points from the plot that would be applied to the main cluster, as shown here:

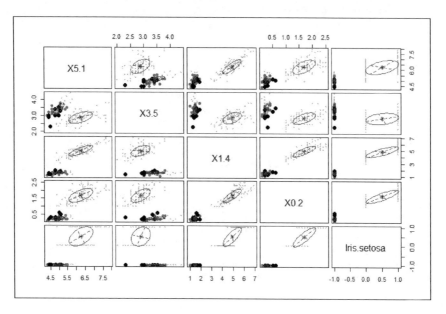

The final, fourth plot gives an *orbital* view of each of the clusters giving a highlight display of where the points might appear relative to the center of each cluster, as shown here:

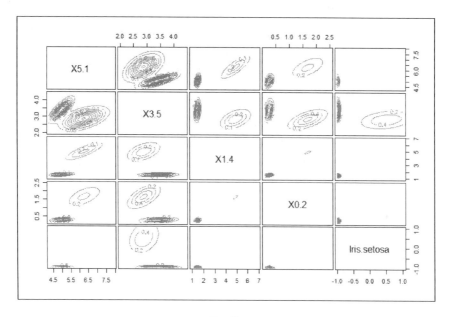

Density estimation

Density estimation is the process of estimating the probability density function of a population given in an observation set. The density estimation process takes your observations, disperses them across a number of data points, runs a FF transform to determine a kernel, and then runs a linear approximation to estimate density.

Density estimation produces an estimate for the unobservable population distribution function. Some approaches that are used to produce the density estimation are as follows:

- **Parzen windows**: In this approach, the observations are placed in a window and density estimates are made based on proximity
- **Vector quantization**: This approach lets you model the probability density functions as per the distribution of observations
- **Histograms**: With a histogram, you get a nice visual showing density (size of the bars); the number of bins chosen while developing the histogram decide your density outcome

Density estimation is performed via the `density` function in R programming. Other functions for density evaluation in R are:

Function	Description
DBSCAN	This function determines clustering for fixed point clusters
OPTICS	This function determines clustering for wide distribution clusters

Usage

The `density` function is invoked as follows:

```
density(x, bw = "nrd0", adjust = 1,
        kernel = c("gaussian", "epanechnikov",
                  "rectangular",
                  "triangular", "biweight",
                  "cosine", "optcosine"),
        weights = NULL, window = kernel, width,
        give.Rkern = FALSE,
        n = 512, from, to, na.rm = FALSE, ...)
```

The various parameters of the `density` function are explained in the following table:

Parameter	Description
x	This is the matrix.
bw	This is the smoothing bandwidth to be used.
adjust	This is the multiplier to adjust bandwidth.
kernel	This is the smoother kernel to be used. It must be one of the following kernels: • gaussian • rectangular • triangular • epanechnikov • biweight • cosine • optcosine
weights	This is a vector of observation weights with same length as x.
window	This is the kernel used.
width	This is the S compatibility parameter.
give.Rkern	If the value of this parameter is TRUE, no density is estimated.
N	This is the number of density points to estimate.
from, to	These are the left and right-most points to use.
na.rm	If the value of this parameter is TRUE, missing values are removed.

The available bandwidths can be found using the following commands:

```
bw.nrd0(x)

bw.nrd(x)

bw.ucv(x, nb = 1000, lower = 0.1 * hmax, upper = hmax, tol = 0.1 *
lower)

bw.bcv(x, nb = 1000, lower = 0.1 * hmax, upper = hmax, tol = 0.1 *
lower)

bw.SJ(x, nb = 1000, lower = 0.1 * hmax, upper = hmax, method =
    c("ste", "dpi"), tol = 0.1 * lower)
```

The various parameters of the bw function are explained in the following table:

Parameter	Description
x	This is the dataset
nb	This is the number of bins
lower, upper	This is the range of bandwidth which is to be minimized
method	The ste method is used to solve the equation or the dpi method is used for direct plugin
tol	This is the convergence tolerance for ste

Example

We can use the iris dataset as follows:

```
> data <- read.csv("http://archive.ics.uci.edu/ml/machine-learning-
databases/iris/iris.data")
The density of the X5.1 series (sepal length) can be computed as
follows:
> d <- density(data$X5.1)
> d

Call:
density.default(x = data$X5.1)

Data: data$X5.1 (149 obs.);  Bandwidth 'bw' = 0.2741

      x                 y
 Min.:3.478    Min.   :0.0001504
 1st Qu.:4.789    1st Qu.:0.0342542
 Median :6.100    Median :0.1538908
 Mean   :6.100    Mean   :0.1904755
 3rd Qu.:7.411    3rd Qu.:0.3765078
 Max.   :8.722    Max.   :0.3987472
```

We can plot the density values as follows:

```
> plot(d)
```

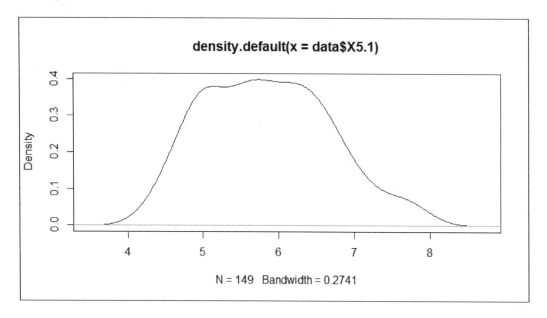

The plot shows most of the data occurring between 5 and 7. So, sepal length averages at just under 6.

Anomaly detection

We can use R programming to detect anomalies in a dataset. Anomaly detection can be used in a number of different areas, such as intrusion detection, fraud detection, system health, and so on. In R programming, these are called outliers. R programming allows the detection of outliers in a number of ways, as listed here:

- Statistical tests
- Depth-based approaches
- Deviation-based approaches
- Distance-based approaches
- Density-based approaches
- High-dimensional approaches

Show outliers

R programming has a function to display outliers: `identify` (in `boxplot`).

The `boxplot` function produces a *box-and-whisker* plot (see following graph). The `boxplot` function has a number of graphics options. For this example, we do not need to set any.

The `identify` function is a convenient method for marking points in a scatter plot. In R programming, box plot is a type of scatter plot.

Example

In this example, we need to generate a 100 random numbers and then plot the points in boxes.

Then, we mark the first outlier with it's identifier as follows:

```
> y <- rnorm(100)
> boxplot(y)
> identify(rep(1, length(y)), y, labels = seq_along(y))
```

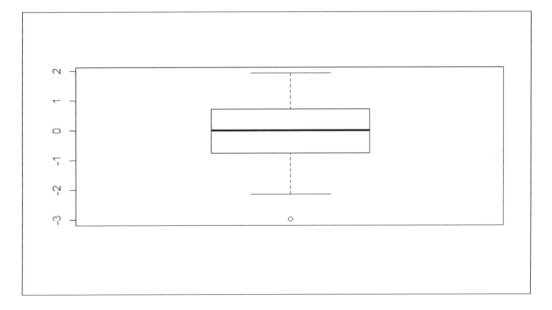

 Notice the **0** next to the outlier in the graph.

Example

The `boxplot` function automatically computes the outliers for a set as well.

First, we will generate a 100 random numbers as follows (note that this data is randomly generated, so your results may not be the same):

```
> x <- rnorm(100)
```

We can have a look at the summary information on the set using the following code:

```
> summary(x)
    Min.  1st Qu.   Median      Mean  3rd Qu.      Max.
-2.12000 -0.74790 -0.20060 -0.01711  0.49930   2.43200
```

Now, we can display the outliers using the following code:

```
> boxplot.stats(x)$out
[1]  2.420850  2.432033
```

The following code will graph the set and highlight the outliers:

```
> boxplot(x)
```

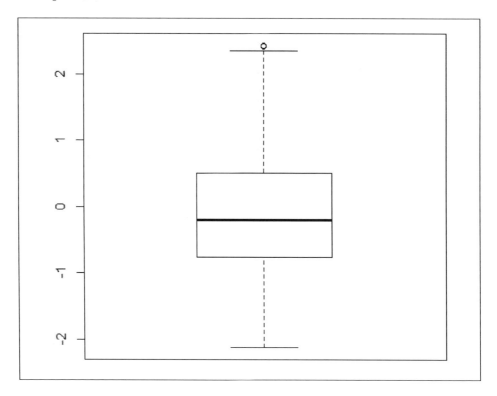

Notice the **0** next to the outlier in the graph.

We can generate a box plot of more familiar data showing the same issue with outliers using the built-in data for cars, as follows:

```
boxplot(mpg~cyl,data=mtcars, xlab="Cylinders", ylab="MPG")
```

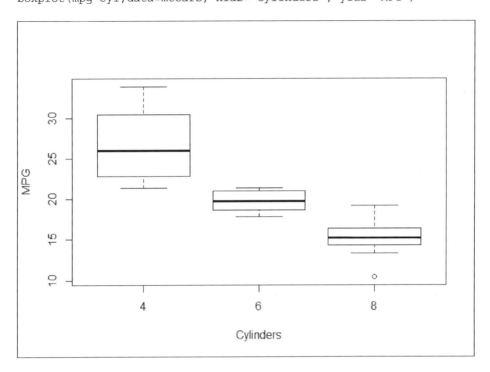

Another anomaly detection example

We can also use box plot's outlier detection when we have two dimensions. Note that we are forcing the issue by using a union of the outliers in x and y rather than an intersection. The point of the example is to display such points. The code is as follows:

```
> x <- rnorm(1000)
> y <- rnorm(1000)
> f <- data.frame(x,y)
> a <- boxplot.stats(x)$out
> b <- boxplot.stats(y)$out
> list <- union(a,b)
> plot(f)
> px <- f[f$x %in% a,]
```

```
> py <- f[f$y %in% b,]
> p <- rbind(px,py)
> par(new=TRUE)
> plot(p$x, p$y,cex=2,col=2)
```

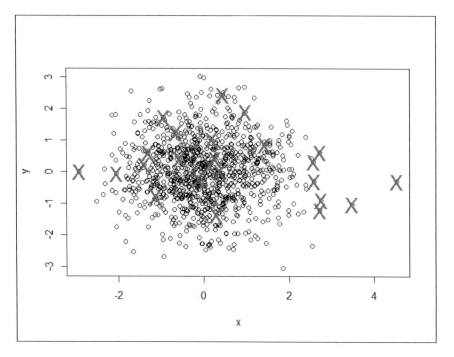

While R did what we asked, the plot does not look right. We completely fabricated the data; in a real use case, you would need to use your domain expertise to determine whether these outliers were correct or not.

Calculating anomalies

Given the variety of what constitutes an anomaly, R programming has a mechanism that gives you complete control over it: write your own function that can be used to make a decision.

Usage

We can use the name function to create our own anomaly as shown here:

```
name <- function(parameters,…) {
  # determine what constitutes an anomaly
  return(df)
}
```

Here, the parameters are the values we need to use in the function. I am assuming we return a data frame from the function. The function could do anything.

Example 1

We will be using the `iris` data in this example, as shown here:

```
> data <- read.csv("http://archive.ics.uci.edu/ml/machine-learning-
databases/iris/iris.data")
```

If we decide an anomaly is present when sepal is under 4.5 or over 7.5, we could use a function as shown here:

```
> outliers <- function(data, low, high) {
>   outs <- subset(data, data$X5.1 < low | data$X5.1 > high)
>   return(outs)
>}
```

Then, we will get the following output:

```
> outliers(data, 4.5, 7.5)
     X5.1 X3.5 X1.4 X0.2     Iris.setosa
8    4.4  2.9  1.4  0.2     Iris-setosa
13   4.3  3.0  1.1  0.1     Iris-setosa
38   4.4  3.0  1.3  0.2     Iris-setosa
42   4.4  3.2  1.3  0.2     Iris-setosa
105  7.6  3.0  6.6  2.1 Iris-virginica
117  7.7  3.8  6.7  2.2 Iris-virginica
118  7.7  2.6  6.9  2.3 Iris-virginica
122  7.7  2.8  6.7  2.0 Iris-virginica
131  7.9  3.8  6.4  2.0 Iris-virginica
135  7.7  3.0  6.1  2.3 Iris-virginica
```

This gives us the flexibility of making slight adjustments to our criteria by passing different parameter values to the function in order to achieve the desired results.

Example 2

Another popular package is DMwR. It contains the `lofactor` function that can also be used to locate outliers. The DMwR package can be installed using the following command:

```
> install.packages("DMwR")
> library(DMwR)
```

We need to remove the species column from the data, as it is categorical against it data. This can be done by using the following command:

```
> nospecies <- data[,1:4]
```

Now, we determine the outliers in the frame:

```
> scores <- lofactor(nospecies, k=3)
```

Next, we take a look at their distribution:

```
> plot(density(scores))
```

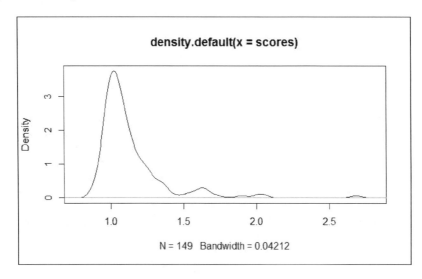

One point of interest is if there is some close equality amongst several of the outliers (that is, density of about 4).

Association rules

Association rules describe associations between two datasets. This is most commonly used in market basket analysis. Given a set of transactions with multiple, different items per transaction (shopping bag), how can the item sales be associated? The most common associations are as follows:

- **Support**: This is the percentage of transactions that contain A and B.
- **Confidence**: This is the percentage (of time that rule is correct) of cases containing A that also contain B.
- **Lift**: This is the ratio of confidence to the percentage of cases containing B. Please note that if lift is 1, then A and B are independent.

Mine for associations

The most widely used tool in R from association rules is `apriori`.

Usage

The `apriori` rules library can be called as follows:

```
apriori(data, parameter = NULL, appearance = NULL, control = NULL)
```

The various parameters of the `apriori` library are explained in the following table:

Parameter	Description
data	This is the transaction data.
parameter	This stores the default behavior to mine, with `support` as 0.1, `confidence` as 0.8, and `maxlen` as 10. You can change parameter values accordingly.
appearance	This is used to restrict items that appear in rules.
control	This is used to adjust the performance of the algorithm used.

Example

You will need to load the `apriori` rules library as follows:

```
> install.packages("arules")
> library(arules)
```

The market basket data can be loaded as follows:

```
> data <- read.csv("http://www.salemmarafi.com/wp-content/
uploads/2014/03/groceries.csv")
```

Then, we can generate rules from the data as follows:

```
> rules <- apriori(data)

parameter specification:
confidenceminvalsmaxaremavaloriginalSupport support minlenmaxlen
target
        0.8    0.1    1 none FALSE              TRUE    0.1        1
10   rules
   ext
  FALSE

algorithmic control:
 filter tree heap memopt load sort verbose
```

```
    0.1 TRUE TRUE   FALSE TRUE    2     TRUE
```

```
apriori - find association rules with the apriori algorithm
version 4.21 (2004.05.09)         (c) 1996-2004    Christian Borgelt
set item appearances ...[0 item(s)] done [0.00s].
set transactions ...[655 item(s), 15295 transaction(s)] done [0.00s].
sorting and recoding items ... [3 item(s)] done [0.00s].
creating transaction tree ... done [0.00s].
checking subsets of size 1 2 3 done [0.00s].
writing ... [5 rule(s)] done [0.00s].
creating S4 object  ... done [0.00s].
```

There are several points to highlight in the results:

- As you can see from the display, we are using the default settings (confidence 0.8, and so on)

- We found 15,000 transactions for three items (picked from the 655 total items available)

- We generated five rules

We can examine the rules that were generated as follows:

```
> rules

set of 5 rules
> inspect(rules)


lhsrhs                    support confidence      lift
1 {semi.finished.bread=} => {margarine=}   0.2278522           1
2.501226
2 {semi.finished.bread=} => {ready.soups=} 0.2278522           1
1.861385
3 {margarine=}           => {ready.soups=} 0.3998039           1
1.861385
4 {semi.finished.bread=,
   margarine=}            => {ready.soups=} 0.2278522           1
1.861385
5 {semi.finished.bread=,
   ready.soups=}          => {margarine=}   0.2278522           1
2.501226
```

The code has been slightly reformatted for readability.

Looking over the rules, there is a clear connection between buying bread, soup, and margarine—at least in the market where and when the data was gathered.

If we change the parameters (thresholds) used in the calculation, we get a different set of rules. For example, check the following code:

```
> rules <- apriori(data, parameter = list(supp = 0.001, conf = 0.8))
```

This code generates over 500 rules, but they have questionable meaning as we now have the rules with 0.001 confidence.

Questions

Factual

- How do you decide whether to use `kmeans` or `kdemoids`?
- What is the significance of the boxplot layout? Why does it look that way?
- Describe the underlying data produced in the outliers for the `iris` data, given the density plot.
- What are the extract rules for other items in the market dataset?

When, how, and why?

- What is the risk of not vetting the outliers that are detected for the specific domain? Shouldn't the calculation always work?
- Why do we need to exclude the `iris` category column from the outlier detection algorithm? Can it be used in some way when determining outliers?
- Can you come up with a scenario where the market basket data and rules we generated were not applicable to the store you are working with?

Challenges

- I found it difficult to develop test data for outliers in two dimensions that both occurred in the same instance using random data. Can you develop a test that would always have several outliers in at least two dimensions that occur in the same instance?
- There is a good dataset on the Internet regarding passenger data on the Titanic. Generate the rules regarding the possible survival of the passengers.

Summary

In this chapter, we discussed cluster analysis, anomaly detection, and association rules. In cluster analysis, we use k-means clustering, k-medoids clustering, hierarchical clustering, expectation-maximization, and density estimation. In anomaly detection, we found outliers using built-in R functions and developed our own specialized R function. For association rules, we used the apriori package to determine the associations amongst datasets.

In the next chapter, we will cover data mining for sequences.

2
Data Mining Sequences

Data mining is frequently used to detect sequences or patterns in data. In this chapter, we are looking for the data to follow a pattern where one event or series of events predicts another data point in a consistent manner.

This chapter describes the different ways to find patterns in your dataset:

- Patterns to look for
- Find patterns in data
- Constraints

We can find patterns in many large datasets. This can range across a number of areas, such as population mix changes, frequency of cell phone use, deterioration of highways, accidents due to age, and so on. It really feels like there are many patterns and sequences just waiting to be discovered.

We can find these patterns using a number of tools in R programming. Most patterns are limited in their extent by constraints, such as time over which the sequence will be meaningful.

Patterns

We will go over several methods of determining patterns in data:

Type of model	How the model works
eclat	This model is used for itemset pattern detection, often used for shopping carts
arules	This model determines the co-occurrence of items in a dataset
apriori	This model learns the association rules in a dataset
TraMineR	This is an R package for mining sequences

Eclat

The Eclat algorithm is used for frequent itemset mining. In this case, we are looking for similar patterns in behavior, as opposed to looking for irregularities (like we did in other data mining approaches).

This algorithm uses intersections in the data to compute the support of candidates for events that frequently occur together, such as shopping cart items. The frequent candidates are then tested to confirm the pattern in the dataset.

Usage

Eclat is used in R programming with the `eclat` function in the `arules` package. The R programming usage of the Eclat algorithm follows this convention:

```
> eclat(data,
  parameter = NULL,
  control = NULL)
```

The various parameters of the `eclat` function are explained in the following table:

Parameter	Description
data	This is the data matrix that will be analyzed
parameter	This is the object of ECParameter or list
control	This is the object of ECControl or list

The common ECParameters are as follows:

Parameter	Description
support	This parameter defines the minimal support of an itemset (default value is 0.1)
minlen	This parameter contains the minimum size of an itemset (default value is 1)
maxlen	This parameter contains the maximum size of an itemset (default value is 10)
target	This parameter defines the type of association to be mined: • Frequent itemsets • Maximally frequent itemsets • Closed frequent itemsets

The common ECControl values are as follows:

Parameter	Description
sort	This parameter can have one of the following values: • 1 implies ascending • -1 implies descending • 0 implies do not sort • 2 implies ascending • -2 implies descending with respect to transaction size sum
verbose	This parameter shows the display progress information

Calling the eclat function returns the frequent itemsets found in the data.

The eclat implementation includes the Adult dataset. The Adult dataset includes approximately 50,000 rows from Census Bureau data.

Using eclat to find similarities in adult behavior

Use the following code to find the similarities in adult behavior:

```
> library("arules")
> data("Adult")
> dim(Adult)
[1] 48842    115
> summary(Adult)
transactions as itemMatrix in sparse format with
 48842 rows (elements/itemsets/transactions) and
 115 columns (items) and a density of 0.1089939
most frequent items:
capital-loss=None            capital-gain=None
46560                        44807
native-country=United-States race=White
43832                        41762
workclass=Private            (Other)
33906                        401333

element (itemset/transaction) length distribution:
sizes
    9    10    11    12    13
   19   971  2067 15623 30162

   Min. 1st Qu.  Median    Mean 3rd Qu.    Max.
```

```
    9.00    12.00    13.00    12.53    13.00    13.00

includes extended item information - examples:
          labels variables        levels
1        age=Young        age       Young
2 age=Middle-aged        age Middle-aged
3       age=Senior        age      Senior

includes extended transaction information - examples:
   transactionID
1              1
2              2
3              3
```

Looking over the summary result, we notice these details:

- As you can see from the summary, we have 48,842 rows and 115 columns
- Also, we have listed the common items of the White race
- There are a number of descriptors, such as age=Young

Finding frequent items in a dataset

Given a dataset, mine the frequent itemsets present using the following code:

```
> data("Adult")
> itemsets <- eclat(Adult)
parameter specification:
 tidLists support minlenmaxlen               target    ext
    FALSE      0.1        1       10 frequent itemsets FALSE
algorithmic control:
 sparse sort verbose
        7   -2     TRUE
eclat - find frequent item sets with the eclat algorithm
version 2.6 (2004.08.16)         (c) 2002-2004    Christian Borgelt
createitemset ...
set transactions ...[115 item(s), 48842 transaction(s)] done [0.03s].
sorting and recoding items ... [31 item(s)] done [0.00s].
creating bit matrix ... [31 row(s), 48842 column(s)] done [0.02s].
writing  ... [2616 set(s)] done [0.00s].
Creating S4 object   ... done [0.00s].
```

The default values have discovered 2,600 frequent sets. If we look for the top-five sets, we will see the following output:

```
> itemsets.sorted <- sort(itemsets)
> itemsets.sorted[1:5]
  items                              support
1 {capital-loss=None}                0.9532779
2 {capital-gain=None}                0.9173867
3 {native-country=United-States}     0.8974243
4 {capital-gain=None,
   capital-loss=None}                0.8706646
5 {race=White}                       0.8550428
```

Here are the observations made on the preceding output:

- Most of the people in the census data did not claim a capital loss or a capital gain (this kind of financial tax event will not be a normal condition)
- Most of the people are from the US
- Most of the people are of the white race

An example focusing on highest frequency

To further prove out the data, we can narrow down to the highest frequency occurring in the dataset (I did this by adjusting the minlen parameter until I ended up with just one set):

```
> itemsets <- eclat(Adult, parameter=list(minlen=9))
> inspect(itemsets)
  items                              support
1 {age=Middle-aged,
   workclass=Private,
   marital-status=Married-civ-spouse,
   relationship=Husband,
   race=White,
   sex=Male,
   capital-gain=None,
   capital-loss=None,
   native-country=United-States}     0.1056673
```

As expected, we have a married, native US, working male filling out the census data form.

arulesNBMiner

In R, `arulesNBMiner` is a package that will look for the co-occurrence of two or more items of a set. The underlying model, the negative binomial model, allows highly skewed frequency distributions that would have otherwise made it difficult to determine a minimum itemset size. We are looking for frequent itemsets in the larger dataset being mined. When deciding to use `arulesNBMiner`, you should have some indication that frequency of itemsets is occurring in subsets of the data.

Usage

`arulesNBMiner` is implemented as a package that must be installed into your R programming environment. A random dataset that can be used to learn how to use the tool is included with the model/function, as shown here:

```
> results <-NBMiner(data, parameter, control = NULL)
```

The various parameters of the `NBMiner` function are explained in the following table:

Parameter	Description
data	This is the data matrix that will be analyzed.
parameter	This is the list of parameters (automatically converted to object of type `NBMinerParameters`).
control	This is the list of controls to apply (automatically converted to `NBMinerControl`). Currently, only the `verbose` and `debug` logicals are available.

`NBMinerParameters` is the parameter block that is used to call `NBMiner`. It is constructed as follows:

```
NBMinerParameters(data, trim = 0.01, pi = 0.99,
    theta = 0.5, minlen = 1, maxlen = 5, rules = FALSE,
    plot = FALSE, verbose = FALSE, getdata = FALSE)
```

The values of `NBMinerParameters` are as follows:

Parameter	Description
data	These are the transactions
trim	This is the fraction of incidences that will be trimmed off the tail of the frequency distribution of the data
pi	This is the precision threshold π
theta	This is the pruning parameter θ

Parameter	Description
`minlen`	This is the minimum number of items found in the itemsets (default value is 1)
`maxlen`	This is the maximum number of items found in the itemsets (default value is 5)
`rules`	This contains a Boolean value to determine whether to mine NB-precise rules instead of NB-frequent itemsets
`plot`	This contains a Boolean value to determine whether to plot the model
`verbose`	This verbose output is used for the estimation procedure
`getdata`	This is used to get the observed and estimated counts also

The `Agrawal` data in the package is available directly. Note that the `Agrawal` data was synthetically generated specifically in order to gather transactions. The code is as follows:

```
> data(Agrawal)
> summary(Agrawal.db)

transactions as itemMatrix in sparse format with
 20000 rows (elements/itemsets/transactions) and
 1000 columns (items) and a density of 0.00997795

most frequent items:
item540 item155 item803 item741 item399 (Other)
   1848    1477    1332    1295    1264  192343
element (itemset/transaction) length distribution:
sizes
   1    2    3    4    5    6    7    8    9   10   11   12   13
  15   88  204  413  737 1233 1802 2217 2452 2444 2304 1858 1492
  14   15   16   17   18   19   20   21   22   23   24   25
1072  706  431  233  138   83   46   19   10    1    1    1

   Min. 1st Qu.  Median    Mean 3rd Qu.    Max.
  1.000   8.000  10.000   9.978  12.000  25.000

includes extended item information - examples:
  labels
1   item1
2   item2
3   item3

includes extended transaction information - examples:
  transactionID
```

```
1          trans1
2          trans2
3          trans3
> summary(Agrawal.pat)
set of 2000 itemsets

most frequent items:
item399 item475 item756 item594 item293 (Other)
     29      29      29      28      26    3960
element (itemset/transaction) length distribution:sizes
   1    2    3    4    5    6
 702 733 385 134   34   12
    Min. 1st Qu.  Median   Mean 3rd Qu.    Max.
    1.00    1.00    2.00   2.05    3.00    6.00

summary of quality measures:
pWeightspCorrupts
Min.:2.100e-08   Min.   :0.0000
 1st Qu.:1.426e-04   1st Qu.:0.2885
 Median :3.431e-04   Median :0.5129
 Mean   :5.000e-04   Mean   :0.5061
 3rd Qu.:6.861e-04   3rd Qu.:0.7232
 Max.   :3.898e-03   Max.   :1.0000

includes transaction ID lists: FALSE
```

Here are the observations made on the preceding output:

- There are 20,000 rows of 1,000 columns
- All columns are named like item399, item475, and so on
- There are 2,000 itemsets skewed towards low numbers of transactions (for example there are 702 of size 1, 733 of size 2, and so on)

Mining the Agrawal data for frequent sets

If we take the Agrawal data and use it in an example, we get the following output:

```
> mynbparameters <- NBMinerParameters(Agrawal.db)
> mynbminer <- NBMiner(Agrawal.db, parameter = mynbparameters)
> summary(mynbminer)
set of 3332 itemsets

most frequent items:
item540 item615 item258 item594 item293 (Other)
```

```
    69      57      55      50      46    6813

element (itemset/transaction) length distribution:sizes
   1    2    3    4    5
1000 1287  725  259   61

   Min. 1st Qu.  Median   Mean 3rd Qu.    Max.
  1.000   1.000   2.000  2.128   3.000   5.000

summary of quality measures:
  precision
 Min.:0.9901
 1st Qu.:1.0000
 Median :1.0000
 Mean   :0.9997
 3rd Qu.:1.0000
 Max.   :1.0000
```

Here are the observations made on the preceding output:

- Items are approximately evenly distributed
- There is a large skew towards itemset length of 1 or 2

Apriori

Apriori is a class algorithm that helps to learn association rules. It works against transactions. The algorithm attempts to find subsets that are common within a dataset. A minimum threshold must be met in order for the association to be confirmed.

The concept of support and confidence for `apriori` is of particular interest. The `apriori` method will return associations of interest from your dataset, such as X when we have Y. Support is the percent of transactions containing X and Y. Confidence is the percentage of transactions that contain X and also contain Y. The default values are 10 percent for support and 80 percent for confidence.

Usage

The `apriori` method can be used as follows:

```
apriori(data, parameter = NULL, appearance = NULL, control = NULL)
```

The various parameters of the `apriori` function are explained in the following table:

Parameter	Description
data	This is the dataset to draw upon.
parameter	This is the list of parameters to control behavior of the process. The default value for support is 0.1, for confidence it's 0.8, and for maxlen it's 10.
appearance	This controls which data values are used.
control	This controls the performance of the algorithm, specifically sorting.

Evaluating associations in a shopping basket

We are looking for associations among the items purchased in a typical shopping basket at the food market. For this, we will perform the following steps:

1. Load the `arules` package as follows:

```
> install.packages("arules")
> library(arules)
```

2. Load our transactions, that is, the Belgian grocery retail data:

```
> tr <- read.transactions("http://fimi.ua.ac.be/data/retail.dat",
format="basket")
```

3. Get an overview of what the data looks like:

```
> summary(tr)

transactions as itemMatrix in sparse format with
 88162 rows (elements/itemsets/transactions) and
 16470 columns (items) and a density of 0.0006257289

most frequent items:
     39      48      38      32      41 (Other)
  50675   42135   15596   15167   14945  770058

element (itemset/transaction) length distribution:
sizes
    1    2    3    4    5    6    7    8    9   10   11   12   13
 3016 5516 6919 7210 6814 6163 5746 5143 4660 4086 3751 3285 2866
   14   15   16   17   18   19   20   21   22   23   24   25   26
 2620 2310 2115 1874 1645 1469 1290 1205  981  887  819  684  586
   27   28   29   30   31   32   33   34   35   36   37   38   39
  582  472  480  355  310  303  272  234  194  136  153  123  115
   40   41   42   43   44   45   46   47   48   49   50   51   52
  112   76   66   71   60   50   44   37   37   33   22   24   21
```

53	54	55	56	57	58	59	60	61	62	63	64	65
21	10	11	10	9	11	4	9	7	4	5	2	2
66	67	68	71	73	74	76						
5	3	3	1	1	1	1						

```
   Min. 1st Qu.  Median   Mean 3rd Qu.   Max.
   1.00    4.00    8.00  10.31   14.00  76.00

includes extended item information - examples:
   labels
1       0
2       1
3      10
```

The following are the observations made on the preceding output:

- We have 80,000 baskets of 16,000 items
- A couple of items are very popular (50,000 of item 39)

4. Let's look at the top frequency items:

```
> itemFrequencyPlot(tr, support=0.1)
```

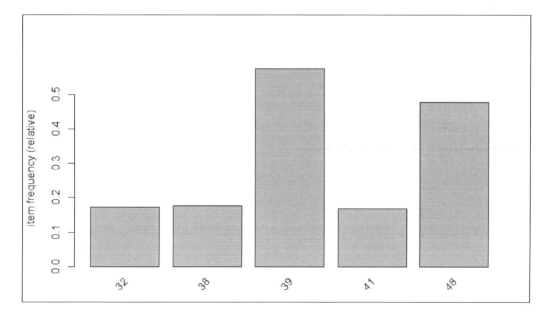

Again, we see a few items with frequency that is higher than normal.

5. Now, build some rules on the associations in place:

```
> rules <- apriori(tr, parameter=list(supp=0.5,conf=0.5))

parameter specification:
confidenceminvalsmaxaremavaloriginalSupport support minlen
        0.5    0.1    1 none FALSE              TRUE     0.5        1
 maxlen target    ext
     10   rules FALSE

algorithmic control:
 filter tree heap memopt load sort verbose
    0.1 TRUE TRUE  FALSE TRUE    2     TRUE

apriori - find association rules with the apriori algorithm
version 4.21 (2004.05.09)        (c) 1996-2004    Christian Borgelt
set item appearances ...[0 item(s)] done [0.00s].
set transactions ...[16470 item(s), 88162 transaction(s)] done
[0.13s].
sorting and recoding items ... [1 item(s)] done [0.01s].
creating transaction tree ... done [0.02s].
checking subsets of size 1 done [0.00s].
writing ... [1 rule(s)] done [0.00s].
creating S4 object  ... done [0.01s].
```

6. After that, we end up with one rule. Look at a summary of the rule(s):

```
> summary(rules)

set of 1 rules

rule length distribution (lhs + rhs):sizes
1
1

     Min. 1st Qu.  Median    Mean 3rd Qu.    Max.
        1       1       1       1       1       1

summary of quality measures:
     support          confidence           lift
 Min.:0.5748    Min.    :0.5748    Min.    :1
 1st Qu.:0.5748    1st Qu.:0.5748    1st Qu.:1
 Median :0.5748    Median :0.5748    Median :1
 Mean    :0.5748    Mean    :0.5748    Mean    :1
```

```
3rd Qu.:0.5748    3rd Qu.:0.5748    3rd Qu.:1
Max.   :0.5748    Max.   :0.5748    Max.   :1

mining info:
datantransactions support confidence
   tr          88162      0.5          0.5
```

The rule has strong support and weak confidence.

7. Let's check what the rule is:

```
> inspect(rules)
lhsrhs     support confidence lift
1 {}  => {39} 0.5747941  0.5747941    1
```

As we would have guessed, most people have item 39 in their basket.

8. We can look for further information on the rule to get a full idea of its impact:

```
> interestMeasure(rules, c("support", "chiSquare", "confidence",
"conviction", "cosine", "leverage", "lift", "oddsRatio"), tr)
          sapply(method, FUN = function(m) interestMeasure(x, m,
transactions, reuse, ...))
support                     0.5747941
chiSquareNaN
confidence                  0.5747941
conviction                  1.0000000
cosine                      0.7581518
leverage                    0.0000000
lift                        1.0000000
oddsRatioNaN
```

These measures are showing complete confidence in the one rule that was derived.

Determining sequences using TraMineR

The TraMineR package is to mine and visualize sequences. The idea is to discover sequences. Graphical devices that produce plots for sequence distribution, sequence frequency, turbulence, and much more are built into the package. Again, there are many naturally occurring items where the data has a repeated sequence, for example, there are many social science venues where the data has naturally recurring items.

In this document, I will walk you through `TraMineR` to produce a series of sequence discovery tools. Which of these tools you select in your mining operation will be up to you.

The `TraMineR` package comes with a couple of built-in datasets for your use:

Dataset	Description
actcal	This dataset contains the individual monthly activity statuses from the year 2000
biofam	This dataset contains the individual family life states between ages 15 and 30
mvad	This dataset contains the individual monthly activity status data

Usage

The `seqdef` function is used to determine the sequences present in your data:

```
seqdef(data, var=NULL, informat="STS", stsep=NULL,
   alphabet=NULL, states=NULL, id=NULL, weights=NULL,
   start=1, left=NA, right="DEL", gaps=NA,
   missing=NA, void="%", nr="*", cnames=NULL,
   xtstep=1, cpal=NULL, missing.color="darkgrey",
   labels=NULL, ...)
```

The various parameters of the `seqdef` function are explained in the following table:

Parameter	Description
data	This is your matrix.
var	This will have a list of columns containing the sequences, or NULL meaning all columns are present.
informat	This contains the format of the original data. It could be any of the following formats: • STS • SPS • SPELL
stsep	This is the separator.
alphabet	This is the list of all possible states.
states	This contains the short state labels.

Determining sequences in training and careers

In this example, we will look at the *sequence* of events in people's lives as they progress from training to becoming fully employed. We are expecting to see a progression from unemployed and untrained to becoming trained, and finally moving to full-time employment.

There are several useful functions in the TraMineR package for sequence analysis. We use seqdef to create a sequence data object for further use by other functions. This is used to set up or hold parameters for the other methods as follows:

```
seqdef(data, var=NULL, informat="STS", stsep=NULL,
    alphabet=NULL, states=NULL, id=NULL, weights=NULL, start=1,
    left=NA, right="DEL", gaps=NA, missing=NA, void="%", nr="*",
    cnames=NULL, xtstep=1, cpal=NULL, missing.color="darkgrey",
    labels=NULL, ...)
```

Most of the arguments can be used with defaults.

As you can see, the seqdata object is the first argument to the plot functions. Instead of xxx, you will use the actual desired plot function, such as seqiplot used in the following code:

```
seqXXXplot(seqdata, group=NULL, type="i", title=NULL,
  cpal=NULL, missing.color=NULL,
  ylab=NULL, yaxis=TRUE, axes="all", xtlab=NULL, cex.plot=1,
  withlegend="auto", ltext=NULL, cex.legend=1,
  use.layout=(!is.null(group) | withlegend!=FALSE),
  legend.prop=NA, rows=NA, cols=NA, ...)
```

Most of the arguments are standard graphical enhancements you might want in a plot; for example, ylab is the label for the *y* axis.

First, we have to get TraMineR loaded into your environment using the following code:

```
> install.packages("TraMineR")
> library ("TraMineR")
```

We will use the inbuilt mvad dataset of the TraMineR package. The mvad dataset tracks 700 individuals in the 1990s as they progress from training to employment. We can use the mvad dataset as follows:

```
> data(mvad)
```

A summary of the data is as follows:

```
> summary(mvad)
```

```
       id              weight          male      catholic  Belfast
 Min.:   1.0   Min.:0.1300    no :342    no :368   no :624
 1st Qu.:178.8   1st Qu.:0.4500   yes:370   yes:344   yes: 88
 Median :356.5   Median :0.6900
 Mean    :356.5   Mean    :0.9994
 3rd Qu.:534.2   3rd Qu.:1.0700
 Max.    :712.0   Max.    :4.4600


 N.EasternSouthern  S.Eastern Western   Grammar   funemp
 no :503    no :497   no :629   no :595   no :583   no :595
 yes:209   yes:215   yes: 83   yes:117   yes:129   yes:117


 gcse5eqfmprlivboth              Jul.93
 no :452    no :537   no :261   school     :135
 yes:260   yes:175   yes:451   FE         : 97
                               employment :173
                               training   :122
                               joblessness:185
                               HE         :  0
```

We can see standard identifiers for weight, sex, religion, and so on.

Picking off the sequence data (we are using columns 17 through 86, as they apply to that person's *state* at the different points of the data survey) and applying that part of the data to the sequence determiner function, we can see the following:

```
> myseq <- seqdef(mvad, 17:86)

 [>] 6 distinct states appear in the data:
     1 = employment
     2 = FE
     3 = HE
     4 = joblessness
     5 = school
     6 = training
 [>] state coding:
       [alphabet]  [label]     [long label]
 1   employmentemploymentemployment
 2   FEFEFE
 3   HEHEHE
 4   joblessnessjoblessnessjoblessness
```

```
5   schoolschoolschool
6   trainingtrainingtraining
 [>] 712 sequences in the data set
 [>] min/max sequence length: 70/70
```

This appears to be correct; we are seeing the states (`joblessness`, `school`, `training`, and `employment`) that we expected from the raw sequence data.

There are several built-in plots that we can use to visualize the sequences that were determined. They are as follows:

- `seqiplot`: This is the index plot
- `seqfplot`: This is the frequency plot
- `seqdplot`: This is the distribution plot

Let's try the index plot:

```
> seqiplot(myseq)
```

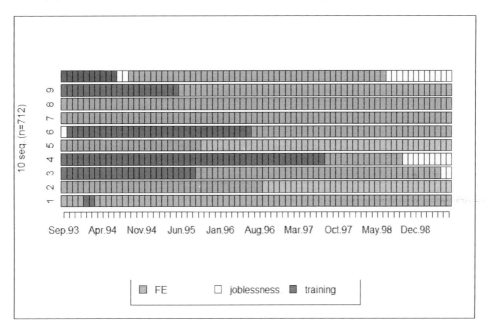

You can see the definite transitions between states of the individuals over time. It makes sense that something like training occurs over several contiguous months. You should verify that the display corresponds with your understanding of your sequence data.

Now, let's try the frequency plot:

```
> seqfplot(myseq)
```

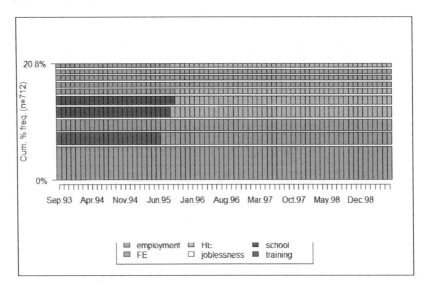

Now, we see the frequency of the sequences over time. Again, it would make sense that we would see sets of people with the same sequences, such as a period of training followed by a period of employment.

Now, we will try the distribution plot:

```
> seqdplot(myseq)
```

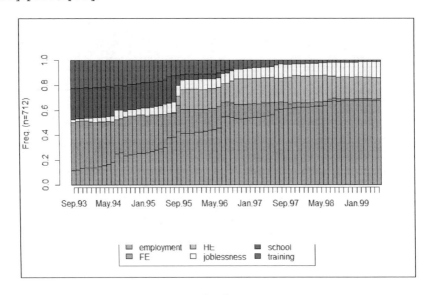

Here, we see the distribution of sequence states over time. On average, people went through school or training and started working. Makes sense!

We can look at the entropy of the sequences using the following command:

```
> seqHtplot(myseq)
```

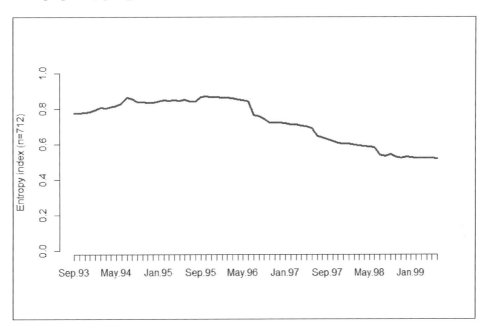

There is a slight increase followed by a marked decline in entropy over time. This corresponds to different people making different choices initially (many states), such as school or training, and then moving into the workforce with employment (one state).

An interesting idea is *turbulence* of the data. **Turbulence** shows how many different subsequent sequences can be derived from a specific sequence instance that we see in the data. We can visualize turbulence with the seqST function. The seqST function takes the sequence data as its argument and returns turbulence data. Let's continue with our example:

```
> myturbulence <- seqSt(myseq)
> hist(myturbulence)
```

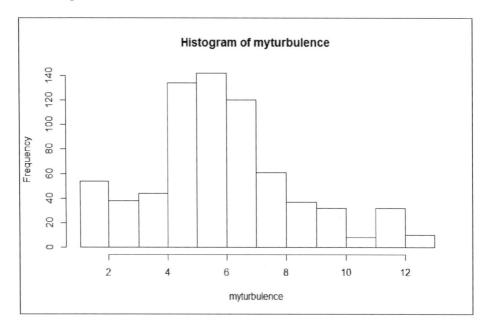

We see an almost standard distribution with a long tail. Most of the states fall into a handful of subsequent states and a few outliers with many or few states.

Similarities in the sequence

The TraMineR package also has the functionality to determine metrics about sequences, such as dissimilarities between different sequences:

- **Longest common prefix (LCP)**: We can compare the longest sequence prefixes that are the same to determine similarity
- **Longest common subsequence (LCS)**: We can look at the longest subsequence, internal to the sequences, that is the same between two sequences for similarity as well
- **Optimal matching (OM) distance**: This is the optimal edit distance for cost in terms of inserts and deletes to produce one sequence from another

All of these functionalities are available using the `seqdist` function in `TraMineR`.

Sequence metrics

We can compute the LCP with `seqdist`.

Usage

The `seqdist` function can be used as follows:

```
seqdist(seqdata, method, refseq=NULL, norm=FALSE,
    indel=1, sm=NA, with.missing=FALSE, full.matrix=TRUE)
```

The various parameters of the `seqdist` function are explained in the following table:

Parameter	Description
`seqdata`	This is the state sequence (defined using `seqdef`)
`method`	This contains the LCP method to be used
`refseq`	This is the optional reference sequence
`norm`	This will normalize the distances
`indl`	This is only used for OM
`sm`	This is the substitution matrix (ignored for LCP)
`with.missing`	This value is TRUE if missing gaps are present
`full.matrix`	If this value is TRUE, a full matrix is returned

Example

Let's see an example of the usage of the `seqdist` function:

1. Use the `famform` sequence data that is built into the package:

   ```
   > data(famform)
   ```

2. Define the sequence object we can use:

   ```
   > seq <- seqdef(famform)
    [>] found missing values ('NA') in sequence data
    [>] preparing 5 sequences
    [>] coding void elements with '%' and missing values with '*'
    [>] 5 distinct states appear in the data:
       1 = M
       2 = MC
       3 = S
       4 = SC
       5 = U
   ```

```
    [>] state coding:
         [alphabet]   [label]   [long label]
1   MMM
2   MCMCMC
3   SSS
4   SCSCSC
5   UUU
    [>] 5 sequences in the data set
    [>] min/max sequence length: 2/5
> seq
       Sequence
[1]  S-U
[2]  S-U-M
[3]  S-U-M-MC
[4]  S-U-M-MC-SC
[5]  U-M-MC
```

3. Determine the LCP that is using sequence 3 and 4:

    ```
    > seqLLCP(seq[3,],seq[4,])
    [1] 4
    ```

    We get four prefix matches (S-U-M-MC compared to S-U-M-MC-SC)

4. We can compute the LCS metric directly:

    ```
    > seqLLCS(seq[1,],seq[2,])
    [1] 2
    ```

    We find the common sequence at 2.

5. The OMD is also determined directly as follows:

    ```
    > cost <- seqsubm(seq, method="CONSTANT", cval=2)
     [>] creating 5x5 substitution-cost matrix using 2 as constant
    value
    > cost
          M-> MC-> S-> SC-> U->
    M->    0    2   2    2    2
    MC->   2    0   2    2    2
    S->    2    2   0    2    2
    SC->   2    2   2    0    2
    U->    2    2   2    2    0
    ```

    The OMD is just 2 (these are very minor sequences that are used to show the concepts).

Questions

Factual

- How will you exclude white people from the `eclat` results?
- Describe the different transitions that occur in the sequence plots.
- In the `TraMineRmvad` data summary, there are marked differences in regional responses. Can you guess why?

When, how, and why?

- Describe what is going on with the few outliers in `seqiplot`. There are several data points that don't seem to fit.
- What would be going on in the data presented in `seqHtplot` when the line curves upward?
- How will you apply the sequence *finding* routines discussed?

Challenges

- Determine what the item numbers represent in the market basket data.
- The `TraMineR` package includes much more than what was covered in this chapter. You could investigate the additional functionality further.

Summary

In this chapter, we discussed different methods of determining patterns in data. We found patterns in a dataset using the `eclat` function looking for similar patterns in a population. We used a `TraMineR` to find frequent sets of items in a market basket. We used `apriori` rules to determine associations among items in a market basket. We used `TraMineR` to determine sequences of career transition among adults and visualized the same with extensive graphics features available for sequence data. Finally, we examined the similarities and differences between the sequences using `seqdist`.

In the next chapter, we will cover text mining or examining datasets that are text-based, rather than numerical or categorical.

3
Text Mining

A large amount of data available is in the form of text, and it is unstructured, massive, and of tremendous variety. In this chapter, we will have a look at the tools available in R to extract useful information from text.

This chapter describes different ways of mining text. We will cover the following topics:

- Examining the text in various ways
    - Converting text to lowercase
    - Removing punctuation
    - Removing numbers
    - Removing URLs
    - Removing stop words
    - Using the stems of words rather than instances
    - Building a document matrix delineating uses

- XML processing, both orthogonal and of varying degrees
- Examples

Packages

While the standard R system has a number of features and functions available, one of the better aspects of R is the use of packages to add functionalities. A package contains a number of functions (and sometimes sample data) that can be used to solve a particular problem in R. Packages are developed by interested groups for the general good of all R developers. In this chapter, we will be using the following packages:

- `tm`: This contains text mining tools
- `XML`: This contains XML processing tools

Text processing

R has built-in functions for manipulating text. These include adjustments to the text to make it more analyzable (such as using word stems or removing punctuation) and developing a document matrix showing usage of words throughout a document. Once these steps are done, we can then submit our documents to analysis and clustering.

Example

In this example, we will perform the following steps:

1. We will take an HTML document from the Internet.
2. We will clean up the document using text processing functions.
3. Then, we will generate a document matrix.
4. Finally, we will analyze the document matrix.

I think it is easiest to walk through an example directly using the Corpus tools. In this case, we will use a recent US Federal Treasury Open Market Committee statement looking for interesting phrases.

I used Barack Obama's latest State of the Union address (which can be found at http://www.whitehouse.gov/the-press-office/2014/01/28/president-barack-obamas-state-union-address) and copied it into a local text file that we read with R:

```
> path <- "state-of-the-union.txt"
```

For processing in R, we need to break this up into chunks or lines using the following code:

```
> install.packages("tm")
> library(tm)
> text <- readLines(path,encoding="UTF-8")
```

The `text` variable is an array of the lines of the statement. There are a number of text functions available that can operate directly on the text in the result, such as converting all the text to lowercase. Some of the common operations include:

- **Convert to lowercase**: This operation allows for cleaner comparisons.
- **Remove punctuation**: This operation is performed to concentrate on the text involved.
- **Remove numbers**: This operation is used to concentrate on the text involved.
- **Remove URLs**: This operation is used to avoid the complication of words appearing in the URLs.
- **Adjust stop words list**: This operation is especially useful when working with an industry-specific text.
- **Work with word stems**: This operation lets you adjust the text so that only the word stems appear. This helps to concentrate the focus on the true terms involved in your text rather than the various forms that appear.

R uses a corpus to manipulate text. A corpus can be created from several sources, including a `VectorSource` (text stream). The following code converts the raw text into a corpus for further processing in R:

```
> vs <- VectorSource(text)
> elem <- getElem(stepNext(vs))
> result <- readPlain(elem, "en", "id1")
> txt <- Corpus(vs)
```

Creating a corpus

We need to convert these lines into a corpus for use within R. A **corpus** is a collection of texts, usually by an author or on a subject. R programming uses the term to encompass a set of texts that you consider to be related.

Now, the text data is in a format that can be readily handled by the text mining package. We can perform the functions on the text mentioned earlier.

Converting text to lowercase

In this section, we will use the document in its R corpus format and convert all of the text to lowercase. This will help to flatten all references to the same usage. The code is as follows:

```
> txtlc <- tm_map(txt, tolower)
> inspect(txt[1])
<<VCorpus (documents: 1, metadata (corpus/indexed): 0/0)>>
[[1]]
```

```
<<PlainTextDocument (metadata: 7)>>
Mr. Speaker, Mr. Vice President, Members of Congress, my fellow
Americans:
> inspect(txtlc[1])
<<VCorpus (documents: 1, metadata (corpus/indexed): 0/0)>>
[[1]]
[1] mr. speaker, mr. vice president, members of congress, my fellow
americans:
```

Removing punctuation

Similarly, we can remove all the punctuation from a corpus. This is a common step
when analyzing text to avoid cases where the same word has different punctuation
applied next to it, but is the same word. The code is as follows:

```
> txtnp <- tm_map(txt, removePunctuation)
> inspect(txt[1])
<<VCorpus (documents: 1, metadata (corpus/indexed): 0/0)>>
[[1]]
<<PlainTextDocument (metadata: 7)>>
Mr. Speaker, Mr. Vice President, Members of Congress, my fellow
Americans:
> inspect(txtnp[1])
<<VCorpus (documents: 1, metadata (corpus/indexed): 0/0)>>
[[1]]
<<PlainTextDocument (metadata: 7)>>
Mr Speaker Mr Vice President Members of Congress my fellow Americans
```

Removing numbers

We can remove all the numbers from a corpus. In most cases, specific numbers in
text are not comparable. There is no context to apply to decide whether a number
(by itself) is being used in the same manner from one instance to another. The code
is as follows:

```
> txtnn <- tm_map(txt, removeNumbers)
> inspect(txt[49])
<<VCorpus (documents: 1, metadata (corpus/indexed): 0/0)>>
[[1]]
<<PlainTextDocument (metadata: 7)>>
Of course, to reach millions more, Congress needs to get on board.
Today, the federal minimum wage is worth about twenty percent
less than it was when Ronald Reagan first stood here.  Tom Harkin
and George Miller have a bill to fix that by lifting the minimum
wage to $10.10.  This will help families.  It will give businesses
customers with more money to spend.  It doesn<U+0092>t involve any
new bureaucratic program.  So join the rest of the country.  Say yes.
Give America a raise.
```

```
> inspect(txtnn[49])
<<VCorpus (documents: 1, metadata (corpus/indexed): 0/0)>>
[[1]]
<<PlainTextDocument (metadata: 7)>>
Of course, to reach millions more, Congress needs to get on board.
Today, the federal minimum wage is worth about twenty percent less
than it was when Ronald Reagan first stood here.  Tom Harkin and
George Miller have a bill to fix that by lifting the minimum wage
to $..  This will help families.  It will give businesses customers
with more money to spend.  It doesn<U+393C><U+3E32>t involve any new
bureaucratic program.  So join the rest of the country.  Say yes.
Give America a raise.
```

Removing words

There is a function available to remove *stop words* from a corpus. This is typically used to remove all the short, English words that bear no additional meaning to your analysis. However, stop words exist in all languages. Stop words are normally removed so that you end up with words of particular meaning from the speaker/author. Stop words are words like "the" and "and"—while necessary, they add no value to your context. You can adjust the standard stop words for the language of interest by just adding them to the collection. The code is as follows:

```
> txtns <- tm_map(txt[1], removeWords, stopwords("english"))
> inspect(txtns)
<<VCorpus (documents: 1, metadata (corpus/indexed): 0/0)>>
[[1]]
<<PlainTextDocument (metadata: 7)>>
Mr. Speaker, Mr. Vice President, Members  Congress,  fellow Americans:
> inspect(txt[1])
<<VCorpus (documents: 1, metadata (corpus/indexed): 0/0)>>
[[1]]
<<PlainTextDocument (metadata: 7)>>
Mr. Speaker, Mr. Vice President, Members of Congress, my fellow
Americans:
```

Removing whitespaces

I think removing whitespaces has little to do with standard text mining; the functions that you are employing will disregard whitespace already. This function provides a way to clean up your intermediary results for better presentation. The code is as follows:

```
> txtnw <- tm_map(txt[30], stripWhitespace)
> inspect(txtnw)
<<VCorpus (documents: 1, metadata (corpus/indexed): 0/0)>>
[[1]]
```

```
<<PlainTextDocument (metadata: 7)>>
The ideas I<U+393C><U+3E32>ve outlined so far can speed up growth and
create more jobs. But in this rapidly-changing economy, we have to
make sure that every American has the skills to fill those jobs.
> inspect(txt[30])
<<VCorpus (documents: 1, metadata (corpus/indexed): 0/0)>>
[[1]]
<<PlainTextDocument (metadata: 7)>>
The ideas I<U+0092>ve outlined so far can speed up growth and create
more jobs.  But in this rapidly-changing economy, we have to make sure
that every American has the skills to fill those jobs.
```

Note that `stripWhitespace` also collapsed the punctuation from two extended characters to one.

Word stems

We can adjust the corpus to use only word stems. A **word stem** is the base or root of a word, regardless of the current inflection or usage. For example, the words "wait", "waiting", "waits", and "waited" all have the same stem:"wait". This allows cleaner comparison of the text with the different radicals that may appear in usage.

In this process, we will perform the following steps:

1. We will need a dictionary for the process to use as a basis for the translation. We will use the original corpus as the dictionary.

2. Create a corpus of the word stem bases.

3. Complete the corpus from the stem bases and the dictionary we have stored.

The code is as follows:

```
> inspect(txt[86])
<<VCorpus (documents: 1, metadata (corpus/indexed): 0/0)>>
[[1]]
<<PlainTextDocument (metadata: 7)>>
My fellow Americans, men and women like Cory remind us that America
has never come easy.  Our freedom, our democracy, has never been
easy.  Sometimes we stumble; we make mistakes; we get frustrated
or discouraged.  But for more than two hundred years, we have put
those things aside and placed our collective shoulder to the wheel
of progress <U+0096> to create and build and expand the possibilities
of individual achievement; to free other nations from tyranny and
fear; to promote justice, and fairness, and equality under the law,
so that the words set to paper by our founders are made real for every
citizen.  The America we want for our kids <U+0096> a rising America
where honest work is plentiful and communities are strong; where
prosperity is widely shared and opportunity for all lets us go as far
```

as our dreams and toil will take us <U+0096> none of it is easy. But
if we work together; if we summon what is best in us, with our feet
planted firmly in today but our eyes cast towards tomorrow <U+0096> I
know it<U+0092>s within our reach.

```
> txtstem <- tm_map(txt, stemDocument)
> inspect(txtstem[86])
<<VCorpus (documents: 1, metadata (corpus/indexed): 0/0)>>
[[1]]
<<PlainTextDocument (metadata: 7)>>
```
My fellow Americans, men and women like Cori remind us that America
has never come easy. Our freedom, our democracy, has never been
easy. Sometim we stumble; we make mistakes; we get frustrat or
discouraged. But for more than two hundr years, we have put those
thing asid and place our collect shoulder to the wheel of progress
<U+393C><U+3E36> to creat and build and expand the possibl of individu
achievement; to free other nation from tyranni and fear; to promot
justice, and fairness, and equal under the law, so that the word set
to paper by our founder are made real for everi citizen. The America
we want for our kid <U+393C><U+3E36> a rise America where honest work
is plenti and communiti are strong; where prosper is wide share and
opportun for all let us go as far as our dream and toil will take us
<U+393C><U+3E36> none of it is easy. But if we work together; if we
summon what is best in us, with our feet plant firm in today but our
eye cast toward tomorrow <U+393C><U+3E36> I know it<U+393C><U+3E32>
within our reach
```
> txtcomplete <- tm_map(txtstem, stemCompletion, dictionary=txt)
> inspect(txtcomplete[86])
```

I have highlighted some of the words that have changed to stems in the
following output:

```
<<VCorpus (documents: 1, metadata (corpus/indexed): 0/0)>>
[[1]]
```
My fellow Americans, men and women like Cori remind us that America
has never come easy. Our freedom, our democracy, has never been easy.
Sometim we stumble; we make mistakes; we get **frustrat** or discouraged.
But for more than two **hundr** years, we have put those **thing asid** and
place our collect shoulder to the wheel of progress to creat and
build and expand the possibl of individu achievement; to free other
nation from tyranni and fear; to promot justice, and fairness, and
equal under the law, so that the word set to paper by our founder
are made real for everi citizen. The America we want for our kid a
rise America where honest work is plenti and communiti are strong;
where prosper is wide share and opportun for all let us go as far as
our dream and toil will take us none of it is easy. But if we work
together; if we summon what is best in us, with our feet plant firm
in today but our eye cast toward tomorrow I know it within our reach
```
content
<NA>
meta
```

I understand that this process produces more readily comparable results. However, the use of stemmed words in a document appears alien when you read the sentences. It will probably be useless to produce a stemmed document for display purposes.

Document term matrix

One of the more interesting tools is the document term matrix. A document term matrix describes the frequency of terms that occur in a collection of documents. So, for each document, it contains the number of times a term occurs within that document. In our case, it contains the frequency of each of the keywords found and their occurrence in each of the documents (or lines/paragraphs).

Once we have a document term matrix, we can then more easily apply statistical analysis to the text that we are analyzing. The document term matrix walks through the text and counts the usage of terms throughout and serves as a holder for these counts. The code is as follows::

```
> dtm <- DocumentTermMatrix(txt)
> dtm
<<DocumentTermMatrix (documents: 87, terms: 2130)>>
Non-/sparse entries: 4615/180695
Sparsity           : 98%
Maximal term length: 19
Weighting          : term frequency (tf)
```

As you look through the matrix, you can see a lot of meaningless words as well, such as "the." You can remove these from the count by transforming the initial dataset.

First, we create a corpus of the text lines we loaded. Then, we can run a transformation function to remove unwanted words from a list from the corpus. As you can tell from the syntax, there are a number of transformations that can be applied to your data:

```
> txt <- tm_map(txt, removeWords, stopwords("English"))
```

We can also reduce the sparsity of the matrix by using the tm package function to remove sparse terms. Notice that we went from 4,600 nonsparse terms down to 1,700. This is a drastic reduction to have an effect. The reduction in sparse entries from 180,000 to 9,000 is also very significant! The code for the tm package function is as follows:

```
> dtm2 <- removeSparseTerms(dtm, 0.94)
> inspect(dtm2)
<<DocumentTermMatrix (documents: 87, terms: 127)>>
Non-/sparse entries: 1719/9330
Sparsity           : 84%
Maximal term length: 11
```

```
Weighting          : term frequency (tf)
...
     Terms
Docs and any are because been believe build business businesses
   1   0   0   0       0    0       0     0        0          0
   2   1   0   0       0    0       0     0        0          0
   3   1   0   0       0    0       0     0        0          1
   4   1   0   0       0    0       0     0        0          0
   5   3   0   0       0    0       0     0        0          0
   6   0   0   0       0    0       0     0        0          0
   7   1   0   1       0    0       0     0        1          0
   8   1   1   0       0    0       1     0        0          0
   9   1   0   2       0    1       0     0        0          0
...
```

There are still several thousand nonsparse terms at work in the matrix. This is just a few of them. I think it is useful to look over the matrix to visually scan for unexpected cases of larger use. In many cases, some of the more frequent words may be surprising at first, but then upon contemplation they fit the context.

We can look for associations of different words as they appear, as shown in the following example:

```
> findAssocs(dtm, "work", 0.15)
           work
and        0.45
most       0.45
hard       0.41
want       0.41
future     0.39
but        0.38
are        0.36
the        0.35
who        0.35
help       0.33
years,     0.33
create     0.32
our        0.32
new        0.31
build      0.29
```

Looks like Obama wants us to work hard for our future.

Using VectorSource

Now that you have seen some of the functions of the `tm` package in action, we can examine their usage more closely. In R programming, when we are dealing with text, the text must have a source. A **source** is the raw text stream that we are analyzing. In this case, we will use a `VectorSource` instance that takes the text and aligns it into a vector (as in a math vector) of words that appear in the source. Once we have a `VectorSource`, it is used for further R processing:

```
VectorSource(x, encoding = "unknown")
```

Here, x is the vector and `encoding` stores the assumed encoding for input strings.

The `getElem` function establishes the source passed for further data access in R:

```
getElem(source)
```

The `stepNext` function updates the position of the source for further use:

```
stepNext(source)
```

A `Corpus` is a collection of data source that can be used for further processing:

```
Corpus(source)
```

A `DocumentTermMatrix` shows the usage of terms across a corpus:

```
dtm <- DocumentTermMatrix(x, control=)
```

The terms appearing in the preceding command are explained as follows:

- x: This is the corpus.
- control: This is the named list of control options. Some options are specific to further uses. The global options available are:
    - bounds: This is the range of corpus to be used
    - weighting: This has the weighting function to be used for the terms encountered

The `tm_map` function is an interface that is used to apply transformations to a corpus:

```
tm_map(x, FUN, ..., lazy=TRUE)
```

The terms appearing in the preceding command are explained as follows:

- x: This is the corpus to which the transformations will be applied
- FUN: This is the transformation to be applied
- lazy: If this is set as TRUE, it allows lazy data access to be performed

The `removeWords` function will remove the words provided from a text document:

```
removewords
```

The `stopWords` set is a list of common English stop words:

```
stopWords
```

The `removeSparseTerms` function is used to remove sparsely populated terms for a document matrix:

```
removeSparseTerms(x, sparse)
```

The terms appearing in the preceding command are explained as follows:

- `x`: This is the corpus.
- `sparse`: This contains the value for maximum sparsity to be allowed. It ranges from greater than 0 to less than 1.

The `findAssocs` function is used to find associations between words in a document matrix:

```
findAssocs(x, terms, corlimit)
```

The terms appearing in the preceding command are explained as follows:

- `x`: This is the corpus
- `terms`: These are the terms for which we have to find associations
- `corlimit`: This contains the lower correlation limits to explore

So, we took some raw text (pretty much straight from the Internet); cleaned up the usage, numbers, and punctuation; drew out the roots of the words; produced a vector of the uses; and performed some preliminary analysis in several fairly short, clear steps.

Text clusters

We can use the same clustering techniques that we saw in *Chapter 2, Data Mining Sequences*, against our text to look for relationships. Clustering is typically used in numerical analysis where we are trying to group together like observations based on commonality or *closeness* of the observation data points. In text analysis, we are repeating the same operation with clusters: trying to determine the relationships between word usage across a document.

We are using k-means clustering in this example. K-means clustering reduces the sum of squares differences between relationships and group/cluster words where the distances are minimized to the thresholds specified, in this case, the number of clusters specified.

We can implement k-means clustering as follows:

```
> library(stats)
> mymeans <- kmeans(dtm,5)
> mymeans
K-means clustering with 5 clusters of sizes 9, 33, 14, 21, 10

Cluster means:
        about      access        all   america\u0092samerica
1 0.11111111 0.22222222 0.55555556      0.00000000 0.55555556
2 0.06060606 0.06060606 0.09090909      0.03030303 0.09090909
3 0.14285714 0.00000000 0.28571429      0.21428571 0.28571429
4 0.09523810 0.09523810 0.19047619      0.04761905 0.23809524
5 0.10000000 0.00000000 0.30000000      0.10000000 0.10000000
americanamericans       and        any        are    because
1 0.3333333 0.0000000 7.888889 0.11111111 1.00000000 0.33333333
2 0.1212121 0.1818182 0.969697 0.03030303 0.03030303 0.09090909
3 0.2142857 0.5714286 3.642857 0.00000000 0.28571429 0.21428571
4 0.3809524 0.2857143 2.428571 0.04761905 0.47619048 0.19047619
5 0.2000000 0.2000000 3.500000 0.30000000 0.40000000 0.20000000


... (many more cluster displays)

Clustering vector:
  1  2  3  4  5  6  7  8  9 10 11 12 13 14 15 16 17 18 19 20 21 22
  2  2  2  2  4  2  4  2  4  4  4  2  3  3  1  4  2  2  3  5  4  5
 23 24 25 26 27 28 29 30 31 32 33 34 35 36 37 38 39 40 41 42 43 44
  4  2  5  3  5  1  1  2  4  3  2  2  4  3  2  2  1  2  4  4  3  4
 45 46 47 48 49 50 51 52 53 54 55 56 57 58 59 60 61 62 63 64 65 66
  3  2  3  3  4  3  4  2  2  2  2  2  2  4  4  2  4  5  2  3  5  5
 67 68 69 70 71 72 73 74 75 76 77 78 79 80 81 82 83 84 85 86 87
  1  5  1  1  3  5  4  2  1  4  4  5  2  2  2  2  3  2  2  1  2

Within cluster sum of squares by cluster:
[1]  407.3333 377.6970 507.1429 723.1429 287.1000
```

```
(between_SS / total_SS =  33.6 %)

Available components:

[1] "cluster"       "centers"     "totss"     "withinss"
[5] "tot.withinss" "betweenss"   "size"      "iter"
[9] "ifault"
```

If you look at the summary data, you will see that we need to remove the sparse entries (600 centers!):

```
> summary(mymeans)
             Length Class  Mode
cluster         87  -none- numeric
centers        635  -none- numeric
totss            1  -none- numeric
withinss         5  -none- numeric
tot.withinss     1  -none- numeric
betweenss        1  -none- numeric
size             5  -none- numeric
iter             1  -none- numeric
ifault           1  -none- numeric
```

We can find the most frequently used terms (mentioned at least 10 times) (which still have stop words, such as ".", "and", and so on):

```
> freq <- findFreqTerms(dtm,10)

> freq

 [1] "all"         "america"     "american"  "americans"
 [5] "and"         "are"         "because"   "businesses"
 [9] "but"         "can"         "congress"  "country"
[13] "every"       "first"       "for"       "from"
[17] "get"         "give"        "has"       "have"
[21] "help"        "here"        "his"       "it\u0092s"
[25] "jobs"        "just"        "keep"      "know"
[29] "last"        "let\u0092s"  "like"      "make"
[33] "more"        "new"         "not"       "one"
[37] "opportunity" "our"         "over"      "people"
[41] "reform"      "some"        "states"    "support"
[45] "than"        "that"        "that\u0092s" "the"
[49] "their"       "they"        "this"      "those"
[53] "time"        "we\u0092re"  "what"      "when"
[57] "who"         "will"        "with"      "work"
[61] "working"     "you"
```

We can plot the cluster dendogram for a picture of the relationships:

```
> m2 <- as.matrix(dtm)
> dm <- dist(scale(m2))
> fit <- hclust(dm, method="ward")
> plot(fit)
```

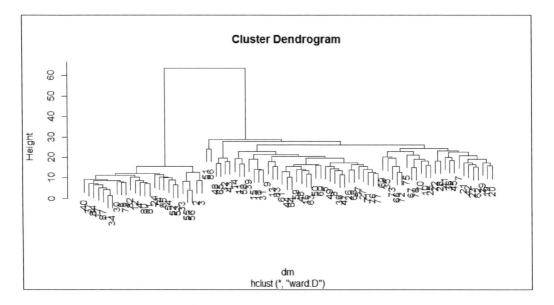

It is interesting that the words line up into two groups. I had expected a wider distribution.

Word graphics

In this section, we will use **FED Open Market comment** (**FOMC**) text (where the previous steps have been performed).

We can plot the (top 10) frequent terms (with a minimum of five uses) and their relationships as they appear in the corpus:

```
> source("http://bioconductor.org/biocLite.R")
> biocLite("Rgraphviz")
> plot(dtm, terms = findFreqTerms(dtm, lowfreq = 5)[1:10],
corThreshold = 0.5)
```

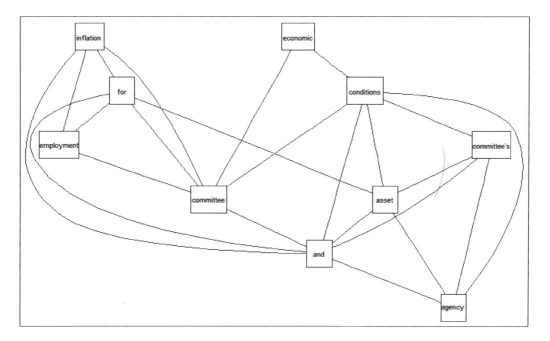

You can see the key concepts: **inflation, economic, conditions, employment,** and the FOMC. This makes sense. This is exactly what you would expect the FOMC to talk about.

We can see a bar graph of the frequent words (with counts over 10) using R:

```
> library(ggplot)
# I had renamed the word frequency object, freq, to wf to make this
example clearer
> p <- ggplot(subset(wf, freq>10), aes(word,freq))
> p <- p + geom_bar(stat="identity")
> p <- p + theme(axis.text.x=element_text(angle=45, hjust=1))
> p
```

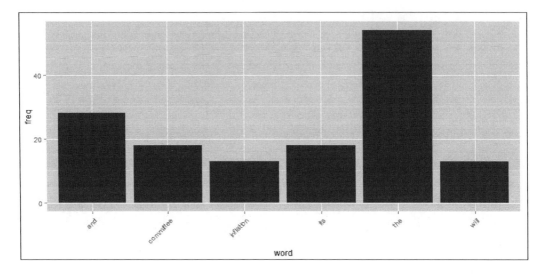

Again, we still have stop words ("and" and "the"). The occurrence of "committee" and "inflation" is significant. This is consistent with prior results.

We can generate a **word cloud** of the frequent words:

```
> install.packages("wordcloud")
> library(wordcloud)
> wordcloud(names(wf), freq, min.freq=10)
```

In this case, we have such a small dataset that we don't see terms that are of much interest. It is curious that the word "market" showed up frequently enough to warrant display.

Analyzing the XML text

In this section, we use R to process XML data. For testing purposes, I am using the sample books' XML, which can be found at `http://msdn.microsoft.com/en-us/library/ms762271%28v=vs.85%29.aspx` and stored in a local XML file.

So, let's load the XML data into R:

```
> install.packages("XML")
> library(XML)
> url <- "books.xml"
> data <- xmlParse(url)
```

The XML package works as and when required. As the source XML file may be large, the functions will not load much data until required. You may find that the `data` object has no content at this point.

Have the XML package parse the entire XML stream and convert it to a list:

```
> df <- xmlToDataFrame(data)
```

Look at the first row in the list (so we can get the column headings):

```
> colnames(df)
[1] "author"        "title"         "genre"
[4] "price"         "publish_date" "description"
```

In this case we had a consistent XML, so the XML converted readily to a data frame. For example, we can compute the average book price using the following code:

```
> mean(as.numeric(df$price))
[1] 3.416667
```

Another interesting case is where the data is not consistent and cannot be easily transformed to a data frame. In this example case, we can use the course listing from the University of Washington (`http://www.cs.washington.edu/research/xmldatasets/data/courses/uwm.xml`).

When working with XML, we need to move into the actual data in the document. This is done by accessing the root of the document as follows:

```
> root <- xmlRoot(data)
```

At this point, `root` maps directly to the XML. The `root` field we have is a collection of the subjects offered, as shown in the following display for the first course offering:

```
> root[1]
$course_listing
<course_listing>
  <note>#</note>
  <course>216-088</course>
  <title>NEW STUDENT ORIENTATION</title>
  <credits>0</credits>
  <level>U</level>
  <restrictions>; ; REQUIRED OF ALL NEW STUDENTS. PREREQ: NONE</
restrictions>
  <section_listing>
    <section_note/>
    <section>Se 001</section>
    <days>W</days>
    <hours>
      <start>1:30pm</start>
      <end/>
    </hours>
    <bldg_and_rm>
      <bldg>BUS</bldg>
      <rm>S230</rm>
    </bldg_and_rm>
    <instructor>Gusavac</instructor>
    <comments>9 WKS BEGINNING WEDNESDAY, 9/6/00 </comments>
  </section_listing>
  <section_listing>
    <section_note/>
    <section>Se 002</section>
    <days>F</days>
    <hours>
      <start>11:30am</start>
      <end/>
    </hours>
    <bldg_and_rm>
      <bldg>BUS</bldg>
      <rm>S171</rm>
    </bldg_and_rm>
    <instructor>Gusavac</instructor>
    <comments>9 WKS BEGINNING FRIDAY, 9/8/00 </comments>
  </section_listing>
</course_listing>

attr(,"class")
[1] "XMLInternalNodeList" "XMLNodeList"
```

We can get a list of the fields that appear in each XML node:

```
> fields <- xmlApply(root, names)
> fields
$course_listing
            note            course            title
          "note"          "course"          "title"
         credits             level      restrictions
       "credits"           "level"    "restrictions"
  section_listing
"section_listing"


... (2000 more)
```

So, as expected, every class has a note, title, and so on. Looking at the data, we can see there is a variety of `section_listing` entries depending on how many sections are offered for a particular subject. The `section_listing` entry is a whole new subtree; hence, it is shown in quotations in the previous code example.

We can verify there are significant differences by checking the XML:

```
> table(sapply(fields, identical, fields[[1]]))
FALSE    TRUE
 1779     333
```

It looks like over 300 subjects have a number of sections offered. This precludes our easily porting the XML tree into a matrix and/or data frame, as the data is not consistent from one node to another.

We can make sure we have the right list of fields (rather than the cursory glance earlier):

```
> unique(unlist(fields))
[1] "note"             "course"           "title"
[4] "credits"          "level"            "restrictions"
[7] "section_listing"
```

So, we want to categorize the data in some manner. What are the different levels that are available for the courses? Let's find out:

```
> unique(xpathSApply(data,"//*/level",xmlValue))
[1] "U"    "G"    "U/G"
```

A standard mechanism of extracting information from XML is the use of a path. A path describes the direction you want to take from the node used as a starting point down to the specific test in mind.

In the case of the previous command, we tell R to start with data or the base of the XML document. From there, go down two levels (the first level is taken up by the base of the document and the second level would be `course_listing`). You should be able to follow along the path specified in the previous sample output. We then look for instances of the `level` field. Each value of the `level` field are put into a result. All of the results are put into a uniqueness test and the output is placed on screen.

We see three levels of classes: graduate (`G`), undergraduate (`U`), and something that appears to be offered as graduate or undergraduate (`U/G`), probably depending on the student taking the subject.

What is the breakdown between the levels? A standard technique in R is to take the raw values found in the path and add them to a table. As the same values are found when added to the table, a simple counter is expanded:

```
> table(xpathSApply(data,"//*/level",xmlValue))

  G     U   U/G
511  1154   447
```

I think this breakdown is probably consistent with other schools: the majority of the subjects are at the undergraduate level. It is interesting that the undergraduate classes almost outnumber the graduate classes.

Which instructor is teaching the most? We use the same approach, following the path down to the instructor and putting the results in a table:

```
> instructors <- table(xpathSApply(data,"///*/instructor",xmlValue))
>instructors
                ... PeteringSurerus
                                  1
                           Peterson
                                 42
                    PetersonFaculty
                                  1
                            Pevnick
                                  2
                        Phillabaum
                                  9
                          Phillips
                                 10 ...
> which.max(instructors)
  TA
1108
> which.min(instructors)
Abler
    3
```

There are built-in mechanisms to get the maximum and minimum values from a table. It is interesting that TA is mentioned the most number of times; maybe there are many subjects that are possible, but not probable.

What course has the most sections? This can be found out by using the following command:

```
> sections <- table(xpathSApply(data,"//*/section_listing",xmlValue))
> which.max(sections)
Se 101To be ArrangedFaculty
                   3739
```

It appears that a majority of the sections are TA. That seems odd.

If we look at the credits offered in various subjects, we see the following result:

```
> credits <- table(xpathSApply(data,"//credits",xmlValue))

> credits

    0   0-1   0@    1 1-12   1-2   1-3   1-4  1-5 1-5H  1-6  1-9 1-9H    1@
    4    2    2  233   84    12   84    27    1    1   51    7    2    16
   12   1H1or2     2 2-10 2-12   2-3   2-4  2-6 2or32or4    3  3-4  3-5
    1    1    5  182    1    2   22    9    7    8    1 1204    1    3
  3-6   3@  3H3or43or6    4    5    6    8    9
    8    1   10    2    9   76    8   23    1    1
```

```
> xpathSApply(data,"//*[credits=12]",xmlValue)
[1] "+930-401THERAPEUTIC RECREATION INTERNSHIP AND SEMINAR12U; ;
PREREQ: MUST HAVE COMPLETED ALL COURSE WORK IN THE THERRECMAJORSe001W9
:00am10:40amEND953Thomas"
```

When we display the generated credits table, we see that a large number of subjects appear to be offered with a range of credits. We also see a standard problem with large data: bad data, such as the 0@ credits.

There is one subject offered with 12 credits, which we can use a slightly different path to find. Here, we move down two levels again, find the credits field, and look for a value of 12. The entirety is returned as a result of the apply function.

 The field values are displayed one after another irrespective of field names.

Questions

Factual

- How does using lowercase help in analyzing text?
- Why are there so many sparse entries? Does this number make sense?
- Determine how to order the instructors matrix.

When, how, and why?

- How would you remove the Unicode sequences from the text?
- In what list of terms would you be interested in finding associations?
- How could you adjust the course credits to be inclusive of the ranges of credits?

Challenges

- Can you determine the benefit of using word stems in the analysis?
- Can you figure out how to display the actual text words in the dendogram rather than their index point?
- Is there a way to convert a non-heterogeneous XML dataset to a matrix?

Summary

In this chapter, we discussed different methods of mining against a text source. We took a raw document, cleaned it up using built-in R functions, and produced a corpus that allowed analysis. We were able to remove sparse terms and stop words to be able to focus on the real value of the text.

From the corpus, we were able to generate a document term matrix that holds all of the word references in a source.

Once the matrix was available, we organized the words into clusters and plotted the data/text accordingly. Similarly, once in clusters, we could perform standard R clustering techniques to the data.

Finally, we looked at using raw XML as the text source for our processing and examined some of the XML processing features available in R.

In the next chapter, we will be covering regression analysis.

Data Analysis – Regression Analysis

4

Regression analysis is one of the first tools used when analyzing your dataset. It involves estimating the relationship between variables, and often it will give you an immediate insight into the organization of your data.

In this chapter, we will look at tools available in R for regression analysis:

- Simple regression
- Multiple regression
- Multivariate regression
- Robust regression

Packages

In R, there are several packages available that provide the programmer with the regression functionality. We will be using the following packages in the examples:

- `chemometrics`: This package has tools to analyze chemometric data (multivariate)
- `MASS`: This package offers modern applied statistics with S

Simple regression

In simple regression, we try to determine whether there is a relationship between two variables. It is assumed that there is a high degree of correlation between the two variables chosen for use in regression.

For this section, we will be using the `iris` dataset. The `iris` dataset has observations of the different characteristics of iris plants. For regression, we are seeing if there is a relationship between one characteristic of iris plants and others. As mentioned, the characteristics tested will have a high degree of correlation. The `iris` dataset is as follows:

```
> data <- read.csv("http://archive.ics.uci.edu/ml/machine-learning-
databases/iris/iris.data")
```

Let's also clean up the data so as to be more readable:

```
>colnames(data) <- c("sepal_length", "sepal_width", "petal_length",
"petal_width", "species")
```

Now, let's look at a summary to get an overall picture:

```
> summary(data)
sepallength     sepal_width      petal_length
 Min.   :4.300   Min.   :2.000   Min.   :1.000
 1st Qu.:5.100   1st Qu.:2.800   1st Qu.:1.600
 Median :5.800   Median :3.000   Median :4.400
 Mean   :5.848   Mean   :3.051   Mean   :3.774
 3rd Qu.:6.400   3rd Qu.:3.300   3rd Qu.:5.100
 Max.   :7.900   Max.   :4.400   Max.   :6.900
petal_width              species
 Min.   :0.100   Iris-setosa    :49
 1st Qu.:0.300   Iris-versicolor:50
 Median :1.300   Iris-virginica :50
 Mean   :1.205
 3rd Qu.:1.800
 Max.   :2.500
```

We can look at plots of the data points to try to determine what variables appear to be related:

```
> plot(data)
```

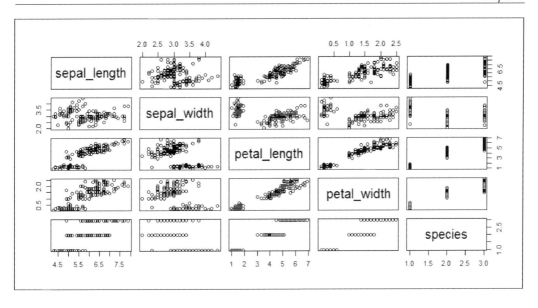

What if we were to use petal length to predict petal width? The two plots show a nice linear relationship. The only concern would be that there appears to be two clusters. Intuitively, there should be a strong relationship between the two. We can check this using R:

```
>cor(data$petal_length,data$petal_width)
[1] 0.9623143
```

And we see a high correlation between the two. If we go ahead and determine the regression between the two, we see:

```
> fit <- lm(data$petal_length ~ data$petal_width)
> fit
Call:
lm(formula = data$petal_length ~ data$petal_width)

Coefficients:
     (Intercept)   data$petal_width
           1.093              2.224
```

We can display the fit information. The fit information displays four charts: **Residuals vs Fitted**, **Normal Q-Q**, **Scale-Location**, and **Residuals vs Leverage**.

If you remember, the residuals are the difference between the observed data and the **fitted** or projected values from the model. So, for the **Residuals vs Fitted** plot, we see some variance.

The Qs stand for quantile, the normalized quantile of the data point versus the actual. I think the **Normal Q-Q** graphic is very typical for plots I have seen — majority of the data is in the same quantile, with some degree of variation at the foot and the head of the plot.

The **Scale-Location** plot shows the square root of the standardized residuals as a function of the fitted values. You can see columns of data points, as there is not enough data to cover a wider area. There is a pretty big variety in the fitted values.

Leverage is the importance of a data point in determining the regression result. The **Residuals vs Leverage** graphic is overlayed with Cook's distance — another measure of importance of a data point. Overall, we see consistent importance of the data points at all levels.

Let's display the fit information:

```
>par(mfrow=c(2,2)) # set the plot area to 2 plots by 2 plots
> plot(fit)
```

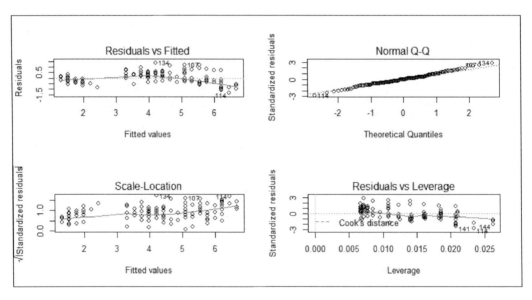

We can use the regression variables in predicting a formula (ordered in the standard $y = mx + c$ format):

petal_length = petal_width * 2.224 + 1.093

We can look at the differences between the observed values and the fitted values using the `residuals()` function:

```
> residuals(fit)
           1            2            3            4
-0.138259922 -0.238259922 -0.038259922 -0.138259922
           5            6            7            8
-0.283118763 -0.360689343 -0.038259922 -0.138259922
           9           10           11           12
 0.184169498 -0.038259922  0.061740078  0.084169498
...
```

There are differences for every data point with valid data (149 data points). A rough scan doesn't reveal any outliers. However, a summary produces meaty results:

```
> summary(fit)

Call:
lm(formula = data$petal_length ~ data$petal_width)

Residuals:
    Min      1Q  Median      3Q     Max
-1.33171 -0.30741 -0.01956  0.25988  1.39259

Coefficients:
                 Estimate Std. Error t value Pr(>|t|)
(Intercept)       1.09340    0.07384   14.81   <2e-16 ***
data$petal_width  2.22429    0.05184   42.91   <2e-16 ***
---
Signif. codes:  0 '***' 0.001 '**' 0.01 '*' 0.05 '.' 0.1 ' ' 1

Residual standard error: 0.4801 on 147 degrees of freedom
Multiple R-squared:  0.926,  Adjusted R-squared:  0.9255
F-statistic:  1841 on 1 and 147 DF,  p-value: <2.2e-16
```

The summary shows us several points about the regression:

- First, it shows what the model is based on (petal length and width).
- It shows the range of residuals. The residuals appear to be in a small range. It is interesting that the upper and lower bounds have the same absolute range.
- The coefficients' (in this case, we are only using one variable, so coefficient) values are presented.

- We see an intercept of 1. I think that is reasonable looking back at the data. The standard error is pretty low. The probability greater than *t* value is very low. I think there is confidence in the estimate.

- We see a petal width estimate of 2.2. Again, this looks good as seen in the raw data, with a similar low standard error and very low estimate of the difference.

The residuals vary from -1 to +1, which appears to be a broad range. Here is the raw data:

	sepal_ length	sepal_ width	petal_ length	petal_ width	species
1	4.9	3.0	1.4	0.2	Iris-setosa
2	4.7	3.2	1.3	0.2	Iris-setosa
3	4.6	3.1	1.5	0.2	Iris-setosa
4	5.0	3.6	1.4	0.2	Iris-setosa
5	5.4	3.9	1.7	0.4	Iris-setosa
(more)					
95	5.7	3.0	4.2	1.2	Iris-versicolor
96	5.7	2.9	4.2	1.3	Iris-versicolor
97	6.2	2.9	4.3	1.3	Iris-versicolor
98	5.1	2.5	3.0	1.1	Iris-versicolor
99	5.7	2.8	4.1	1.3	Iris-versicolor
100	6.3	3.3	6.0	2.5	Iris-virginica
101	5.8	2.7	5.1	1.9	Iris-virginica
102	7.1	3.0	5.9	2.1	Iris-virginica

We can see that such residual values are too extreme, at least for Iris-setosa. The other two varieties might show a better fit or at least different regressions. We can remove the setosa observations from the data with the following command:

```
> data2<- subset(data, data$species!='Iris-setosa')
```

We can see how the various plots look:

```
> plot(data2)
```

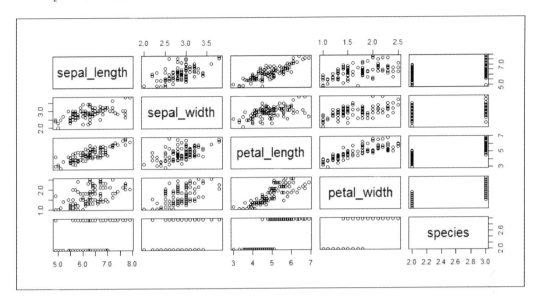

We can see a more clustered relationship between petal length and petal width. The setosa data was definitely responsible for the extra cluster that appeared in the earlier plots. Unfortunately, the data does appear to be more scattered.

Let's run the regression against the subset produced:

```
>cor(data2$petal_length,data2$petal_width)

[1] 0.8233476

> fit <- lm(data2$petal_length ~ data2$petal_width)

> summary(fit)

Call:
lm(formula = data2$petal_length ~ data2$petal_width)

Residuals:
     Min       1Q   Median       3Q      Max
 -0.9842  -0.3043  -0.1043   0.2407   1.2755

Coefficients:
                  Estimate Std. Error t value Pr(>|t|)
```

```
(Intercept)           2.2240      0.1926    11.55    <2e-16 ***
data2$petal_width     1.6003      0.1114    14.36    <2e-16 ***
---
Signif. codes:  0 '***' 0.001 '**' 0.01 '*' 0.05 '.' 0.1 ' ' 1

Residual standard error: 0.4709 on 98 degrees of freedom
Multiple R-squared:  0.6779,  Adjusted R-squared:  0.6746
F-statistic: 206.3 on 1 and 98 DF,  p-value: <2.2e-16
```

The correlation dropped from 0.96 to 0.82 — this is not good.

While the residual standard error has not changed, we have reduced our degrees of freedom from 147 to 98. Reducing the standard error on the regression is a good thing — it means we are closer to the observed data points with our modeled data. However, the R-squared dropped significantly from 0.926 to 0.6779.

The f-statistic dropped from 1800 to 200 with the p-value unchanged with a good, small value. Overall, I don't think we can exclude setosa from the evaluation.

I think it is important to try to test different subsets of your data to make sure they are all truly in agreement.

Multiple regression

In multiple regression, we are using more than one predictor to predict a variable.

For the multiple regression, we will be using obesity data from the Austrian Department of Public Health, which can be found at http://www.biostat.au.dk/teaching/postreg/AllData.htm.

First, let's load the data into R. We start with the Excel file at http://www.biostat.au.dk/teaching/postreg/obese.xls, save it locally as a CSV file, and then read the CSV file in normally to R:

```
> data <- read.csv("obese.csv")
```

We should always get an idea of the data ranges with a summary:

```
> summary(data)

      sex              sbp              dbp
 Min.   :1.000    Min.   : 80.0    Min.   : 40.00
 1st Qu.:1.000    1st Qu.:116.0    1st Qu.: 74.00
 Median :2.000    Median :130.0    Median : 80.00
 Mean   :1.564    Mean   :132.8    Mean   : 82.53
 3rd Qu.:2.000    3rd Qu.:144.0    3rd Qu.: 90.00
```

```
Max.    :2.000   Max.    :270.0   Max.    :148.00

scl              age              bmi              id
 Min.   :115.0    Min.   :30.00    Min.   :16.20    Min.   :    1
 1st Qu.:197.0    1st Qu.:39.00    1st Qu.:22.80    1st Qu.:1174
 Median :225.0    Median :45.00    Median :25.20    Median :2350
 Mean   :228.3    Mean   :46.03    Mean   :25.63    Mean   :2349
 3rd Qu.:255.0    3rd Qu.:53.00    3rd Qu.:28.00    3rd Qu.:3524
 Max.   :568.0    Max.   :66.00    Max.   :57.60    Max.   :4699
 NA's   :32

     obese
 Min.   :0.0000
 1st Qu.:0.0000
 Median :0.0000
 Mean   :0.1281
 3rd Qu.:0.0000
 Max.   :1.0000
```

We have six possible variables to predict obesity (where 1 is for obese and 0 is for not obese):

- sex: 1 represents male and 2 represents female
- sbp: This represents systolic blood pressure
- dbp: This represents dystolic blood pressure
- scl: This represents serum cholesterol level
- age: This represents the age of the patient
- bmi: This represents body mass index

Assuming all these variables have an effect on obesity, we create a model based on the variables:

```
> model <- lm(data$obese ~ data$sex + data$sbp + data$dbp + data$scl +
data$age + data$bmi)
```

Let's look at the standard x/y plots for the various data items:

```
> plot(data)
```

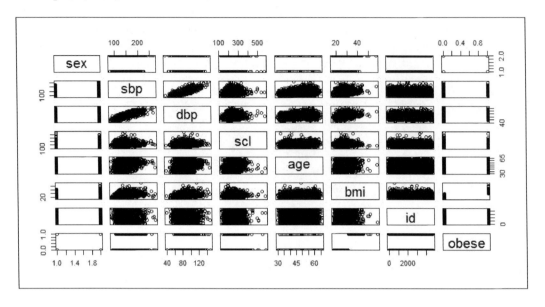

Most of the data looks like a large blob covering all data points. The only correlation appears to exist with sbp and dbp.

Let's look at the summary statistics for a quick check:

```
> summary(model)

Call:
lm(formula = data$obese ~ data$sex + data$sbp + data$dbp + data$scl +
data$age + data$bmi)

Residuals:
     Min       1Q    Median       3Q      Max
-1.01539 -0.16764 -0.03607  0.11271  0.68603

Coefficients:
              Estimate Std. Error t value Pr(>|t|)
(Intercept) -1.389e+00  3.390e-02 -40.970   <2e-16 ***
data$sex     6.479e-02  7.118e-03   9.101   <2e-16 ***
data$sbp     1.030e-04  2.630e-04   0.392   0.6954
data$dbp    -7.374e-06  4.562e-04  -0.016   0.9871
data$scl    -1.229e-04  8.258e-05  -1.488   0.1368
data$age    -1.121e-03  4.625e-04  -2.425   0.0154 *
```

```
data$bmi      5.784e-02  9.287e-04  62.285   <2e-16 ***
---
Signif. codes:  0 '***' 0.001 '**' 0.01 '*' 0.05 '.' 0.1 ' ' 1

Residual standard error: 0.2382 on 4651 degrees of freedom
  (32 observations deleted due to missingness)
Multiple R-squared:  0.4922,  Adjusted R-squared:  0.4915
F-statistic: 751.2 on 6 and 4651 DF,  p-value: <2.2e-16
```
All of the coefficients are very small; large degrees of freedom; small standard error; small f-statistic p-value: looks ok.

We will gather some more statistics on the relationship.

The residuals look mixed. The range is varying from about -1 to 1. The planned data should only be from 0 to 1. We can take a look at the residual as follows:

```
>resid(model)

-0.3593690076 -0.0520330610 -0.1306809185 -0.0785678149
         4656          4657          4658          4659
-0.0475088136 -0.3754792745 -0.0542681627 -0.3179715071
         4661          4662          4663          4664
-0.0710123758  0.0397175807  0.5118121778 -0.3075321204
         4665          4666          4667          4668
-0.1689782711 -0.1014993845  0.4396866832  0.6248164103
         4669          4670          4671          4672
(more)
```

Similarly, the fitted predictions are not particularly accurate either:

```
>fitted(model)

 0.0710123758 -0.0397175807  0.4881878222  0.3075321204
         4665          4666          4667          4668
 0.1689782711  0.1014993845  0.5603133168  0.3751835897
         4669          4670          4671          4672
 0.2272450653  0.2090975000 -0.1165723642  0.2486420151
         4673          4674          4675          4676
-0.0950795821  0.0363646586 -0.3369085204  1.0129235885
         4677          4678          4679          4680
(more)
```

The graphs for the fit look like this:

```
>par(mfrow=c(2,2))
```

```
> plot(model)
```

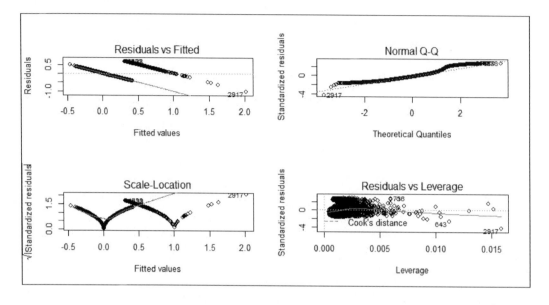

We see the scale-location standardized residual versus fitted values has an unusual shape. This is due to the predicted value, obesity, being just 0 or 1.

Similarly, the **Residual vs Fitted** graph points to the binary obesity value.

The **Normal Q-Q** graph does not show much of interest.

The **Residuals vs Leverage** graph is very heavily weighted towards small values, as we saw with the previous small coefficients.

I think we don't have a great regression to predict obesity using all the variables.

What happens if we just use the blood pressure values? Let's find out:

```
> model <- lm(data$obese ~ data$sbp + data$dbp)
```

```
> summary(model)
```

```
Call:
lm(formula = data$obese ~ data$sbp + data$dbp)
```

```
Residuals:
```

```
      Min       1Q    Median       3Q       Max
 -0.60924 -0.15127 -0.10049 -0.04029   1.02968


Coefficients:
               Estimate Std. Error t value Pr(>|t|)
(Intercept) -0.4299333  0.0314876 -13.654   <2e-16 ***
data$sbp     0.0012021  0.0003334   3.605 0.000315 ***
data$dbp     0.0048283  0.0005972   8.085 7.85e-16 ***
---
Signif. codes:  0 '***' 0.001 '**' 0.01 '*' 0.05 '.' 0.1 ' ' 1

Residual standard error: 0.3234 on 4687 degrees of freedom
Multiple R-squared:  0.06419,  Adjusted R-squared:  0.06379
F-statistic: 160.7 on 2 and 4687 DF,  p-value: <2.2e-16
```

We see a similar standard error and f-statistic. Most importantly, the R-squared value has dropped from about one half to 0.06. I think we are on the right track using just these two values.

Plotting the fit gives more credence to this assumption:

```
> plot(model)
```

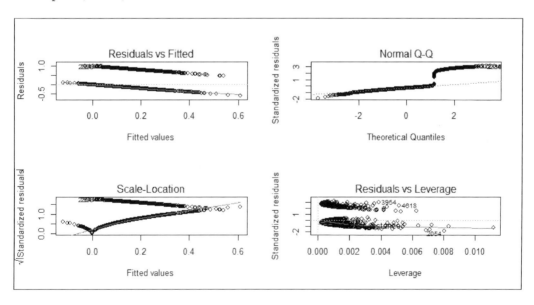

We see the **Residuals vs Leverage** graph is lining up directly on the 0 and 1 obesity scores. We also see similar reinforcement with the concentrations in the **Residuals vs Fitted** graph and the **Scale-Location** graph.

My issue is the small coefficients. We end up with the formula:

obesity = -0.43 + 0.001 * sbp + 0.004 * dbp

I think that these are not the variables needed to predict obesity.

We tried using the entire dataset and we also tried narrowing down the dataset to likely candidates. The result was unexpected.

Multivariate regression analysis

Multivariate regression is a technique that estimates a single regression model with more than one outcome variable.

For multivariate regression, we will be using the chemometrics package. Chemometrics is the science of extracting information from chemical systems using the data present. However, the data normally has a small number of observations with a large number of variables.

There are three problems in using chemometrics:

1. We can only graph three of the *n* variables as this is a limitation of the package.
2. The variables are all highly correlated, which eliminates the possibility of using statistics to separate out the more interesting values.
3. Again, there are a small number of observations to work with.

So, let us load the chemometrics package into R:

```
>install.packages('chemometrics')

>library('chemometrics')
```

 This is a large package that loads a number of dependencies.

We will be using the Auto MPG dataset from University of California, Irvine, data archive. This data is taken from the link http://archive.ics.uci.edu/ml/datasets/Auto+MPG. The summary is as follows:

```
>data <- read.table("http://archive.ics.uci.edu/ml/machine-learning-
databases/auto-mpg/auto-mpg.data")
> colnames(data) <- c("mpg", "cylinders", "displacement",
"horsepower", "weight", "acceleration", "model.year", "origin", "car.
name")

>summary(data)
```

```
        mpg              cylinders          displacement         horsepower
 Min.   : 9.00    Min.    :3.000    Min.   : 68.0    150      : 22
 1st Qu.:17.50    1st Qu.:4.000    1st Qu.:104.2    90       : 20
 Median :23.00    Median :4.000    Median :148.5    88       : 19
 Mean   :23.51    Mean    :5.455    Mean   :193.4    110      : 18
 3rd Qu.:29.00    3rd Qu.:8.000    3rd Qu.:262.0    100      : 17
 Max.   :46.60    Max.    :8.000    Max.   :455.0    75       : 14
                                                     (Other) :288
        weight           acceleration        model.year           origin
 Min.   :1613    Min.    : 8.00    Min.   :70.00    Min.    :1.000
 1st Qu.:2224    1st Qu.:13.82    1st Qu.:73.00    1st Qu.:1.000
 Median :2804    Median :15.50    Median :76.00    Median :1.000
 Mean   :2970    Mean    :15.57    Mean   :76.01    Mean    :1.573
 3rd Qu.:3608    3rd Qu.:17.18    3rd Qu.:79.00    3rd Qu.:2.000
 Max.   :5140    Max.    :24.80    Max.   :82.00    Max.    :3.000

car.name
 ford pinto     :  6
amc matador     :  5
 ford maverick :  5
toyota corolla:  5
amc gremlin     :  4
amc hornet      :  4
 (Other)        :369
```

We can see the following details from the summary:

- A wide range of mpg
- It is interesting that some cars had three cylinders
- The cars range from year 1970 to 1982
- The displacement varies a lot
- The weight also varies tremendously

We will be trying to predict the values for mpg, acceleration, and horsepower using the other data values present. We will use R to produce our model and the results.

So, first we specify the model using the variables in the observation we want to apply:

```
> m <- lm(cbind(data$mpg,data$acceleration,data$horsepower) ~
data$cylinders + data$displacement + data$weight + data$model.year)

> summary(m)
Response data$mpg :
```

The summary reiterates our model variables:

```
Call:
lm(formula = `data$mpg` ~ data$cylinders + data$displacement +
data$weight + data$model.year)
```

We see a range of residuals from -9 to 14. This is a large divergence from the mpg we are trying to model:

```
Residuals:
    Min      1Q  Median      3Q     Max
-8.9756 -2.3327 -0.1833  2.0587 14.3889
```

Some of the estimate values are very small; they are not particularly applicable to our model.

Also, some of the probabilities $> t$ are significant; this is again not a good indicator for a model:

```
Coefficients:
                    Estimate Std. Error t value Pr(>|t|)
(Intercept)       -1.371e+01  4.052e+00  -3.383 0.000789 ***
data$cylinders    -2.516e-01  3.285e-01  -0.766 0.444212
data$displacement  4.739e-03  6.707e-03   0.707 0.480223
data$weight       -6.751e-03  5.716e-04 -11.811  <2e-16 ***
data$model.year    7.595e-01  5.061e-02  15.007  <2e-16 ***
---
Signif. codes:  0 '***' 0.001 '**' 0.01 '*' 0.05 '.' 0.1 ' ' 1

Residual standard error: 3.441 on 393 degrees of freedom
Multiple R-squared:  0.8082,  Adjusted R-squared:  0.8062
F-statistic: 413.9 on 4 and 393 DF,  p-value: <2.2e-16


Response data$acceleration :

Call:
lm(formula = `data$acceleration` ~ data$cylinders + data$displacement
+
data$weight + data$model.year)

Residuals:
    Min      1Q  Median      3Q     Max
-5.7550 -1.5625 -0.1788  1.1564  7.6315

Coefficients:
```

```
                    Estimate Std. Error t value Pr(>|t|)
(Intercept)        10.7368193  2.6069139   4.119 4.65e-05 ***
data$cylinders      0.0867985  0.2113795   0.411    0.682
data$displacement  -0.0314665  0.0043155  -7.291 1.70e-12 ***
data$weight         0.0021690  0.0003678   5.897 7.97e-09 ***
data$model.year     0.0526444  0.0325637   1.617    0.107
---
Signif. codes:  0 '***' 0.001 '**' 0.01 '*' 0.05 '.' 0.1 ' ' 1

Residual standard error: 2.214 on 393 degrees of freedom
Multiple R-squared:  0.3621,  Adjusted R-squared:  0.3556
F-statistic: 55.77 on 4 and 393 DF,  p-value: <2.2e-16


Response data$horsepower :

Call:
lm(formula = `data$horsepower` ~ data$cylinders + data$displacement +
data$weight + data$model.year)

Residuals:
    Min      1Q  Median      3Q     Max
-71.033  -6.323   3.624  13.999  68.302

Coefficients:
                    Estimate Std. Error t value Pr(>|t|)
(Intercept)       160.507707  29.361062   5.467 8.17e-08 ***
data$cylinders    -15.329261   2.380718  -6.439 3.51e-10 ***
data$displacement   0.144583   0.048605   2.975  0.00311 **
data$weight        -0.006605   0.004142  -1.595  0.11160
data$model.year    -0.445283   0.366758  -1.214  0.22544
---
Signif. codes:  0 '***' 0.001 '**' 0.01 '*' 0.05 '.' 0.1 ' ' 1

Residual standard error: 24.93 on 393 degrees of freedom
Multiple R-squared:  0.3132,  Adjusted R-squared:  0.3062
F-statistic: 44.79 on 4 and 393 DF,  p-value: <2.2e-1
```

We told R to predict the three variables so that it produced results of the predictions for each of these variables:

- For all three variables, we get a wide range of residuals
- For mpg, the errors are very small
- For acceleration, we see the same small errors
- For horsepower, we have a high standard error; there appears to be a mismatch, except that the true horsepower value can be pretty large

To get a better picture of the fit, we can use the manova function. The manova function measures the multivariate analysis of variance when we have more than one dependent variable. We generate the manova instance, mm, using the existent regression model we developed already, m:

```
> mm <- manova (m)

> mm
Call:
manova (m)

Terms:
data$cylinders data$displacement data$weight
resp 1                  14581.60            1133.12      1219.53
resp 2                    771.23             125.33       183.81
resp 3                 103934.57            4639.37      1895.38
Deg. of Freedom              1                   1            1
data$model.year Residuals
resp 1               2666.07    4652.25
resp 2                 12.81    1925.94
resp 3                916.33  244304.99
Deg. of Freedom            1        393


Residual standard errors: 3.440609 2.213731 24.93273
Estimated effects may be unbalanced

> summary (mm)
Df   Pillai approx F num Df den Df     Pr (>F)
data$cylinders       1 0.78618    479.21      3     391 <2.2e-16
data$displacement    1 0.24844     43.08      3     391 <2.2e-16
data$weight          1 0.27474     49.37      3     391 <2.2e-16
data$model.year      1 0.37086     76.83      3     391 <2.2e-16
Residuals          393

data$cylinders       ***
```

```
data$displacement ***
data$weight       ***
data$model.year   ***
Residuals
---
Signif. codes:  0 '***' 0.001 '**' 0.01 '*' 0.05 '.' 0.1 ' ' 1
```

Looking at the manova results, we find the following details:

- We see very large initial manova result residuals of 3, 2, and 24
- The degrees of freedom show a good fit for all variables
- The only bigger Pillai's trace is for the number of cylinders
- Also, we see a very large F statistic for the number of cylinders

The results are still very rough, but we do have a model for predicting the outcomes.

If we drop the car's model name, car.name (so we just have numeric data in the data frame), we can produce a correlation matrix:

```
data$car.name<- NULL
```

Also, we need to account for the missing horsepower values by coercing them to NA:

```
>data$horsepower[data$horsepower=='?'] <- NA
```

```
>data$horsepower<- as.numeric(data$horsepower)
```

Now, we can generate some statistics:

```
>cor(data)
                     mpg  cylinders displacement horsepower
mpg            1.0000000 -0.7753963   -0.8042028         NA
cylinders     -0.7753963  1.0000000    0.9507214         NA
displacement  -0.8042028  0.9507214    1.0000000         NA
horsepower            NA         NA           NA          1
weight        -0.8317409  0.8960168    0.9328241         NA
acceleration   0.4202889 -0.5054195   -0.5436841         NA
model.year     0.5792671 -0.3487458   -0.3701642         NA
origin         0.5634504 -0.5625433   -0.6094094         NA

                  weight acceleration model.year     origin
mpg           -0.8317409    0.4202889  0.5792671  0.5634504
cylinders      0.8960168   -0.5054195 -0.3487458 -0.5625433
displacement   0.9328241   -0.5436841 -0.3701642 -0.6094094
```

horsepower	NA	NA	NA	NA
weight	1.0000000	-0.4174573	-0.3065643	-0.5810239
acceleration	-0.4174573	1.0000000	0.2881370	0.2058730
model.year	-0.3065643	0.2881370	1.0000000	0.1806622
origin	-0.5810239	0.2058730	0.1806622	1.0000000

As expected (with the data used for most multivariate regressions), most of the values are highly correlated to each other.

Similarly, we can generate the covariance values:

```
>cov(data)
```

	mpg	cylinders	displacement	weight
mpg	61.089611	-10.3089111	-655.40232	-5505.2117
cylinders	-10.308911	2.8934154	168.62321	1290.6956
displacement	-655.402318	168.6232137	10872.19915	82368.4232
weight	-5505.211745	1290.6955749	82368.42324	717140.9905
acceleration	9.058930	-2.3708422	-156.33298	-974.8990
model.year	16.741163	-2.1934990	-142.71714	-959.9463
origin	3.532185	-0.7674772	-50.96499	-394.6393

	acceleration	model.year	origin
mpg	9.0589297	16.7411630	3.5321849
cylinders	-2.3708422	-2.1934990	-0.7674772
displacement	-156.3329756	-142.7171373	-50.9649887
weight	-974.8990108	-959.9463438	-394.6393302
acceleration	7.6048482	2.9381049	0.4553536
model.year	2.9381049	13.6724428	0.5357898
origin	0.4553536	0.5357898	0.6432920

We see strong negative covariance between mpg, displacement, and weight. This makes sense; as the vehicle size increases, the mpg would decrease. There is some positive covariance with year the vehicle was made. I assume this is the influence of the government on manufacturers to increase mpg. It is interesting that acceleration has a positive covariance, but I am not sure why that would occur.

Robust regression

With multivariate data, we need to trim down to the primary predictors. In R, we can use the prcomp function. The prcomp function will determine the measure of the importance of a variable in predicting the result.

I removed the horsepower column first as the NA values threw errors. The columns we end up with are mpg, cylinders, and so on, corresponding to PC1 to PC7 in the original data:

```
> data <- subset(data, select = -c('horsepower'))

>prcomp(data)

Standard deviations:
[1]  852.4479181   37.3631951    4.9556049    2.3653826    2.1999725
[6]    0.6098103    0.5167486

Rotation:
                        PC1           PC2           PC3
mpg            0.0076298796    0.01595015  -0.823189547
cylinders     -0.0017911340   -0.01431314   0.001739055
displacement  -0.1143223782   -0.99241700  -0.028635762
weight        -0.9934108142    0.11443292  -0.003865543
acceleration   0.0013574785    0.03157265  -0.051883472
model.year     0.0013349862    0.02327853  -0.564552619
origin         0.0005475619    0.00395091  -0.010461439
                        PC4           PC5           PC6
mpg           -0.565406878    0.010097475   0.0434064695
cylinders      0.007700936   -0.005506178  -0.2872920842
displacement   0.010966214   -0.029120056  -0.0016527831
weight        -0.004479662    0.002214055   0.0003840199
acceleration   0.053644868   -0.994906897  -0.0556398264
model.year     0.820238828    0.077102184  -0.0412980324
origin        -0.066677775    0.056836279  -0.9543452938
PC7
mpg           -1.937340e-02
cylinders     -9.576860e-01
displacement   1.574545e-02
weight        -2.328483e-05
acceleration   2.227407e-02
model.year     1.716564e-02
origin         2.853479e-01
```

We can see that the origin value has no correlation with the rest of the data. All of the other variables have some cross-correlation that works. So, we didn't find anything unexpected that should be dropped from our model (from the previous code, m <- lm(cbind(data$mpg,data$acceleration,data$horsepower) ~ data$cylinders + data$displacement + data$weight + data$model.year).

We can further analyze the data for Cook's distance. Cook's distance measures the influence of a data point on our regression. Using the R `cooks.distance` function, we can analyze the data as follows:

```
>d1<- cooks.distance(m)
>d1
          [,1]           [,2]
1   2.436506e-03 3.581308e-04
2   4.833923e-04 2.656062e-04
3   1.732134e-03 8.401681e-04
```

Now, we can look at the regression points that could be used:

```
> r <- stdres(m)

> a <- cbind(data, d1, r)

> a[d1> 4/398, ]
```

	mpg	cylinders	displacement	weight	acceleration	model.year
6	15.0	8	429	4341	10.0	70
7	14.0	8	454	4354	9.0	70
8	14.0	8	440	4312	8.5	70
9	14.0	8	455	4425	10.0	70
14	14.0	8	455	3086	10.0	70

```
(more)
```

	origin	1	2	r
6	1	0.0316915655	1.450126e-03	1.1988501
7	1	0.0124784451	1.405378e-03	0.9504220
8	1	0.0216278941	7.612076e-03	0.8921663
9	1	0.0153827261	1.326945e-04	1.0686089
14	1	0.1542750769	4.265531e-02	-1.2473311
40	1	0.0119925188	4.304444e-04	0.9951620
43	1	0.0121565950	2.303933e-03	1.3432769
44	1	0.0200318228	6.303327e-04	1.2192432

```
(more)
```

We can now move towards a robust regression analysis:

```
>rlm(data$mpg ~ data$cylinders + data$displacement + data$weight +
data$model.year)

Call:
rlm(formula = data$mpg ~ data$cylinders + data$displacement +
```

```
data$weight + data$model.year)

Converged in 6 iterations

Coefficients:
      (Intercept)      data$cylinders data$displacement
     -9.870815146         -0.363931540       0.006499224
data$weight    data$model.year
    -0.006625956         0.705663002

Degrees of freedom: 398 total; 393 residual
Scale estimate: 3.15
```

We started out with the previous formula:

```
> m <- lm(cbind(data$mpg,data$acceleration,data$horsepower) ~
data$cylinders + data$displacement + data$weight + data$model.year)
```

We removed acceleration, horsepower, displacement, and vehicle weight. Now we can derive a simplified formula:

mpg = -9.8 – cylinders / 3 + .7 * the model year

The intercept is about -9.8. The cylinders correlation is about – 1/3. The model year coefficient is about 0.7.

This just says that if we wait long enough, the government's directions to the auto industry will force better mileage. Surprising!

We can also use **Modern Applied Statistics in S+ (MASS)** methods for robust regression. The idea is that we have larger errors than expected, but still want to try and use the data points we have. We try using the rlm (which stands for robust fitting of linear models) function:

```
> library(MASS)
> m <- rlm(mpg ~ cylinders + displacement + weight + model.year, data)

> m
Call:
rlm(formula = mpg ~ cylinders + displacement + weight + model.year,
    data = data)
Converged in 6 iterations

Coefficients:
  (Intercept)     cylinders displacement        weight
-9.870815146 -0.363931540  0.006499224 -0.006625956
```

```
model.year
 0.705663002


Degrees of freedom: 398 total; 393 residual
Scale estimate: 3.15
```

We end up with the following formula:

mpg = - cylinders/3 + .7 * model year

Some change to account for the cylinders, but the time effect of government intervention is still the overwhelming factor.

We can also try the `ltsreg` (which stands for least trim squares) function in MASS. This method is normally used when there are a lot of outlier values in the data. We aren't really in that state here, but just to try it out.

Note, the method is nondeterministic, so in our case I ran the function three times:

```
>m2<- ltsreg(mpg ~ cylinders + displacement + weight + model.year,
data)
>m2
Call:
lqs.formula(formula = mpg ~ cylinders + displacement + weight +
model.year, data = data, method = "lts")

Coefficients:
  (Intercept)    cylinders  displacement       weight
    -0.787503    -1.230076      0.011049    -0.003729
model.year
     0.503659


Scale estimates 2.787 2.870


(run second time)
>ltsreg(mpg ~ cylinders + displacement + weight + model.year, data)
Call:
lqs.formula(formula = mpg ~ cylinders + displacement + weight +
model.year, data = data, method = "lts")

Coefficients:
  (Intercept)    cylinders  displacement       weight
     2.079872    -0.901353      0.002364    -0.004555
model.year
```

```
     0.505625

Scale estimates 2.789 2.783

(run third time)
>ltsreg(mpg ~ cylinders + displacement + weight + model.year, data)
Call:
lqs.formula(formula = mpg ~ cylinders + displacement + weight +
model.year, data = data, method = "lts")

Coefficients:
 (Intercept)      cylinders  displacement         weight
   13.899925      -1.023310      0.019264      -0.005873
model.year
    0.366595

Scale estimates 2.670 2.725
```

You can see different values for each iteration:

Intercept	cylinders	displacement	weight	model.year
-.8	-1.2	0.01	0	0.5
2	-0.9	0	0	0.5
13.9	-1	0.01	0	0.3

Weight and displacement are consistently unimportant, while model year and cylinders are definite coefficients. Curiously, the intercept varies widely between iterations.

The data we use does not really have a large number of outliers in the results. I was using both robust methods to test whether the two factors, displacement and weight, were really not important to the calculation. We have proved this.

We also verified that cylinders are a factor. This makes sense: a car with more cylinders will get less mileage. It is interesting that the robust methods assign slightly less importance to government intervention.

Questions

Factual

- What is the best way to handle NA values when performing a regression?
- When will the quantiles graph for a regression model not look like a nice line of fit?
- Can you compare the anova versus manova results? Aside from the multiple sections, is there really a difference in the calculations?

When, how, and why?

- Why does the **Residuals vs Leverage** graph show such a blob of data?
- Why do we use 4 as a rounding number in the robust regression?
- At what point will you feel comfortable deciding that the dataset you are using for a regression has the right set of predictors in use?

Challenges

- Are there better predictors available for obesity than those used in the chapter?
- How can multilevel regression be used for either the obesity or mpg datasets?
- Can you determine a different set of predictors for mpg that does not reduce it to simple government fiat?

Summary

In this chapter, we discussed how to perform regression analysis using R. We performed simple regression and analyzed fit, residuals, and other factors. We used multiple regression, including selecting and using a set of predictor values. We tried to determine a set of values from predictors using multivariate regression. Lastly, we used robust regression to overcome possible problems in the predictors and to build a reliable model. In the next chapter, we will be covering correlation.

5
Data Analysis – Correlation

Correlation is a good technique to use on your dataset. Correlation helps us to establish basic relationships between data items.

In this chapter, we look at tools available in R for correlation:

- A basic correlation
- Visualizing correlations
- Covariance
- Pearson correlation
- Polychoric correlation
- Tetrachoric correlation
- A heterogeneous correlation matrix
- Partial correlation

Packages

In R, there are several packages that provide the correlation functionality to the programmer. We will be using the following packages in this chapter:

- `corrgram`: This is the tool to graphically display correlations
- `Hmisc`: This contains a variety of miscellaneous R functions
- `polycor`: This contains functions to compute polychoric correlations
- `ggm`: This contains functions for analyzing and fitting graphical Markov models

Correlation

Basic correlation is performed in R using the `cor` function. The `cor` function is defined as follows:

```
cor(x, y = NULL,
   use = "everything",
   method = c("pearson", "kendall", "spearman"))
```

The various parameters of this function are described in the following table:

Parameter	Description
x	This is the dataset.
y	This is the dataset that is compatible with x.
use	This is the optional method for computing the covariance of missing values assigned. The choices are: • `everything` • `all.obs` • `complete.obs` • `na.or.complete` • `pairwise.complete.obs`
method	This parameter stores which correlation method is to be used in order to estimate a rank-based measure of the associations computed. The choices are: • `pearson` • `kendall` (Kendall's tau) • `spearman` (Spearman's rho)

Example

Let's use the historical data of stock, bonds, and treasuries' returns from NYU, which is available at `http://people.stern.nyu.edu/adamodar/New_Home_Page/data.html`. We produce a dataset that we can load in as follows:

```
> install.packages("xlsx")
> library(xlsx)
> url <- "http://www.stern.nyu.edu/~adamodar/pc/datasets/histretSP.xls"
> download.file(url, destfile="histretSP.xls")
> data <- read.xlsx("histretSP.xls", 1, startRow=12, endRow=98, headers=TRUE)
```

We can take a cursory look at the data items with a `summary` command:

```
> summary(data)

      Year                SP500              TBill3Mos
 Min.    :1928     Min.    :-43.840     Min.    : 0.030
 1st Qu.:1949     1st Qu.: -1.205     1st Qu.: 1.022
 Median :1970     Median : 14.520     Median : 3.135
 Mean    :1970     Mean    : 11.505     Mean    : 3.573
 3rd Qu.:1992     3rd Qu.: 25.720     3rd Qu.: 5.228
 Max.    :2013     Max.    : 52.560     Max.    :14.300


  TBond10Year
 Min.    :-11.120
 1st Qu.:  1.012
 Median :  3.450
 Mean    :  5.213
 3rd Qu.:  8.400
 Max.    : 32.810
```

The data has columns for the following elements:

- Year
- S&P 500 returns for that year (in percentage)
- 3-month T-Bill returns
- 10-year T-Bond returns

We can see wildly fluctuating returns for stocks and bonds over the years.

Graphing the data points against each other produces a variety of scatter plots using the `splom()` (scatter plot matrices) function. The `splom()` function has a number of optional arguments:

```
splom(x,
      data,
      auto.key = FALSE,
      aspect = 1,
      between = list(x = 0.5, y = 0.5),
      panel = lattice.getOption("panel.splom"),
      prepanel,
      scales,
      strip,
      groups,
      xlab,
      xlim,
```

```
        ylab = NULL,
        ylim,
        superpanel = lattice.getOption("panel.pairs"),
        pscales = 5,
        varnames = NULL,
        drop.unused.levels,
        ...,
        lattice.options = NULL,
        default.scales,
        default.prepanel = lattice.getOption("prepanel.default.splom"),
        subset = TRUE)
```

The various parameters of the `splom` function are described in the following table:

Parameter	Description
x	This is the object to be affected, usually a data frame
data	This contains formula method values
...	Many more options

Once we have loaded the library, we can invoke the `splom` function:

```
> library(lattice)
```

```
> splom(~data[2:4])
```

There is no apparent relationship between the data points so far. Although, there are congregations of data points around central points.

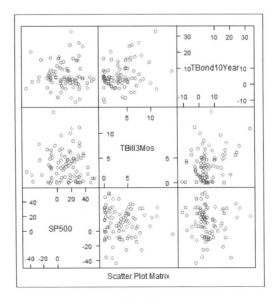

Scatter Plot Matrix

Similarly, we can use the `scatterplotMatrix()` function to draw out the different datasets. The `scatterplotMatrix` function automatically adds trendlines, as shown in the following output:

```
> install.packages("car")
> library(car)

> scatterplotMatrix(data)
```

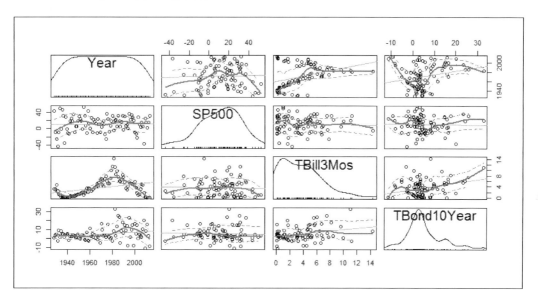

In these plots, we at least start to see some trending in the data as compared to a plain scatter diagram.

A standard correlation test produces the following output:

```
> cor(data)
                 Year        SP500     TBill3Mos  TBond10Year
Year       1.00000000  0.03968668   0.34819233   0.23669464
SP500      0.03968668  1.00000000  -0.03139095  -0.02981359
TBill3Mos  0.34819233 -0.03139095   1.00000000   0.29873018
TBond10Year 0.23669464 -0.02981359  0.29873018   1.00000000
```

You can see that the data points have perfect correlation against themselves with the 1.0 values. I had expected a strong relationship between stock and bond returns. The results show a high relationship between T-Bills and T-Bonds; this makes sense as they are similar investments. There is a slightly negative correlation between stocks and bonds. This probably makes sense as well, as people will favor one or the other depending on the investment climate at the time.

Visualizing correlations

We can visualize a correlation using the `corrgram()` function:

```
> install.packages('corrgram')

> library(corrgram)
> corrgram(data)
```

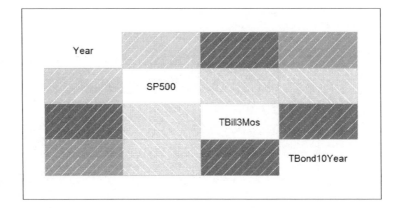

The results are color-coded to distinguish correlations: red for negative and blue for positive. In this case, the strong blue points (T-Bills and T-Bonds) are highly correlated. The red color is used to show negative correlation, so the pink shows some degree of negative correlation for S&P 500 and T-Bills and T-Bonds.

Let's look at a scatter plot of the bill and bond returns:

```
> plot(data$SP500,data$TBill3Mos)
```

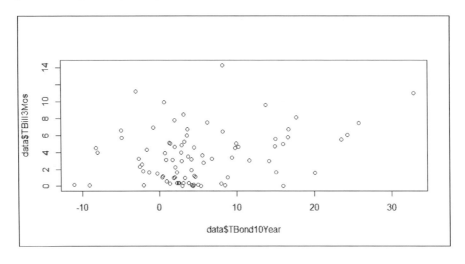

As you can tell from the previous graph, there is really no clearly distinguished relationship between the 3-month T Bill rate and the 10-year T Bond rate.

We could use regression to try to see the relationship better by adding a regression line to the graphic:

```
> abline(lm(data$TBill3Mos ~ data$TBond10Year))
```

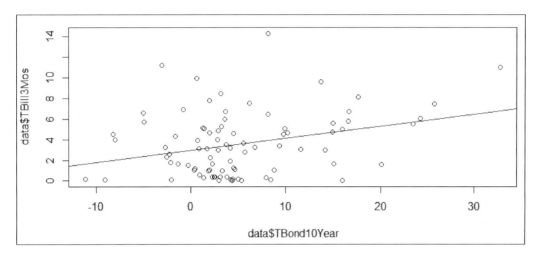

At least we can now visualize the relationship between the two.

There is another R package that has a correlation graphing function; the `chart.Correlation()` function is available in the `PerformanceAnalytics` package. The function call is shown in the following code:

```
chart.Correlation(R,
    histogram = TRUE,
    method = c("pearson", "kendall", "spearman"),
...)
```

The various parameters of the `chart.Correlation` function are described in the following table:

Parameter	Description
R	This contains the correlation values that will be plotted
histogram	This has a Boolean value to denote whether the chart includes a histogram

Parameter	Description
method	This will contain one of the following methods: • pearson • kendall • spearman
...	Any other pass through arguments to the pairs function

We load the PerformanceAnalytics package, load our dataset, and produce a chart of the correlations using the following code:

```
> install.packages("PerformanceAnalytics")

> library(PerformanceAnalytics)

> data <- read.csv("returns.csv")

> chart.Correlation(cor(data), histogram=TRUE)
```

The following graph provides a lot of information about the correlation in one nice plot:

- Along the diagonal, we have a smoothed plot of the data points
- Along the lower-left corner, we have (x,y) scatter plots of the fields
- The top-right corner just displays the correlation between the fields, and the size of the numeric is indicative of the amount of correlation present between the two fields

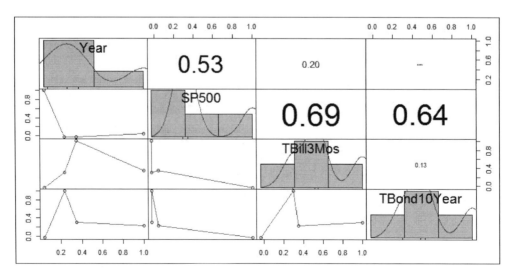

Covariance

As a further test, we can measure the covariance of the data elements using the cov function. Correlation and covariance are very similar terms. Correlation tells you the degree to which variables change together. Covariance measures how two variables change together (assuming they were random), whether positive (in the same direction) or negative. The cov function operates similar to the cor function:

```
> cov(data)
                  Year        SP500 TBill3Mos TBond10Year
Year         623.50000   19.835706 26.578824    46.387059
SP500         19.83571  400.653816 -1.920823    -4.683701
TBill3Mos     26.57882   -1.920823  9.345373     7.167499
TBond10Year   46.38706   -4.683701  7.167499    61.599953
```

As a rough measure of the scale, we can see a large number for year against itself—perfect covariance. In contrast, we find covariance values less than 10 for stocks and bonds. Again, we see very little of a relationship between the data values.

We can prove the correlation between two of the factors using the cor.test function. The cor.test function tests for an association between paired samples:

```
cor.test(x, y,
         alternative = c("two.sided", "less", "greater"),
         method = c("pearson", "kendall", "spearman"),
         exact = NULL, conf.level = 0.95, continuity = FALSE, ...)
```

The various parameters of the cor.test function are described in the following table:

Parameter	Description
x	This is a numerical vector
y	This is a numerical vector
alternative	This is the alternative hypothesis and it must be one of these: • two.sided • greater • less
method	This contains the correlation coefficient to be used: • pearson • kendall (Kendall's tau) • spearman (Spearman's rho)
exact	This defines the exact p-value to be used
continuity	If this is set to TRUE, continuity correction is used
...	These are the pass through arguments to subordinate functions

We can use two of the preceding factors in our dataset:

```
> cor.test(data$SP500, data$TBill3Mos)


    Pearson's product-moment correlation

data:  data$SP500 and data$TBill3Mos
t = -0.2878, df = 84, p-value = 0.7742
alternative hypothesis: true correlation is not equal to 0
95 percent confidence interval:
 -0.2416590  0.1816928
sample estimates:
        cor
-0.03139095
```

The 95 percent confidence level for a correlation between the S&P 500 returns and the 3-month T-Bill returns ranges from -0.24 to 0.18. We have a high p-value. The correlation estimate was -0.03, so we do have a correlation!

We can plot the various relationships at once using the `pairs` function. The `pairs` function plots each variable against every other variable on one graph:

```
> pairs(data)
```

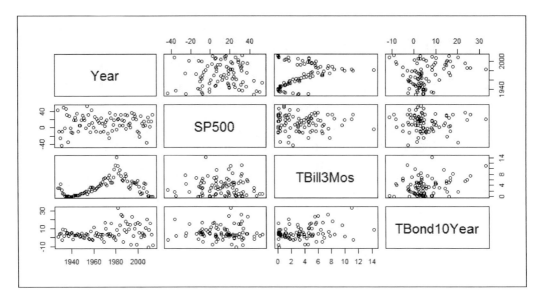

From these graphs, we can see a few points of interest:

- 3-month T Bills appear to have a marked relationship over time
- T Bonds have some kind of relationship with bills
- There is some relationship between bonds and S&P
- There doesn't appear to be any other relationships at all, and the other graphs are very scattered

Pearson correlation

We can also use the `rcorr` function in the `Hmisc` package to produce the set of Pearson correlations between all pairs. The Pearson correlation is a measure of the linear correlation between two variables ranging from -1 to 1, where -1 is pure negative, 1 is pure positive, and 0 meaning none. The only slight hiccup is the `rcorr` function expects a matrix rather than a data frame. The function call looks like:

```
rcorr(x, y, type=c("pearson","spearman"))
```

The various parameters of the `rcorr` function are described in the following table:

Parameter	Description
x	This is a numeric matrix with at least five rows and two columns (if y is absent).
y	This is a numeric vector or matrix that will be concatenated to x. If y is omitted for `rcorr`, x must be a matrix.
type	This specifies the type of correlations to compute. Spearman correlations are the Pearson linear correlations computed on the ranks of elements present, using midranks for ties.
...	These are the pass through arguments for the function.

We first load the package and library, and then we can invoke the function:

```
> install.packages('Hmisc')

> library(Hmisc)

> rcorr(as.matrix(data))
          Year SP500 TBill3Mos TBond10Year
Year      1.00  0.04      0.35        0.24
SP500     0.04  1.00     -0.03       -0.03
TBill3Mos 0.35 -0.03      1.00        0.30
```

```
TBond10Year 0.24 -0.03      0.30         1.00

n= 86


P
            Year    SP500   TBill3Mos TBond10Year
Year                0.7168  0.0010      0.0282
SP500       0.7168          0.7742      0.7852
TBill3Mos   0.0010  0.7742              0.0052
TBond10Year 0.0282  0.7852  0.0052
```

We see the same 1.0 correlation values in the axes. The correlation values have similar low correlations across the set. You can see there were 86 data points.

The p-values show the slightly negative relationship between S&P 500 returns and bills or bonds. The strong relationship between the bonds and bills is also shown in the p-values.

Polychoric correlation

R programming also provides a polychoric correlation function in the `polycor` package. Polychoric correlation is an estimate of the correlation between two normally distributed, continuous variables from two observed ordinal variables.

Polychoric correlation is used when the data items have a small number of options. The smaller the number of responses available, the more the correlation between the continuous variables.

We are using the self-esteem responses for online personality tests, which is available at http://personality-testing.info/_rawdata/. There are a few steps that are necessary to make the data readable in R. The top entry in the previous table references a ZIP file located at http://personality-testing.info/_rawdata/16PF.zip. Download this file to your workspace and extract the `data.csv` file as `poly.csv` in your workspace. Subjects were rated based on their replies for questions like, "I am a person of worth" on a scale from 1 (strongly disagree) to 4 (strongly agree). The code is as follows:

```
> data <- read.table("poly.csv", sep="\t")
> library(psych)
> result <- polychoric(data)
> plot(data)
```

In this example, we are measuring the correlation between the first two questions in the survey:

- I feel that I am a person of worth, at least on an equal plane with others.
- I feel that I have a number of good qualities.

In the following graph, we can see that most of the data points are matched with every other data point between the two factors. This just shows that we have clean data.

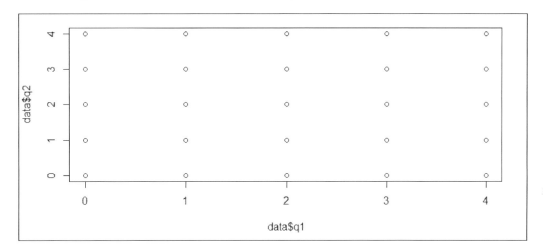

Again, to make sure that we have a good idea of what the data looks like, let's take a look at the histograms of the two questions:

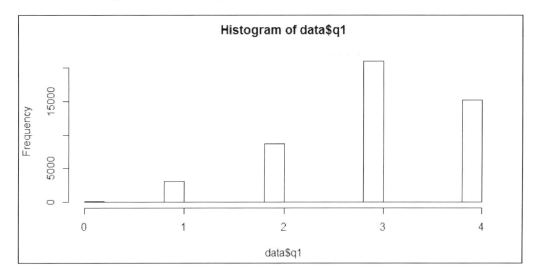

We see remarkable similarities between the responses for the two questions: a majority of people picked option 3, followed by 4, 2, and then 1. It is unfortunate that the survey questions were worded so similarly.

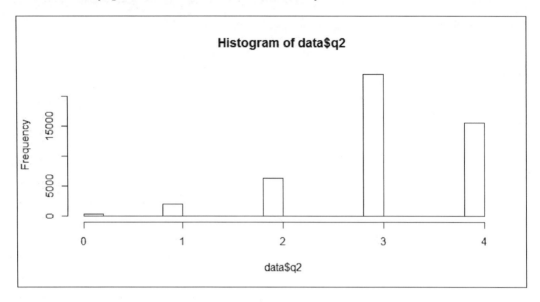

I thought it was interesting that the counts appeared to be very close between the two.

First, we need to load the `polycor` package:

```
> install.packages('polycor')
```

```
> library('polycor')
```

If we run a simple correlation between the two, we get a very high correlation value:

```
> cor(data$q1, data$q2)
[1] 0.6609112
```

Running `polychor` against the same values reveals an even higher correlation. Remember, the polychoric correlation takes into account the small number of possible options available.

 The `polychor` function can take some time.

The `polychor` function is as follows:

```
polychor(x,
smooth=TRUE,
global=TRUE,
polycor=FALSE,
ML = FALSE,
        std.err=FALSE,
weight=NULL,
progress=TRUE,
na.rm=TRUE,
delete=TRUE)
```

The various parameters of the `polychor` function are described in the following table:

Parameter	Description
x	This is the input, and normally this is a 2 x 2 matrix
smooth	If this is set to TRUE and the tetrachoric matrix is not positively definite, then apply a simple smoothing algorithm using cor.smooth
global	This defines whether to use global values or local values
polycor	This defines whether to use the polychor function
ML	This defines whether to compute maximum likelihood
std.err	This defines whether to report standard error
weight	This contains weights for observations
progress	This defines whether to show the progress bar
na.rm	This defines whether to delete the missing data
delete	This defines whether to delete cases with no variance

We can now run a polychoric correlation between the two using the following code:

```
> polychor(data$q1, data$q2)
[1] 0.7514105
```

Lastly, we run a full test using a maximum likelihood (`ML = TRUE`) estimate and return the estimated variance of the correlation (`std.err=TRUE`):

```
> polychor(data$q1, data$q2, ML=TRUE, std.err=TRUE)

Polychoric Correlation, ML est. = 0.7589 (0.002599)
Test of bivariate normality: Chisquare = 4875, df = 15, p = 0

   Row Thresholds
   Threshold Std.Err.
```

```
1      -2.741 0.027410
2      -1.499 0.008698
3      -0.695 0.006135
4       0.465 0.006006


   Column Thresholds
   Threshold Std.Err.
1    -2.3130 0.016130
2    -1.6450 0.009412
3    -0.9196 0.006595
4     0.4464 0.005983
```

We have a maximum likelihood estimate of 0.7589, which is very close to our `polychor` correlation of 0.7514.

With the high chi-square and large number of degrees of freedom, we cannot reject the null hypothesis. This makes sense; we estimated a high degree of correlation between the two, so we could predict one value using the other.

The thresholds for each variable are estimated along with the maximum likelihood. However, the threshold values computed are a large portion of the possible values. On the other hand, the standard errors are very small.

Overall, it looks like we really do have a high correlation between the two factors.

Tetrachoric correlation

Tetrachoric correlation is used for binary data in the same manner as polychoric correlation (covered in the previous section of this chapter) is used for categorical values.

For this test, we are using the Titanic survival information from the site `http://biostat.mc.vanderbilt.edu/wiki/Main/DataSets`. The binary data used is the survival characteristic. Various attributes of the passengers, such as age, ticket class, sex, and so on, are included in the dataset.

Once the dataset is loaded, we can view a summary:

```
> data <- read.csv("titanic3.csv")

> summary(data)

     pclass          survived
 Min.   :1.000   Min.   :0.000
 1st Qu.:2.000   1st Qu.:0.000
 Median :3.000   Median :0.000
 Mean   :2.295   Mean   :0.382
```

```
3rd Qu.:3.000    3rd Qu.:1.000
Max.    :3.000    Max.    :1.000


                              name              sex
Connolly, Miss. Kate          :    2    female:466
Kelly, Mr. James              :    2    male  :843
Abbing, Mr. Anthony           :    1
Abbott, Master. Eugene Joseph :    1
Abbott, Mr. Rossmore Edward   :    1
Abbott, Mrs. Stanton (Rosa Hunt):  1
(Other)                       :1301


      age              sibsp             parch
Min.   : 0.17    Min.   :0.0000    Min.    :0.000
1st Qu.:21.00    1st Qu.:0.0000    1st Qu.:0.000
Median :28.00    Median :0.0000    Median :0.000
Mean   :29.88    Mean   :0.4989    Mean    :0.385
3rd Qu.:39.00    3rd Qu.:1.0000    3rd Qu.:0.000
Max.   :80.00    Max.   :8.0000    Max.    :9.000
NA's   :263


      ticket            fare                  cabin
CA. 2343: 11    Min.   :  0.000              :1014
1601    :  8    1st Qu.:  7.896    C23 C25 C27  :    6
CA 2144 :  8    Median : 14.454    B57 B59 B63 B66:  5
3101295 :  7    Mean   : 33.295    G6           :    5
347077  :  7    3rd Qu.: 31.275    B96 B98      :    4
347082  :  7    Max.   :512.329    C22 C26      :    4
(Other) :1261   NA's   :1          (Other)      : 271

embarked      boat           body
 :  2         :823    Min.   :  1.0
C:270    13   : 39    1st Qu.: 72.0
Q:123    C    : 38    Median :155.0
S:914    15   : 37    Mean   :160.8
         14   : 33    3rd Qu.:256.0
         4    : 31    Max.   :328.0
         (Other):308  NA's   :1188


            home.dest
                 :564
New York, NY     : 64
London           : 14
```

```
Montreal, PQ          : 10
Cornwall / Akron, OH:  9
Paris, France         :  9
(Other)              :639
```

To run the tetrachoric correlation, we need to load the `psych` package:

```
> install.packages("psych")
```

```
> library(polycor)
```

The `tetrachoric` function is as follows

```
tetrachoric(x,
    y=NULL,
    correct=TRUE,
    smooth=TRUE,
    global=TRUE,
    weight=NULL,
    na.rm=TRUE,
    delete=TRUE)
```

The various parameters of the `tetrachoric` function are described in the following table:

Parameter	Description
x	This is the input, which is usually a 2 x 2 matrix
y	This contains discrete scores
correct	If this is set to TRUE, continuity correction is used
smooth	This is used to apply a smoothing algorithm
global	This defines whether to use global values or local
weight	This contains weights that will be applied
na.rm	This is used to delete missing values
delete	This is used to delete cases with missing covariance

The tetrachoric correlation is based on a 2 x 2 matrix of the applicable data points. In this case, we are looking at those who survived and what sex they were. We can use the `subset` and `nrow` functions to gather these counts:

```
> nrow(subset(data, survived==1 & sex=='male'))
[1] 161
> nrow(subset(data, survived==1 & sex=='female'))
[1] 339
> nrow(subset(data, survived==0 & sex=='male'))
```

```
[1] 682
> nrow(subset(data, survived==0 & sex=='female'))
[1] 127
```

Now, we have the data needed to run the tetrachoric correlation. Let's run the tetrachoric correlation:

```
> tetrachoric(matrix(c(161,339,682,127),2,2))

Call: tetrachoric(x = matrix(c(161, 339, 682, 127), 2, 2))
tetrachoric correlation
[1] -0.75


 with tau of
[1]   0.37 -0.30
```

We can get a visual of the correlation with the `draw.tetra` function using the following command:

```
> draw.tetra(-0.75, 0.37, -0.30)
```

We can see that the data is localized to the lower-left corner of the positive quadrant in the graph. As we only had values of 0, 1, and 2, that was expected. The function also highlighted the apparent alignment of the data into a normal distribution (as you can see from the highlighted section of the normal distribution graphics on the top and right hand side of the tetra diagram).

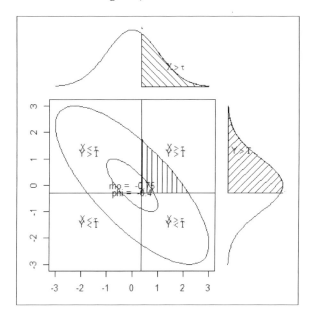

A heterogeneous correlation matrix

We can also generate a heterogeneous correlation matrix using R. (This example is right out of the manual, but shows the actual data points.) We are using random data, so set the seed and generate the correlations and the data in a normal distribution.

To generate a heterogeneous correlation matrix, we perform the following steps:

1. We are using random numbers here. So, in order to reproduce the results, we set the random number seed to a specific value:

```
> set.seed(12345)
```

2. We will create a 4 x 4 matrix of zeroes:

```
> R <- matrix(0, 4, 4)
```

3. Then, we generate random numbers in a uniform distribution:

```
> R[upper.tri(R)] <- runif(6)
```

4. Let's set the diagonal of the matrix to 1s:

```
> diag(R) <- 1
```

5. Now, we'll compute the correlation matrix:

```
> R <- cov2cor(t(R) %*% R)
> round(R, 4)   # population correlations

          [,1]    [,2]    [,3]    [,4]
[1,]  1.0000  0.5848  0.5718  0.6233
[2,]  0.5848  1.0000  0.7374  0.6249
[3,]  0.5718  0.7374  1.0000  0.5923
[4,]  0.6233  0.6249  0.5923  1.0000


> data <- rmvnorm(1000, rep(0, 4), R)
> round(cor(data), 4)
          [,1]    [,2]    [,3]    [,4]
[1,]  1.0000  0.5577  0.5648  0.5948
[2,]  0.5577  1.0000  0.7410  0.6203
[3,]  0.5648  0.7410  1.0000  0.5959
[4,]  0.5948  0.6203  0.5959  1.0000
```

6. So, we have the parameters needed to invoke the function:

```
> x1 <- data[,1]
> x2 <- data[,2]
> y1 <- cut(data[,3], c(-Inf, .75, Inf))
> y2 <- cut(data[,4], c(-Inf, -1, .5, 1.5, Inf))
```

```
> data <- data.frame(x1, x2, y1, y2)
> hetcor(data)

Two-Step Estimates

Correlations/Type of Correlation:
        x1       x2          y1          y2
x1       1 Pearson Polyserial Polyserial
x2 0.5577        1 Polyserial Polyserial
y1 0.5538  0.7479          1 Polychoric
y2 0.6299   0.627     0.6051          1


Standard Errors:
        x1       x2       y1
x1
x2 0.02181
y1 0.03286 0.02288
y2 0.01992 0.01991 0.03484


n = 1000


P-values for Tests of Bivariate Normality:
        x1      x2      y1
x1
x2 0.9934
y1 0.8882 0.5964
y2  0.765 0.4645 0.5452
```

The standard error values are pretty low, the correlations are solid, and the normality numbers are spot on. We generated highly correlated data points—this was expected.

7. We can generate the ML estimate as well:

```
> hetcor(x1, x2, y1, y2, ML=TRUE)

Maximum-Likelihood Estimates

Correlations/Type of Correlation:
        x1       x2          y1          y2
x1       1 Pearson Polyserial Polyserial
x2 0.5577        1 Polyserial Polyserial
y1 0.5537  0.7484          1 Polychoric
```

```
y2 0.6301   0.6274       0.6052              1

Standard Errors:
        x1       x2       y1
x1
x2 0.02181
y1 0.03299    0.023
y2 0.02044 0.02043 0.03593

n = 1000

P-values for Tests of Bivariate Normality:
        x1       x2       y1
x1
x2 0.9934
y1 0.8861 0.5878
y2 0.7558 0.4649 0.5485
```

Partial correlation

We can produce a partial correlation between the variables in R as well. Partial correlation is the degree of association between random variables removing the controlling variables from the following equation:

```
> install.packages('ggm')

> library(ggm)

> pcor(c("SP500","TBill3Mos"),var(data))
[1] -0.03139095
```

This exactly matches the previous correlation matrix value.

Excluding the 10-year bond makes little difference in the results:

```
> pcor(c("SP500","TBill3Mos","TBond10Year"),var(data))
[1] -0.02357104
```

Questions

Factual

- How can you decide whether to use Pearson, Kendall, or Spearman as a method for correlation?
- When would you want to see a small degree of freedom in the correlation results?
- Most of the examples used common default parameters. Explore the same examples with nondefault parameters.

When, how, and why?

- Why do the polychoric functions take so long to process?
- Why are the values chosen in the polychoric responses correlated?
- Explain the threshold values that were calculated.

Challenges

- Is there an easier way to develop the 2 x 2 matrix needed as input to the tetrachoric function?
- How could you account for trends in investment vehicles when analyzing stock market returns versus fixed instruments?

Summary

In this chapter, we discussed different aspects of correlation using R. We determined the correlations between datasets using several methods and generated the corresponding graphics to display the correlation values. We were able to determine the correlations among binary data observations. Similarly, we computed the correlations between observations with a small number of responses. Lastly, we determined partial correlations.

In the next chapter, we will learn about clustering.

6
Data Analysis – Clustering

Clustering is the process of trying to make groups of objects that are more similar to each other than objects in other groups. Clustering is also called cluster analysis.

R has several tools to cluster your data (which we will investigate in this chapter):

- K-means, including optimal number of clusters
- Partitioning Around Medoids (PAM)
- Bayesian hierarchical clustering
- Affinity propagation clustering
- Computing a gap statistic to estimate the number of clusters
- Hierarchical clustering

Packages

For R, there are several packages available that provide clustering functionality for the programmer. We will use the following packages in the examples:

- `NbClust`: This is the number of cluster indices
- `fpc`: This contains flexible procedures for clustering
- `vegan`: This is the Community Ecology Package
- `apcluster`: This package performs affinity propagation clustering
- `pvclust`: This package performs hierarchical clustering

K-means clustering

K-means is the process of assigning objects to groups so that the sum of the squares of the groups is minimized. R has the `kmeans` function available for cluster analysis. K-means is a method of determining clusters based on partitioning the data and assigning items in the dataset to the nearest cluster.

K-means clustering is done in R using the `kmeans` function. The `kmeans` function is defined as follows:

```
kmeans(x, centers, iter.max = 10, nstart = 1,
    algorithm = c("Hartigan-Wong", "Lloyd", "Forgy","MacQueen"),
trace=FALSE)
```

The various parameters of this function are described in the following table:

Parameter	Description
x	This is the dataset.
centers	This contains the number of centers/clusters to find.
iter.max	This stores the maximum number of iterations allowed.
nstart	This contains the number of random clusters to find.
algorithm	This contains the algorithm to be used to determine clusters. Hartigan-Wong is the default. Lloyd and Forgy are the same algorithm.
trace	This parameter produces trace information on algorithm progress to determine centers. This is only applicable to Hartigan-Wong.

Example

In our example of k-means clustering, I am using the wine quality data from UCI Machine Learning Repository at `http://www.ics.uci.edu/~mlearn/MLRepository.html`.

First, we load the data (note that this is not a standard CSV file; it uses the semicolon as a column separator) as follows:

```
> data <- read.csv("https://archive.ics.uci.edu/ml/machine-learning-
databases/wine-quality/winequality-white.csv", sep=";")
```

There are close to 5,000 observations in the dataset. Here's a summary of the data that provides an overview:

```
> summary(data)

 fixed.acidityvolatile.aciditycitric.acid
 Min.   : 3.800   Min.   :0.0800   Min.   :0.0000
 1st Qu.: 6.300   1st Qu.:0.2100   1st Qu.:0.2700
 Median : 6.800   Median :0.2600   Median :0.3200
 Mean   : 6.855   Mean   :0.2782   Mean   :0.3342
 3rd Qu.: 7.300   3rd Qu.:0.3200   3rd Qu.:0.3900
 Max.   :14.200   Max.   :1.1000   Max.   :1.6600

 residual.sugar     chlorides       free.sulfur.dioxide
 Min.   : 0.600   Min.   :0.00900   Min.   :  2.00
 1st Qu.: 1.700   1st Qu.:0.03600   1st Qu.: 23.00
 Median : 5.200   Median :0.04300   Median : 34.00
 Mean   : 6.391   Mean   :0.04577   Mean   : 35.31
 3rd Qu.: 9.900   3rd Qu.:0.05000   3rd Qu.: 46.00
 Max.   :65.800   Max.   :0.34600   Max.   :289.00

 total.sulfur.dioxide    density           pH
 Min.   :  9.0     Min.   :0.9871   Min.   :2.720
 1st Qu.:108.0     1st Qu.:0.9917   1st Qu.:3.090
 Median :134.0     Median :0.9937   Median :3.180
 Mean   :138.4     Mean   :0.9940   Mean   :3.188
 3rd Qu.:167.0     3rd Qu.:0.9961   3rd Qu.:3.280
 Max.   :440.0     Max.   :1.0390   Max.   :3.820

   sulphates         alcohol          quality
 Min.   :0.2200   Min.   : 8.00    Min.   :3.000
 1st Qu.:0.4100   1st Qu.: 9.50    1st Qu.:5.000
 Median :0.4700   Median :10.40    Median :6.000
 Mean   :0.4898   Mean   :10.51    Mean   :5.878
 3rd Qu.:0.5500   3rd Qu.:11.40    3rd Qu.:6.000
 Max.   :1.0800   Max.   :14.20    Max.   :9.000
```

I am not a wine connoisseur, but these sound like reasonable attributes that can be used to determine wine quality. It is surprising that the range of the data is so great. Several of the attributes vary from close to zero to a two- or three-digit number.

We can plot the data to get a bird's-eye view of the apparent relationships present. Here's how the plotted data looks:

```
> plot(data)
```

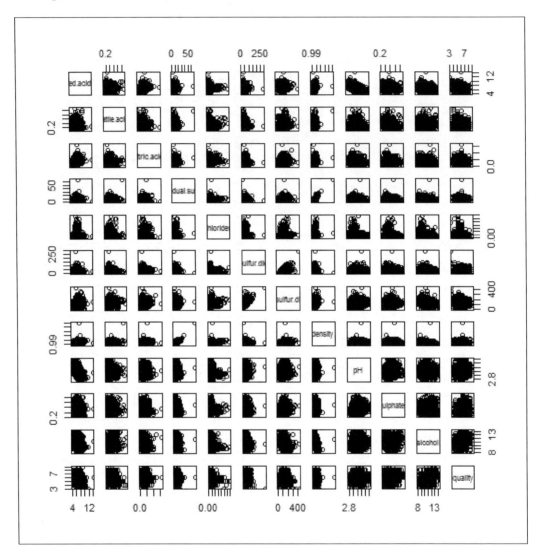

There appear to be many strong relationships among the attributes present—as can be seen by the wide, dark areas present in almost every subgraph.

The `kmeans` function returns an object that provides details on the clusters and the object assignments that are being prescribed, such as which cluster each item is assigned, the total number of squares, and the iterations that took place.

Our first k-means cluster analysis reveals the following:

```
> kmeans(data,5)


K-means clustering with 5 clusters of sizes 993, 718, 392, 1276, 1519

Cluster means:
   fixed.acidityvolatile.aciditycitric.acidresidual.sugar
1      6.960524       0.2855388     0.3537160      8.824018
2      6.813370       0.2799025     0.3158357      3.450557
3      7.010969       0.3073980     0.3557908     10.033801
4      6.840321       0.2724726     0.3359326      7.006975
5      6.777090       0.2700066     0.3230678      4.734200

     chlorides free.sulfur.dioxidetotal.sulfur.dioxide   density
1 0.05114804            47.02971            179.05690 0.9959135
2 0.04015042            18.86212             77.53482 0.9918326
3 0.05228571            55.29847            221.74617 0.9968072
4 0.04732367            37.70415            145.32367 0.9944275
5 0.04193153            28.24753            113.13989 0.9927783

         pH sulphates   alcohol  quality
1 3.183112 0.5075831  9.831101 5.629406
2 3.175864 0.4691086 11.255687 5.903900
3 3.178265 0.5180357  9.541582 5.522959
4 3.198770 0.4855643 10.397542 5.938088
5 3.191257 0.4843779 10.959480 6.069124

Clustering vector:
    [1] 1 5 5 1 1 5 4 1 5 5 2 5 2 4 1 5 5 2 1 4 2 5 5 1 4 3 4 4 5
   [30] 5 4 2 5 5 1 5 4 4 4 4 1 1 4 4 4 1 3 3 4 4 1 5 2 5 4 1 3 4
   [59] 2 5 5 4 4 2 5 5 5 1 5 5 3 3 1 2 5 5 2 2 5 5 5 1 1 3 4 4 4
   [88] 3 4 4 4 3 4 4 4 3 4 2 2 4 1 1 1 1 1 5 1 1 1 1 1 3 1 4 4 5
  [117] 4 2 1 1 2 4 4 4 4 4 5 3 1 1 2 3 3 1 3 1 5 4 5 2 2 4 5 5 2
  [146] 5 1 2 2 5 4 4 5 5 2 1 1 5 5 5 5 4 2 1 3 1 1 5 4 5 4 2 2 4
  [175] 1 4 2 1 5 1 1 1 1 3 3 3 1 5 5 3 3 1 5 5 1 1 1 3 3 3 1 3 3
  [204] 4 5 4 5 5 2 1 2 5 5 5 5 4 1 4 1 4 1 1 5 4 4 4 1 3 1 4 4 1
... (many more lines of data)
[4873] 1 5 5 5 5 2 2 1 1 5 4 4 1 1 5 2 5 5 5 5 5 2 1 5 5 5

Within cluster sum of squares by cluster:
[1] 394416.5 241930.9 388646.0 381855.0 346222.3
 (between_SS / total_SS =  83.1 %)
```

Running the same analysis using 10 clusters yields a much smaller sum of squares (and we also increased our percentage of between versus total from 83 to 90), as follows:

```
> kmeans(data,10)
…
Within cluster sum of squares by cluster:
 [1]  69530.92  86524.22 101918.82 224437.86  80365.61 114842.79
 [7] 112139.31  89575.63  83942.30 100867.45
 (between_SS / total_SS =  89.8 %)
Using 15 we see a further movement:
> kmeans(data,15)

…
Within cluster sum of squares by cluster:
 [1]  47054.21  19357.85  43750.34  44484.13  73327.35  43978.19
 [7]  53886.56  47845.73  39506.90  32966.08 184764.12  58340.23
[13]  53868.83  33703.61  35534.54
 (between_SS / total_SS =  92.2 %)
```

And lastly, at 20 clusters, we see the following:

```
> kmeans(data,20)
Within cluster sum of squares by cluster:
 [1] 37184.486 47160.578 32028.939  7341.079 28065.158 31830.439
 [7] 35303.537 25278.525 28224.605 21418.290 33523.032 62025.326
[13] 15794.070 37469.911 37145.145 21650.444 36625.103 22344.633
[19] 29586.005 23591.604
 (between_SS / total_SS =  94.1 %)
```

I think running the analysis using somewhere near 10 clusters yields the most useful data, as beyond 10 we get a marginal improvement in the sum of squares, but the data should not have such a wide number of cases. Beyond that, the data appears to be very fractured.

We can use the data from five clusters in order to evaluate the results:

- For each of the attributes, we get cluster values.
- The cluster values are in the order of association with data points rather than the numerical order. That makes sense. For some reason, I just expect things to be in numerical order in such a table.
- It is interesting that a couple of the attributes, sugar and dioxides, have larger clusters that are not evenly distributed.

Optimal number of clusters

We can have R figure out the optimal number of clusters using the `NbClust` package. The `NbClust` function runs over each of the number of clusters proposed using a series of indices (30) that measure the centers and distances, tallying a **vote** of each index set for a preferred number of clusters. The results clearly point to a majority decision, such as "*n* indices recommend *m* clusters."

The `NbClust` function looks like the following:

```
NbClust(data, diss = NULL, distance = "euclidean",
min.nc = 2, max.nc =15,
   method = "ward.D2", index = "all", alphaBeale = 0.1)
```

The various parameters of this function are described in the following table:

Parameter	Description
data	This is the dataset.
diss	This is the dissimilarity matrix. The default is NULL.
distance	This is the distance metric to be used.
min.nc	This is the minimum number of clusters.
max.nc	This is the maximum number of clusters.
method	This is the cluster method to be used. It must be one of the following methods: ward, single, complete, average, mcquitty, median, centroid, or kmeans.
index	This is the index to be calculated. Many choices are available.
alphaBeale	This contains a significance value for the Beale index.

We can run the function against our dataset as the following code. We ask `NbClust` to run through all of the cluster sizes from 10 to 15 and provide a recommendation for the number of clusters to use. The function will use the `kmeans` method to determine the optimal number, as follows:

```
> install.packages("NbClust")
> library(NbClust)
> set.seed(2365)
> nc <- NbClust(data, min.nc=10, max.nc=15, method="kmeans")
```

 We set the seed for random selection. The process is not deterministic. Providing a specific seed for random functionality allows the process to be reproducible. Also, this process might take a while depending on the range of minimum and maximum that you provide.

All 4,898 observations were used. Here's the result of running the code:

```
*********************************************************************
* Among all indices:
* 2 proposed 10 as the best number of clusters
* 14 proposed 11 as the best number of clusters
* 2 proposed 13 as the best number of clusters
* 2 proposed 14 as the best number of clusters
* 3 proposed 15 as the best number of clusters

                  ***** Conclusion *****

* According to the majority rule, the best number of clusters is 11
*********************************************************************
```

We can see the results a little clearer with a histogram of the clusters:

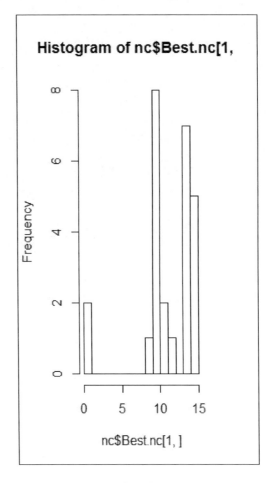

The function automatically generates the following graphs (showing clearly the *best* choice for the specified number of clusters):

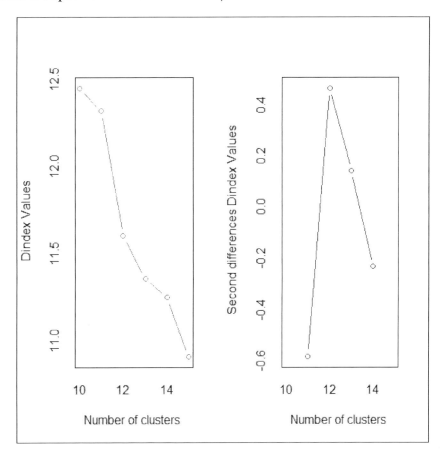

In the graph, we usually look for the **elbow**. Above and below that point, it is not efficient to use that number of clusters. In this case, we can take the lowest value from the second difference graph as the primary motivator for the selected number of clusters, as that corresponds to the elbow that appears slightly in the top-left corner of the first graph.

Medoids clusters

There is another package available to estimate the number of clusters using medoids, called `fpc`. Medoids use minimal dissimilarity to all objects in a cluster as the determinant (as opposed to distance in `kmeans`). The `pamk` function looks like the following:

```
pamk(data, krange=2:10, criterion="asw",  usepam=TRUE,
     scaling=FALSE, alpha=0.001, diss=inherits(data, "dist"),
     critout=FALSE, ns=10, seed=NULL, ...)
```

The various parameters of this function are described in the following table:

Parameter	Description
data	This is the dataset.
krange	This is the number of clusters compared to the average silhouette. The default range is 2 to 10.
criterion	This is the average silhouette method. This should be one of the following: asw, multiasw, or ch. The default is asw.
usepam	This is a logical flag. We can use pam if set to TRUE, else clara. clara is recommended for large datasets. The default value is TRUE.
scaling	This is a logical flag. If set to TRUE, then variables are divided by the root mean square. The default is FALSE.
alpha	This is the tuning constant for the dudahart method. The default value is 0.001.
diss	This is a logical flag about using the dissimilarity matrix.
critout	This is a logical flag about the print criteria for each cluster. The default value is FALSE.
ns	This is a pass through parameter to the distcritmulti function if criterion="multisaw". The default is 10.
seed	This is a pass through parameter to the distcritmulti function if criterion="multisaw". The default is NULL.

Using the `pamk` function against our dataset yields the following result:

```
> install.packages("fpc")
> library(fpc)
> best <- pamk(data)

> best
```

```
$pamobject
Medoids:
        ID fixed.acidityvolatile.aciditycitric.acid
[1,] 3331             6.7              0.23         0.33
[2,] 1149             7.0              0.17         0.37
     residual.sugar chlorides free.sulfur.dioxide
[1,]            8.1     0.048                   45
[2,]            5.7     0.025                   29
     total.sulfur.dioxide density   pH sulphates alcohol
[1,]                  176 0.99472 3.11     0.52     10.1
[2,]                  111 0.99380 3.20     0.49     10.8
     quality
[1,]       6
[2,]       6
Clustering vector:
   [1] 1 2 2 1 1 2 2 1 2 2 2 2 2 1 1 2 2 2 1 2 2 2 2 1 2 1 1 2 2
  [30] 2 2 2 2 2 1 2 1 2 1 1 1 1 1 1 1 1 1 1 1 1 2 2 2 2 1 1 1
  [59] 2 2 2 1 1 2 2 2 2 1 2 2 1 1 1 2 2 2 2 2 2 2 2 1 1 1 1 1 1
  [88] 1 1 1 1 1 2 2 1 1 1 2 2 1 1 1 1 1 1 2 1 1 1 1 1 1 1 1 1 2
 [117] 2 2 1 1 2 2 2 2 1 1 2 1 1 1 2 1 1 1 1 2 1 2 2 2 1 2 2 2
...
[4873] 1 2 2 2 2 2 2 1 1 2 1 1 1 1 2 2 2 2 2 2 2 2 2 1 2 2 2
Objective function:
   build       swap
28.42058 24.79196

Available components:
 [1] "medoids"    "id.med"     "clustering" "objective"
 [5] "isolation"  "clusinfo"   "silinfo"    "diss"
 [9] "call"       "data"

$nc
[1] 2

$crit
 [1] 0.0000000 0.5060017 0.3976270 0.3643445 0.3372835 0.2963456
 [7] 0.2724782 0.2885286 0.2923836 0.2898382
```

Unexpectedly, the pamk method selected two clusters. The results show the breakdown among the parameters, including which cluster each data point is applied to.

We can plot the results as well for better visualization, as follows:

```
> library(cluster)
> plot(pam(data, best$nc))
```

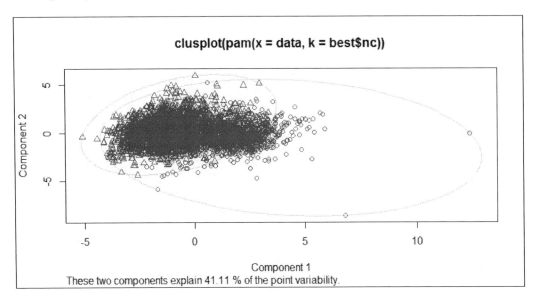

You can see the two clusters that were categorized by the pam function. This makes some sense, as it is similar to the original, dense subplots shown here.

The cascadeKM function

We can also use the cascadeKM function within the vegan package. The cascadeKM function is a wrapper to a kmeans implementation that traverses a range of cluster sizes and produces results that can be used to determine the optimal cluster size.

The function looks as shown in the following code:

```
cascadeKM(data, inf.gr, sup.gr, iter = 100, criterion = "calinski")
```

The various parameters of this function are described in the following table:

Parameter	Description
data	This is the data matrix.
inf.gr	This is the lower bound.
sup.gr	This is the upper bound.
iter	This is the number of iterations.

Parameter	Description
criterion	This is the criterion to select clusters. calinski and ssi are the recommended methods.

We run the function against our data over 100 iterations and plot the results (I ran into a memory issue running the test 1,000 times):

```
> install.packages("vegan")
> library(vegan)
> fit <- cascadeKM(scale(data, center=TRUE, scale=TRUE), 10, 15)
> plot(fit, sortg=TRUE, grmts.plot=TRUE)
```

 This is another memory-intensive function. It takes a long time to run, even over just 100 (the default) iterations.

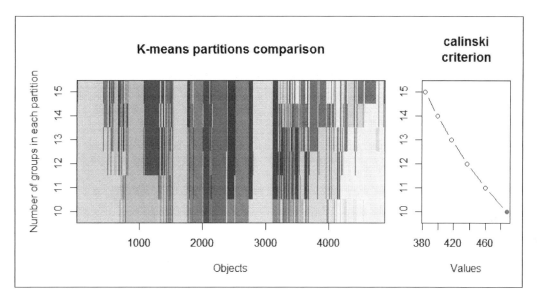

The result is a graph that shows the number of groups in each partition versus the number of objects. The idea is to determine the size of the dataset you have and select the best number of clusters. In this case, we have just about 5,000 observations. Reading into the (color) graph and over to the **calinski criterion** graph, we will use 10 clusters.

Selecting clusters based on Bayesian information

Another method in R to select clusters is the `Mclust` function in the `mclust` package. The `Mclust` function selects the optimal cluster size based on Bayesian information present in the data.

We run the function against our dataset (the white wine data from the previous section) using the same range of 10 to 15 clusters and then plot the results:

```
> library(mclust)
> d <- Mclust(as.matrix(data), G=10:15)
> plot(d)
```

The function produces three different graphs:

- The first graph compares the Bayesian information against the number of clusters (components) as follows:

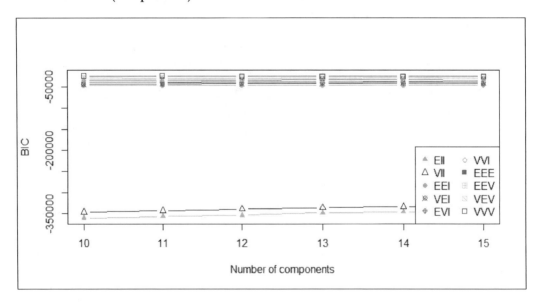

The graph starts with the lowest point at **10**. I am using 10 as optimal as further breakdown increases BIC.

- The second demonstrates each of the subgraphs, comparing each attribute against each other in a plot, as follows:

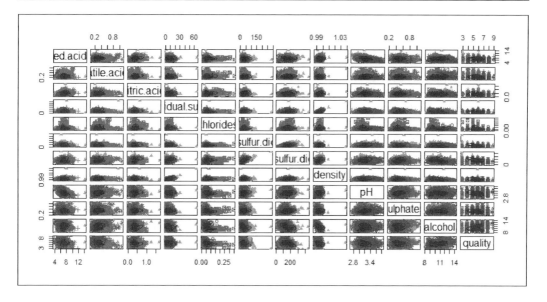

Here, we see a similar graph to the previous one, which shows a high degree of correlation between the components.

- The third graph shows log density contour plots for each of the attribute comparisons, as follows:

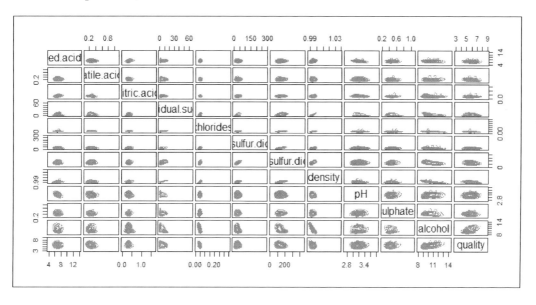

The contour graphs show that some of the attributes are of less interest. The more interesting attributes are more dense (pH versus sulphate versus alcohol).

Just looking at the resulting object summary also produces interesting information, as follows:

```
> summary(d)
-------------------------------------------------------
Gaussian finite mixture model fitted by EM algorithm
-------------------------------------------------------

MclustVVV (ellipsoidal, varying volume, shape, and orientation) model
with 11 components:

 log.likelihood    n   dfBIC        ICL
     -7739.467 4898 1000 -23975.52 -25496.66

Clustering table:
    1    2    3    4    5    6    7    8    9   10   11
  648  729 1103  483   54  335  540  232  587  139   48
```

We see the number of observations (4898) and the number of iterations (1000). We have a Bayesian Information Criterion value of -23975. We will use the BIC computed with one cluster of a particular size against another cluster size for a comparative value. The BIC presented in the summary is for the optimal clusters selected.

The clustering table shows optimum at 11 clusters. It is interesting that just 5 clusters is a close second choice.

Affinity propagation clustering

R programming has a function for affinity propagation clustering, apcluster. Affinity propagation clustering works by comparing the various values for information about what cluster to assign. The apcluster function looks as shown in the next piece of code.

We can run the aplcuster function against the data as follows:

```
> install.packages("apcluster")
> library(apcluster)
> neg <- negDistMat(data, r=2)
> ap <- apcluster(neg)
> ap

APResult object

Number of samples     =   4898
```

```
Number of iterations   =   410
Input preference       =   -2160.385
Sum of similarities    =   -214614.5
Sum of preferences     =   -174991.2
Net similarity         =   -389605.7
Number of clusters     =   81


Exemplars:
    111 163 185 276 400 422 444 460 495 513 658 675 731 747 782 798 814
873 922
    930 1058 1206 1297 1312 1418 1476 1548 1557 1592 1689 1755 1764
1806 1862
    1893 1932 2056 2127 2182 2204 2249 2308 2379 2517 2568 2573 2674
2782 2841
    2892 2919 2955 2983 3037 3073 3196 3248 3380 3496 3497 3523 3598
3600 3752
    3763 3787 3815 3824 4086 4123 4164 4215 4241 4278 4348 4373 4434
4516 4746
    4807 4848
Clusters:
    Cluster 1, exemplar 111:
        41 42 102 107 111 219 348 395 402 480 681 752 852 857 860 1015
1086 1105
        1127 1138 1207 1304 1316 1508 1908 1956 2099 2109 2319 2369 2659
2878
        2976 3214 3266 3428 3511 3599 3794 3898 4067 4069 4073 4177 4227
4301
        4430 4530 4531 4532 4672 4673 4680 4700 4701 4769 4770 4771 4772
4849
        4851 4880 4881 4886
...
> summary(ap)
  Length    Class      Mode
      81 APResultS4
> length(ap@clusters)
[1] 81
```

So, we end up with a completely different value for the optimal number of clusters: 81!. This implies that the data has high affinity. We can display the affinity data in a graph (which generates all the subgraphs as in the previous graph). The graph does show high affinity between most of the variables involved:

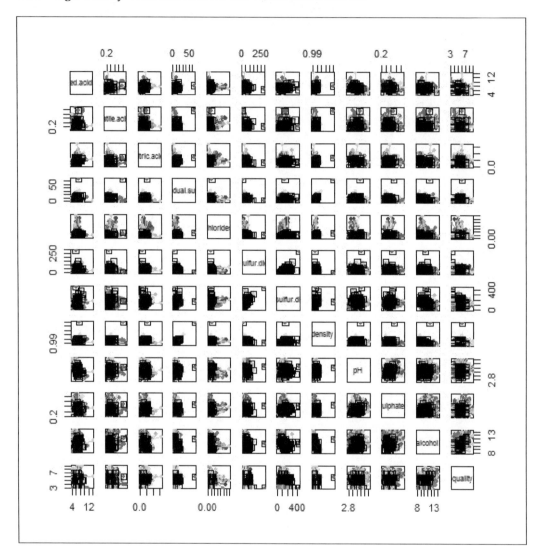

I think it is a little amazing that all of the variables involved in the dataset are so correlated.

Gap statistic to estimate the number of clusters

Another tool available is the `clusGap` function in the cluster library. The `clusGap` function calculates a goodness-of-clustering measure or gap statistic for a range of cluster values and reports on the results.

Interestingly, the function will also provide feedback as the algorithm progresses on its status.

The function call looks as shown in the following code:

```
clusGap(x, FUNcluster, K.max, B = 100, verbose = interactive(), ...)
```

The various parameters of this function are described in the following table:

Parameter	Description
x	This is the dataset.
FUNcluster	This is the clustering function.
K.max	This is the maximum number of clusters to consider.
B	This is the number of Monte Carlo samples to use.
verbose	This tells whether to produce progress output.

Execution (using the interactive feature) against the wine dataset produces this output:

```
> library(cluster)
> clusGap(data, kmeans, 15, B=100, verbose=interactive())
Clustering k = 1,2,..., K.max (= 15): .. done
Bootstrapping, b = 1,2,..., B (= 100)  [one "." per sample]:
.............................................. 50
.............................................. 100
Clustering Gap statistic ["clusGap"].
B=100 simulated reference sets, k = 1..15
 --> Number of clusters (method 'firstSEmax', SE.factor=1): 4
logWE.logW       gap       SE.sim
 [1,] 11.107738 12.39454 1.286797 0.004752362
 [2,] 10.661378 11.96485 1.303473 0.004227228
 [3,] 10.457735 11.79927 1.341531 0.011813389
 [4,] 10.317094 11.69955 1.382453 0.005451640
 [5,] 10.233403 11.60180 1.368400 0.005028345
 [6,] 10.175547 11.50335 1.327803 0.004041562
 [7,] 10.102540 11.43084 1.328297 0.003767100
 [8,] 10.062713 11.37084 1.308128 0.008152799
```

```
[9,]  10.000954  11.32524  1.324286  0.005380141
[10,]   9.963436  11.28827  1.324830  0.006042356
[11,]   9.936529  11.25665  1.320121  0.005529404
[12,]   9.898593  11.22739  1.328794  0.004627005
[13,]   9.869964  11.19813  1.328167  0.004508561
```

From the results, the clusGap function is telling us to use four clusters—as can be seen by the highest gap between logW and E.logW in the table of results. The first number in the table is the number of clusters indexed (the function always starts with two clusters, and we asked it to proceed to 15 and hence the number ranges from 1 to 13).

If we instead store the results in a variable and graph the results, we can see:

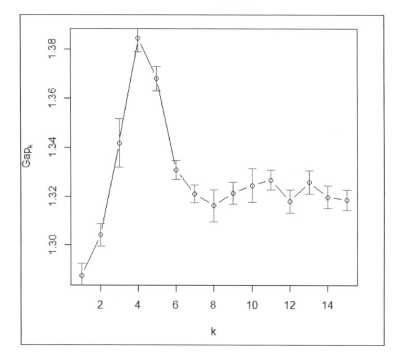

The table display emphasizes **4** as the best number of clusters. It wasn't clear looking at the data values in the table that there was such a large variance between the number of clusters at **4** and the other values.

Hierarchical clustering

We can also use the pvclust function for hierarchical clustering. Hierarchical clustering is available in R using the pvclust function in the pvclust package. The pvclust function looks like the following code:

```
pvclust(data, method.hclust="average",
    method.dist="correlation", use.cor="pairwise.complete.obs",
    nboot=1000, r=seq(.5,1.4,by=.1), store=FALSE, weight=FALSE)
```

The various parameters of this function are described in the following table:

Parameter	Description
data	This is the matrix or data frame.
method.hclust	This is the agglomerative method of hierarchical clustering. This should be one of the following methods: • average • ward • single • complete • mcquitty • median • centroid The default is average.
method.dist	This is the distance measure to be used. This should be one of the following values: • correlation • uncentered • abscor The default is correlation.
use.cor	This is the method to be used to compute the correlation for missing values. This should be one of the following methods: • all.obs • complete.obs • pairwise.complete.obs
nboot	This is the number of bootstrap replications. The default is 1000.

Parameter	Description
r	This is the relative sample size.
store	This is a logical flag about storing bootstraps in the result.
weight	This is a logical flag about computing association by the weight vector.

We need to load the package for `pvclust`, which can be done as follows:

```
> install.packages("pvclust")
> library(pvclust)
```

Using the wine data as the source for the function, we see results like the following:

```
> pv <- pvclust(data)
Bootstrap (r = 0.5)... Done.
Bootstrap (r = 0.6)... Done.
Bootstrap (r = 0.7)... Done.
Bootstrap (r = 0.8)... Done.
Bootstrap (r = 0.9)... Done.
Bootstrap (r = 1.0)... Done.
Bootstrap (r = 1.1)... Done.
Bootstrap (r = 1.2)... Done.
Bootstrap (r = 1.3)... Done.
Bootstrap (r = 1.4)... Done.
```

The summary is uninteresting, whereas the actual data is meaningful:

```
> pv

Cluster method: average
Distance      : correlation

Estimates on edges:

      au    bpse.ause.bp     v       c    pchi
1   1.000 1.000 0.000 0.000  0.000  0.000 0.000
2   1.000 1.000 0.000 0.000  0.000  0.000 0.000
3   1.000 1.000 0.000 0.000  0.000  0.000 0.000
4   1.000 1.000 0.000 0.000  0.000  0.000 0.000
5   1.000 1.000 0.000 0.000  0.000  0.000 0.000
6   0.793 0.999 0.737 0.002 -2.002 -1.184 1.000
7   0.992 0.992 0.005 0.001 -2.415 -0.006 0.653
8   1.000 1.000 0.000 0.000  0.000  0.000 0.000
9   0.992 0.997 0.007 0.001 -2.581 -0.167 0.309
10  0.998 0.994 0.001 0.001 -2.721  0.186 0.854
11  1.000 1.000 0.000 0.000  0.000  0.000 0.000
```

The first values (1:11) correspond to the attributes present in the dataset. Most of the variables have a very high effect on the data except for the sixth—free sulphur dioxide. This is curious as the said compound is an additive to wine to prevent microbe growth and oxidation. I wouldn't expect such an additive to add flavor to wine.

And the plot highlights the hierarchy present in the data—we can see the less-affecting attributes pushed down the hierarchy. The following code plots the data:

```
> plot(pv)
```

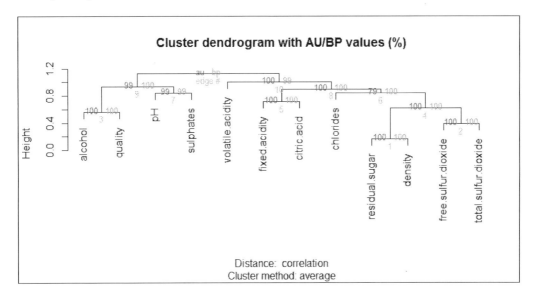

Questions

Factual

- Attempt to use an array of iterations when determining the clusters present.
- Try using some of the other, non-default methods to determine clusters.
- Which clustering method would work best with your data?

When, how, and why?

- From package to package, we arrived at a different number of proposed clusters. How would you decide the number of clusters to use with your data?
- Several of the methods appeared to be overwhelmed by the contributions of the various data points in the wine data (as can be seen by many of the subgraphs that are nearly completely filled in). Is there a way to make the clustering more discriminatory?

Challenges

- Many of the clustering methods are memory-intensive. It was necessary to store the data being used in the R format on the disk and reload in order to free up some space. R does have memory management functions available that might have made that process easier. Investigate being able to use the raw CSV file.

- With such an array of values available for the wine clustering, we used all of the data. Investigate using a subset of the values for clustering.

Summary

In this chapter, we discussed different aspects of clustering using R. We used a couple of different methods to select the number of clusters. We used k-means clustering, which appears to be the most prevalent tool in use. We used medoids clustering, another popular choice. We also looked into Bayesian clustering, an interesting choice for this type of data. Lastly, we looked at affinity clustering.

In the next chapter, we will cover the graphics functionality available in R.

7
Data Visualization – R Graphics

Data visualization in R is typically performed using a graphic to display the characteristics of the data. As a result, the attributes become easier to understand or interpret. This chapter focuses on several graphics that can be used in R to achieve that goal.

R has several tools for visualization. In this chapter, we will cover the following topics:

- Interaction with robust graphics packages to manipulate a graphic once it is created from R
- Various mapping tools

Packages

In R, there are several packages that provide the visualization functionality to the programmer. We will use the following packages in the examples of this chapter:

- `classIn`: This contains univariate class intervals
- `ggplot2`: This has a large number of graphical features
- `gpclib`: This is used for polygon clipping
- `hexbin`: This is used for bivariate data manipulation
- `latticist`: This is an interface between R and the Latticist program
- `mapdata`: This has data that can be added directly to maps
- `maps`: This contains maps of various geographical areas
- `maptools`: This has the access mechanisms to use the maps

- `playwith`: This contains the interface between R and other programs, such as GTK+
- `RColorBrewer`: This is used for map shading
- `RgoogleMaps`: This contains the maps from Google for use in R

Interactive graphics

The R programming system interfaces with the GTK+ toolkit to allow the programmer to interactively modify a graphic. You can invoke the GTK+ toolkit using the `playwith` function. The `playwith` function is used to pass a number of parameters from the R programming space to the GTK+ space. The `playwith` function is called as follows:

```
playwith(expr,
new = playwith.getOption("new"),
title = NULL,
labels = NULL,
data.points = NULL,
viewport = NULL,
parameters = list(),
tools = list(),
init.actions = list(),
preplot.actions = list(),
update.actions = list(),
...,
width = playwith.getOption("width"),
height = playwith.getOption("height"),
pointsize = playwith.getOption("pointsize"),
eval.args = playwith.getOption("eval.args"),
on.close = playwith.getOption("on.close"),
modal = FALSE,
link.to = NULL,
playState = if (!new) playDevCur(),
plot.call,
main.function)
```

The various parameters of the `playwith` function are described in the following table:

Parameter	Description
expr	This contains the expression to create a plot.
title	This is the optional window title.

Parameter	Description
labels	This is a character vector of labels. It will be determined from data if it is not provided.
data.points	This is the vector of data points.
viewport	This is the viewport representing the data space.
parameters	This contains the simple controls (typing) for data.
tools	This is a list of GTK+ tools.
init.actions	This is a list of actions to be run at the start.
prepplot. actions	This is a list of actions to be run before plotting.
update.actions	This is a list of actions to be run after plotting.
width	This is the initial width of plot device in inches.
height	This is the initial height of plot device in inches.
pointsize	This is the default point size for text.
eval.args	This contains a Boolean value and evaluates the plot.call arguments.
on.close	This has the function to call when user closes the plot window.
modal	This contains a Boolean value and determines whether plot window is modal.
linkto	This contains a set of brushed points that will be linked.
playstate	This is the object which will store the playstate of the graphic.
plot.call	This is the plot call (this can be used instead of expr).
main.function	This contains the name of the main function to be used.

The steps required to invoke GTK+ are as follows.

Install and start using the playwith library:

```
> install.packages("playwith")
> library("playwith")
```

Now, depending on the operating system you are using to run R, you will be prompted to install GTK+. You can choose any option as per your requirements.

 If you do not install GTK+, then the playwith package will not work. Also, once you have GTK+ installed, you must restart R in order to use this functionality.

Let's load some data to display. This is the same wine quality data we referenced in the previous chapter:

```
> data <- read.csv("https://archive.ics.uci.edu/ml/machine-learning-
databases/wine-quality/winequality-white.csv", sep=";")
```

We display a simple plot of the fixed acidity in the wine samples (for example):

```
> plot(data$fixed.acidity)
```

The display will look like this:

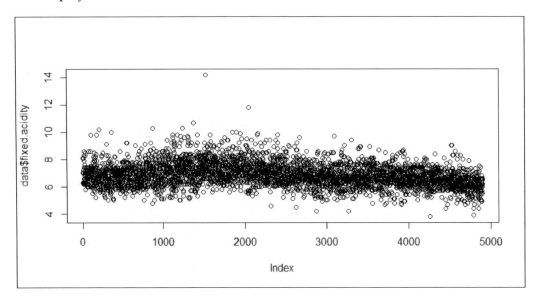

Now, we invoke the `playwith` function passing the plot over as an argument:

```
> playwith(plot(data$fixed.acidity))
```

You should have a display that looks like this:

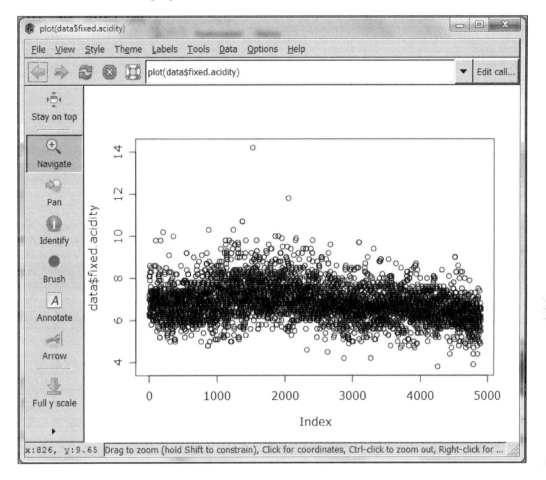

Now, you can use any of the GTK+ toolkits to manipulate your graphic. GTK+, or the GIMP toolkit, is a multiplatform toolkit to create graphical user interfaces. You can perform the following functions in GTK+:

- Zoom in and out of the graphic
- Rotate the graphic (if it is 3D)
- Make annotations
- Add arrow markers
- Change the scale

There are many more standard graphical devices, labels, fonts, styles, and so on.

The latticist package

The `latticist` package works just like the GTK+ package in that it provides a separate interface to manipulate an R graphic. The steps to invoke `latticist` are as follows:

```
> install.packages("latticist")
> library("latticist")
> latticist(data$fixed.acidity)
```

Note, `latticist` assumes that a third-party graphical toolkit is available. GTK+ is one of the toolkits that work with `latticist` (hence, you can see that a very similarly styled image editor is invoked in the following screenshot).

The resulting `latticist` display for the same plot is as follows:

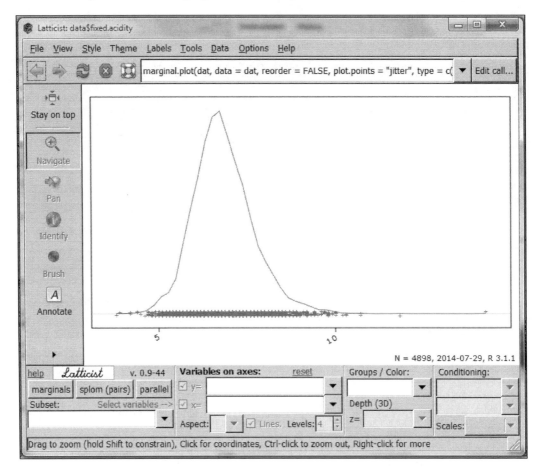

The `latticist` application allows you to manipulate the dataset passed over from R in the following ways:

- Choose variables and expressions for the axes
- Build groups (for display)
- Make subsets

 Note, the `latticist` package is not compatible with the current version of R. Given its usefulness, I would expect the package to be updated to support the user base.

Bivariate binning display

We can use the `hexbin` function/library to group and organize bivariate data. The `hexbin` function looks like this:

```
hexbin(x, y, xbins = 30, shape = 1,
       xbnds = range(x), ybnds = range(y),
       xlab = NULL, ylab = NULL)
```

The various parameters of this function are described in the following table:

Parameter	Description
x, y	These are the vectors of the bivariate data that will be used
xbins	This is the number of bins for the x scale
shape	This is the shape of the plotting regions, where *Shape = y height / x width*
xbnds, ybnds	These are the horizontal and vertical limits
xlab, ylab	These are the optional horizontal and vertical labels

For an example, we will use airport data from the Washington University survey at http://faculty.washington.edu/kenrice/sisg-adv/airportlocations. csv. The data contains the longitude and latitude of 13,000 airports. We can use the `hexbin` function to collate the coordinates and plot their relative positions:

```
> data <- read.csv("http://faculty.washington.edu/kenrice/sisg-adv/
airportlocations.csv")

> summary(data)

  locationID      Latitude         Longitude
 00AK   :   1   Min.   : 5.883   Min.   : 64.80
 00AL   :   1   1st Qu.:34.475   1st Qu.: 83.71
```

```
00AZ     :     1     Median :39.433    Median : 92.38
00C      :     1     Mean   :39.414    Mean   : 96.05
00CA     :     1     3rd Qu.:42.993    3rd Qu.:101.89
00CO     :     1     Max.   :71.286    Max.   :177.38
(Other):13423
```

So, the data consists of call signs for the airports and their latitude and longitude. There are 13,000 entries. (I didn't realize there were that many.)

We install the hexbin package as follows:

```
> install.packages("hexbin")
> library(hexbin)
```

Using the coordinates of the airports as our x and y variables, we see that the binning operation of hexbin produces the following result:

```
> bin <- hexbin(data$Latitude,data$Longitude)
> bin
'hexbin' object from call: hexbin(x = data$Latitude, y =
data$Longitude)
n = 13429  points in nc = 229  hexagon cells in grid dimensions  36 by
31
```

Starting with 13,000 data points, we end up with 229 bins in a 36 x 31 matrix. We can get a visual of the bins using a standard plot:

```
> plot(bin)
```

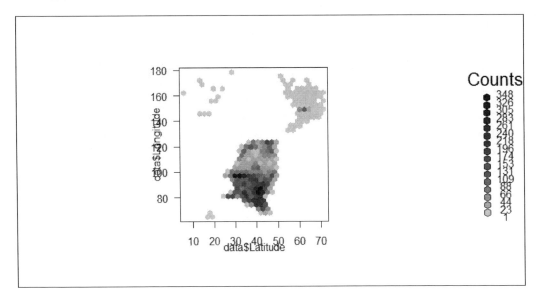

The plot shows higher density as darker areas on the grid. The highest density appears to be near 40 degrees latitude and 90 degrees longitude—somewhere in the far east.

Mapping

There are several packages that provide mapping information for R. We can produce standard maps using the `maps` package. To produce a map of USA, we use the following code:

```
> install.packages("mapdata")
> map(database="usa", col="gray90", fill=TRUE)
```

This produces the following plot:

This is a fairly standard plot. There are quite a few additional parameters available when mapping the `map` call. The `map` function is called as follows:

```
map(database = "world", regions = ".", exact = FALSE,
boundary = TRUE, interior = TRUE, projection = "", parameters = NULL,
orientation = NULL,
   fill = FALSE, col = 1, plot = TRUE, add = FALSE,
namesonly = FALSE, xlim = NULL, ylim = NULL,
wrap = FALSE, resolution = if(plot) 1 else 0,
   type = "l", bg = par("bg"),
mar = c(4.1, 4.1, par("mar")[3], 0.1),
   myborder = 0.01, ...)
```

The various parameters of this function are described in the following table:

Parameter	Description
database	This will contain one of the world, usa, state, or county database. The default database is world.
regions	This is a vector of polygons to draw. It can include multiple polygons with the following naming convention: north:boston.
exact	This takes a Boolean value, where TRUE means only exact region matches are to be used. The default is FALSE.
boundary	This takes a Boolean value, where TRUE means boundaries are to be drawn. The default is FALSE.
interior	This takes a Boolean value, where TRUE means interior segments are drawn. The default is TRUE.
projection	This contains the character string of projection to use. It includes many options, but the standard is mercator.
parameters	These are the parameters for projection.
orientation	This is the vector to be used for plotting the map, and it includes latitude, longitude, and rotation.
fill	This takes a Boolean value, where TRUE means filling the map. The default is FALSE.
col	This has the fill color that will be used.
plot	This takes a Boolean value, and it is used to determine whether to return a plot from function call.
add	This takes a Boolean value, and it is used to determine whether to add the plot points of the map to the current plot.
namesonly	This takes a Boolean value, and it is used to determine whether to return vector of region names.
xlim, ylim	These are the ranges of longitude and latitude.
wrap	This takes a Boolean value, and it is used to determine whether to omit lines that go off screen.
resolution	This is the resolution to be used when drawing the map.
bg	This takes a Boolean value, and it is used to determine whether to draw background.
mar	This contains the margins to be used.
myborder	This contains a vector of coordinates for border.

Plotting points on a map

We have maps and we have data (with location information). We can combine the two using standard map functions.

First, let's load the various packages that are invoked (some invoked indirectly by our coding):

```
> library(maps)
> library(maptools)
> library(RColorBrewer)
> install.packages("classInt")
> library(classInt)
> install.packages("gpclib")
> library(gpclib)
> library(mapdata)
```

Plotting points on a world map

```
> map("worldHires")
```

The words "world" and "worldHires" are synonyms. The word "worldHires" was the name of the company that originally produced the map information.

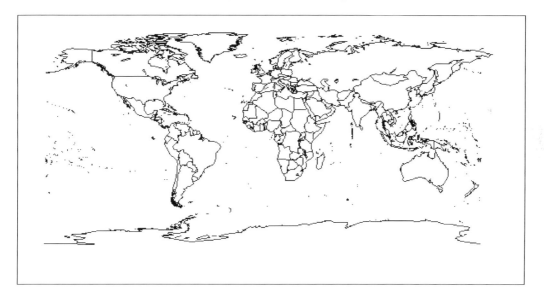

Let's plot our airport locations against the map. For this, we use the `points` function:

```
> points(data$Longitude,data$Latitude,pch=16,col="red",cex=1)
```

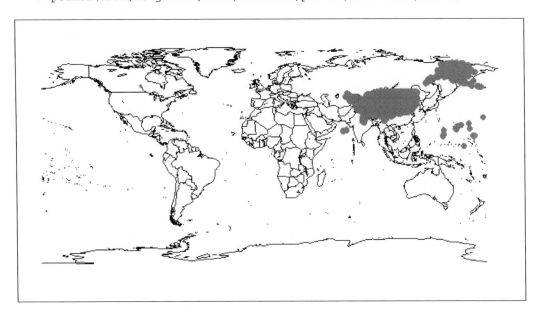

We can see a pretty solid coverage all over the far east.

The `points` function looks like this:

```
points(x, ...)
```

The various parameters of this function are described in the following table:

Parameter	Description
x	These are the points to be plotted on the current graphic. It should contain *x* and *y* coordinates of each point.
pch	This is used to plot the character to be used for each point. The period character, ".", specially handles a rectangle of at least one pixel depending on the `cex` parameter.
col	This is the color of each point.
bg	This is the background color of each point.
cex	This is the expansion factor, for example, to make some points larger than others.
lwd	This is the line width (used when drawing symbols from pch).

Let's work to get a map that just shows the areas of interest. For this, we will be using earthquake data from the `quakes` library. This data is built into the `quakes` package. Load the data, produce a world map, and show earthquakes of interest.
The data appears as follows:

```
> require(graphics)
> head(quakes)
      lat    long depth mag stations
1 -20.42 181.62   562 4.8       41
2 -20.62 181.03   650 4.2       15
3 -26.00 184.10    42 5.4       43
4 -17.97 181.66   626 4.1       19
5 -20.42 181.96   649 4.0       11
6 -19.68 184.31   195 4.0       12
> mean(quakes$mag)
[1] 4.6204
```

As you can see, the quakes are very localized to the southwest Pacific (further in the following graphic). Data is verified by multiple stations. All appear to be fairly strong with an average magnitude of 4.6.

If we display the data on the complete world map, we get the following graph:

```
> map()
> points(quakes$long,quakes$lat,pch=".",col="red",cex=1)
```

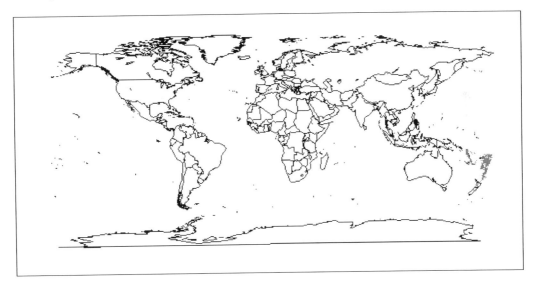

As you can see, we only have earthquake data for the southwest Pacific region. If we change the parameters of the map function call, we can focus on that region in the display (and ignore anything outside of that region):

```
> lon <- mean(quakes$lon)
> lat <- mean(quakes$lat)
> orient <- c(lat,lon,0)
> x <- c(min(quakes$lon)/2,max(quakes$lon)*1.5)
> y <- c(min(quakes$lat)-10,max(quakes$lat)+10)
> map(database= "world", ylim=y, xlim=x, col="grey80", fill=TRUE)
> points(quakes$long,quakes$lat,pch=".",col="red",cex=quakes$mag/2)
```

We localize the boundaries of the map display to be within the range of the quake data. Adjusting the longitude and latitude is necessary to account for changes in the area you are dealing with due to the negative numbers present.

I also adjusted the quake magnitude a little to give an indication of the magnitude of each quake.

The resulting plot looks like this:

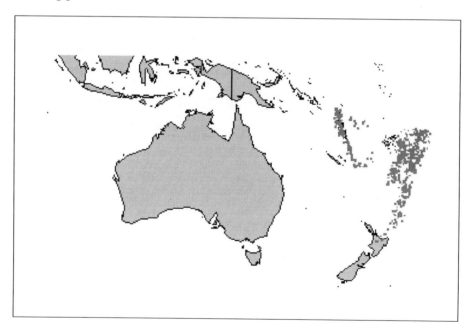

Given the previous seismic data graphic, the shapes of eastern Australia, New Zealand, and Micronesia become more apparently in line with the underlying geological situation.

Google Maps

There is an R package to interface with Google Maps, called `RgoogleMaps`. Here is example coding to produce the initial terrain map (note that the maps are produced directly to file rather than being displayed in the R viewer):

```
> library(RgoogleMaps)
> terrain <-
GetMap(center=c(lat,lon),zoom=5,maptype="terrain",destfile="terrain.
png",scale=c(320,320)
```

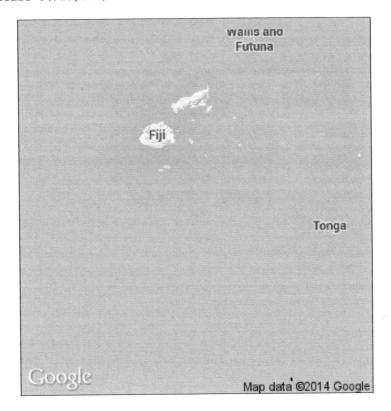

I have scaled the display to fit within this document. It would have been interesting to get the undersea terrain map, but that does not appear to be available.

If we were to plot our quake data atop this graphic, we use the following commands:

```
> markers <- cbind.data.frame(quakes$lat,quakes$long,"small","red","")
> names(markers) <- c("lat","lon","size","col","char")
> terrain <- GetMap.bbox(center=c(lat,lon),z
oom=5,maptype="terrain",destfile="terrain2.
png",lonR=range(quakes$long),latR=range(quakes$lat),markers=markers)
```

However, there appears to be severe memory constraints using the Google Maps product beyond a handful of data points, and I could not get the display to work. Maybe a later version of the software will be corrected.

The ggplot2 package

The ggplot2 package is one of the standard visualization tools available in R. We can produce scatter plots using ggplot2. We will use the Fiji quake data mentioned in the previous section:

```
> qplot(lat,long,data=quakes,color=mag)
```

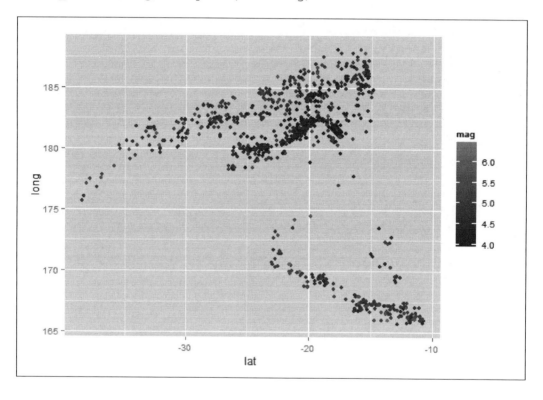

We can add more information to the graph by making the size of the points correspond to some other attribute, such as depth:

```
> qplot(lat,long,data=quakes,color=mag,size=depth)
```

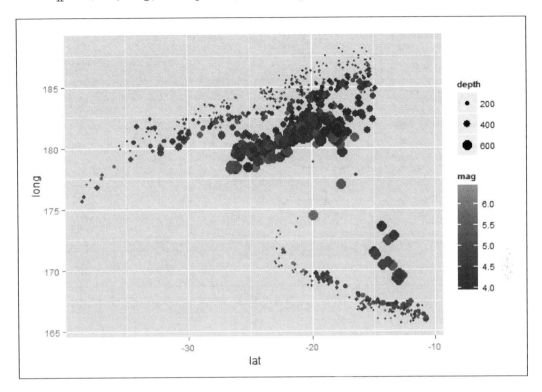

There is a distinction between the various magnitudes of the quakes—they appear to be widely distributed in scale.

We can reduce the effect of the collisions with the globs of color where data points overlap by adjusting the alpha factor (in this case, we are using 0.5):

```
qplot(lat,long,data=quakes,color=mag,size=depth, alpha=0.5)
```

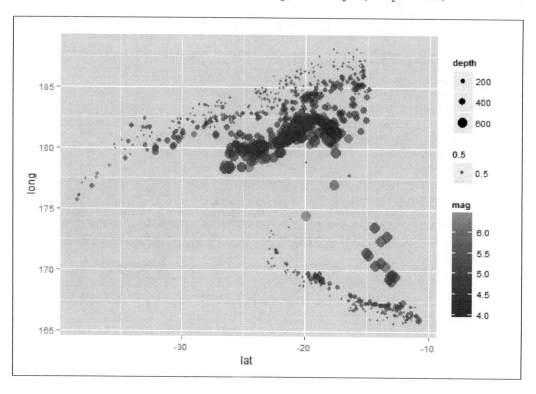

Now, we can more clearly see the independent points.

The `ggplot` function has other geom (geometric methods available). We can generate a line graph (using the women dataset) as follows:

```
qplot(height,weight,data=women,geom="line")
```

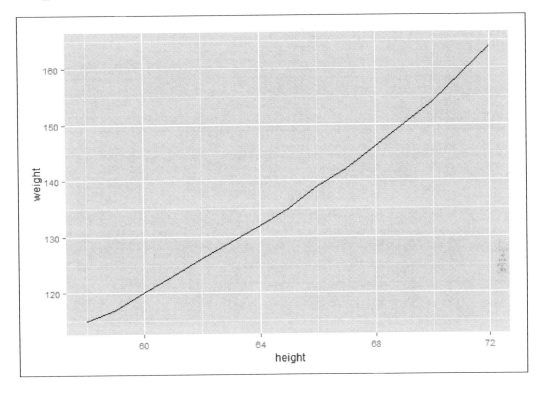

A bar chart geom against the MASS dataset of the eighteenth century painters can be generated using the following code:

```
> qplot(School,data=painters,geom="bar")
```

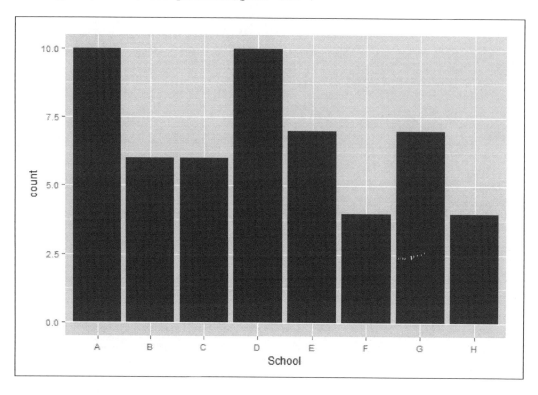

We can draw on facets within the data using the ggplot function. Using wine quality data referenced earlier, we get the following output:

```
> ggplot(data, aes(x=residual.sugar, y=alcohol))
Error: No layers in plot
```

Unlike the other plotting functions in R, ggplot needs to save its plot information into a variable for further manipulation first, as shown here:

```
> sa <- ggplot(data, aes(x=residual.sugar, y=alcohol))
```

Then, we specify the geom we want to apply to the data as follows:

```
> sa <- sa + geom_line()
```

The resulting graph is shown here:

```
> sa
```

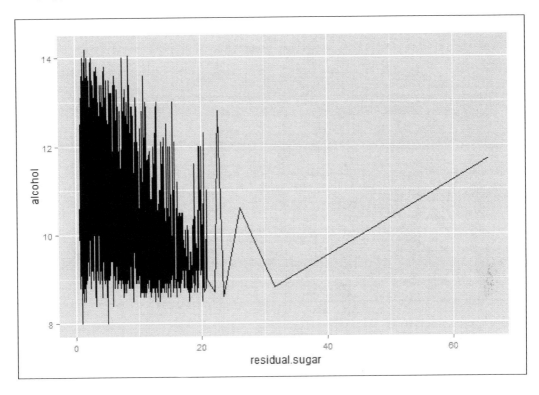

It looks like most of the data has a value of less than 20 for residual sugar with just a few outliers. I was curious whether the quality of the wine had any basis for the sugar/alcohol relationship.

We can split up the data using one of the characteristics as a facet. In this case, we are generating separate graphs for the sugar/alcohol relationship based on the quality level of the wine:

```
> sa + facet_grid(. ~ quality)
```

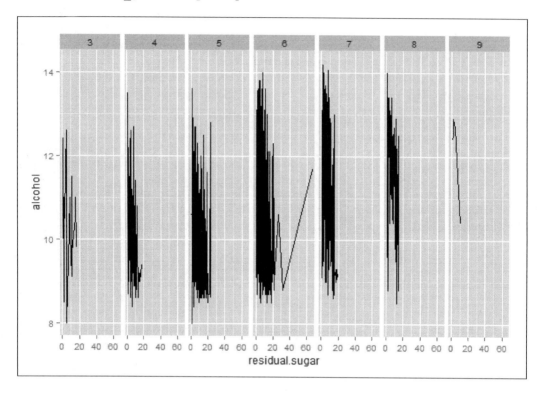

Overall, there appears to be a slightly positive correlation between the alcohol level and the wine quality level. I am not sure if an alcohol level of 0.11 versus 0.12 is significant from a taste point of view.

The `facet_grid` function call can either start with a period or end with a period. Starting with a period gives a horizontal layout to the graphs. Ending with a period presents a vertical layout, as shown in the following example:

```
> sa + facet_grid(quality ~ .)
```

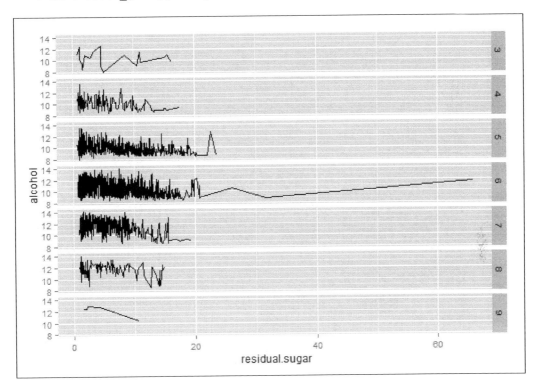

It is interesting that we can see a decrease in the alcohol level as the sugar value increases. I had not expected that. Maybe it is a good idea to play with the layouts of the plots to make sure you are getting all the aspects/information you can out of your data.

We can add a visual smoothing factor to our graph as well use the geom_smooth function:

```
> sa <- ggplot(data, aes(x=residual.sugar, y=alcohol))
> sa <- sa + geom_line()
> sa <- sa + geom_smooth()
> sa
```

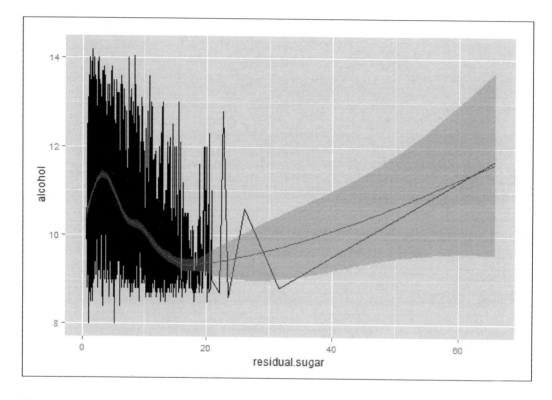

Now, we can see a pronounced decrease in the alcohol level with the increase in sugar. The wide tail is due to such sparse data.

We can use ggplot to produce a histogram of the same data:

```
> ggplot(data, aes(x=residual.sugar)) + geom_histogram(binwidth=.5)
```

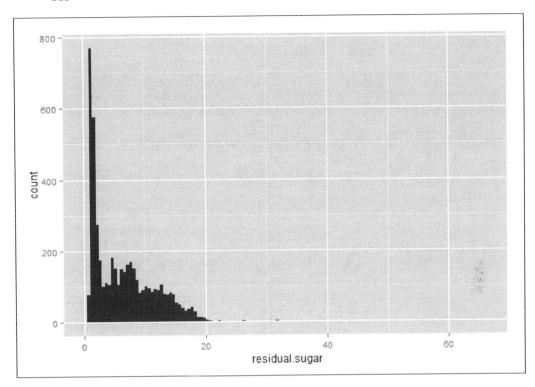

It is interesting that a clear majority of the wines have a very low sugar count, but notice that the graph goes out to 0.06 – almost 20 times the mean value.

Using the same data, we can produce a density graph using `ggplot` via the following code:

```
> ggplot(data, aes(x=residual.sugar)) + geom_density()
```

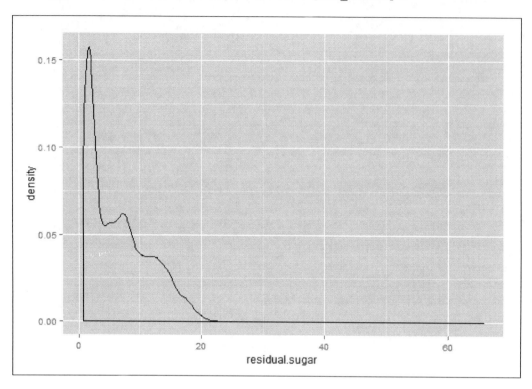

Of course, this graph just mimics the graph we saw just previously with summary information.

Lastly, we can use the `boxplot` feature of `ggplot` (using the same data as the previous section):

```
> bp <- ggplot(data, aes(x=residual.sugar, y=alcohol))
> bp <- bp + geom_boxplot()
> bp + facet_grid(. ~ quality)
```

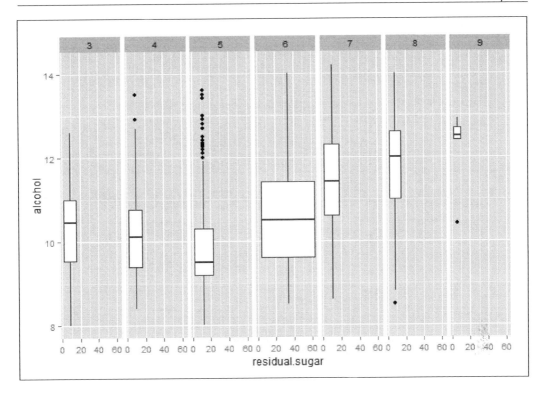

You can now see a marked increase in alcohol/sugar levels with the higher quality of the wines in the box plot graphic.

Questions

Factual

- Use of `hexbin` to manipulate bivariate data has shown several tools. What bivariate data do you have that would benefit from an application using `hexbin`?
- The `ggplot`has function has several other features that I did not explore in this chapter. Familiarize yourself with them.

When, how, and why?

- The `map` functionality appears to be very robust. How might you change the `map` function calls used in the chapter to result in a clearer graphic presentation?
- In the sugar/alcohol graphics, should we exclude the outlier values?

Challenges

- Explore the use of the `playwith` tools to get a good idea about how the interaction works, especially the transfer of data between the external tool and R.

- It was difficult to get any results from `RgoogleMaps` without running out of memory. I have to believe there is something worthwhile there to use.

Summary

In this chapter, we discussed different aspects of visualization using R. We used the interactive, third-party packages to manipulate a graphics display with GTK+ and `latticist`. We saw the display of bivariate data using `hexbin`. There were built-in packages and external packages (`GoogleMaps`) to apply data points to geographical maps. Finally, we touched upon some of the features of the `ggplot` toolkit.

In the next chapter, we will discuss plotting.

8
Data Visualization – Plotting

A key visualization technique in R is a plot, whether it is a scatter plot, bar histogram, or even a word cloud. The R system provides quite an array of plotting mechanisms, both built into the basic R system and available in a variety of packages.

This chapter will cover plotting in the following ways:

- Scatter plots
- Bars and histograms
- Word clouds

Packages

In R, there are several packages available that provide plotting functionalities to the programmer. We will use the following packages in the examples:

- car: With a name that is an acronym for **Companion to Applied Regression**, this package provides the regression tools
- lattice: This package provides high-level data visualization
- gclus: This package has functions to create scatter plots
- MASS: This has support functions and datasets for Venables and Ripley's MASS
- ggplot2: This contains the grammar of graphics

Scatter plots

A scatter plot is a basic plotting device comparing datasets with two axes. A basic scatter plot is provided with the `plot` function built into the R system.

 Several objects available in R and packages have their own `plot` function in order to effectively portray the data associated.

The `plot` function looks as follows:

```
plot(x,
     y,
     type,
     main,
     sub,
     xlab,
     ylab,
     asp)
```

The various parameters of this function are described in the following table:

Parameter	Description
x	This is an independent variable.
y	This is a dependent variable.
type	This defines the type of plot. It should be one of the following types: • p for points • l for lines • b for both • c for the lines part alone of b • o for both overplotted • h for histogram-like (or high-density) vertical lines • s for stair steps • S for other steps, see details below • n for no plotting (not sure why this is a choice as it ends up with no information plotted)
main	This is the title of the plot.
sub	This is the subtitle of the plot.
xlab	This is the x axis label.
ylab	This is the y axis label.
asp	This is the aspect ratio.

In this example, we will portray parts of the `iris` dataset:

```
> data <- read.csv("http://archive.ics.uci.edu/ml/machine-learning-
databases/iris/iris.data")
```

Let's also clean up the data so as to make it more readable:

```
> colnames(data) <- c("sepal_length", "sepal_width", "petal_length",
"petal_width", "species")
```

Now, let's look at a summary to get an overall picture:

```
> summary(data)
  sepallength       sepal_width       petal_length
 Min.   :4.300    Min.   :2.000    Min.   :1.000
 1st Qu.:5.100    1st Qu.:2.800    1st Qu.:1.600
 Median :5.800    Median :3.000    Median :4.400
 Mean   :5.848    Mean   :3.051    Mean   :3.774
 3rd Qu.:6.400    3rd Qu.:3.300    3rd Qu.:5.100
 Max.   :7.900    Max.   :4.400    Max.   :6.900

  petal_width                species
 Min.   :0.100    Iris-setosa    :49
 1st Qu.:0.300    Iris-versicolor:50
 Median :1.300    Iris-virginica :50
 Mean   :1.205
 3rd Qu.:1.800
 Max.   :2.500
```

For this plot, we will use `sepal_length` versus `petal_length` (there should be a positive relationship):

```
> plot(data$sepal_length, data$petal_length)
```

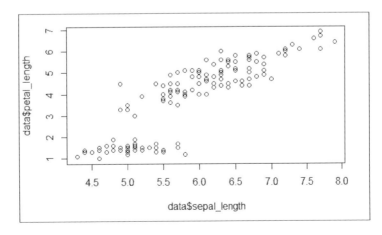

As expected, it's a very ordinary plot. We can adjust some of the items available by changing the parameters to the call. Many of the line plots do not really help visualize this dataset. I thought the choices for step (s) and histogram (h) were somewhat interesting.

First, let's produce the steps diagram with the following code:

```
> plot(data$sepal_length, data$petal_length, type="s")
```

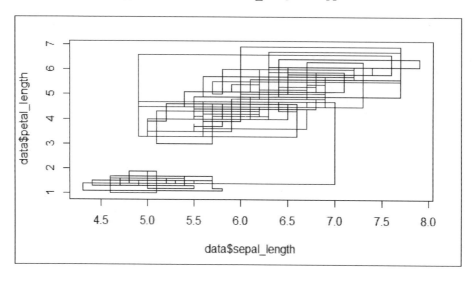

Now, we can also generate a histogram of the data using the following code:

```
> plot(data$sepal_length, data$petal_length, type="h")
```

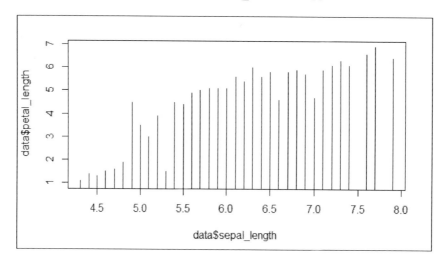

Regression line

Once we have a plot, we can add a regression line to the plot using the `abline` function. The `abline` function adds a straight line to a current plot. (If you attempt to just draw the line first, R complains there is no plot currently in use). The function call looks as shown here:

```
abline(a=NULL,
    b=NULL,
    untf=FALSE,
    h=NULL,
    v=NULL,
    coef=NULL,
    reg=NULL,
    ...)
```

The parameters for the function call are as follows:

Parameter	Description
a	This is the intercept. The default value is NULL.
b	This is the slope. The default value is NULL.
untf	This is a logical flag to determine the "untransforming" of the data. The default value is FALSE.
h	This is to draw Y values for horizontal lines. The default value is NULL.
v	This is to draw X values for vertical lines. The default value is NULL.
coef	This is the vector containing just the intercept and slope. The default value is NULL.
reg	This is the object from the coef function. The default value is NULL.
...	This parameter contains the other values to pass along to the subsidiary functions. The default value is NULL.

For our plot, we invoke the function providing a linear model to use in order to define the intercept, as follows:

```
> abline(lm(data$petal_length~data$sepal_length), col="red")
```

We end up with the regression line (drawn in red as per this command) added at the top of the scatter plot that we produced earlier. I think using a color really highlights and distinguishes the line from all the other points in the scatter plot, especially if the scatter plot is very dense, as shown in the following graph:

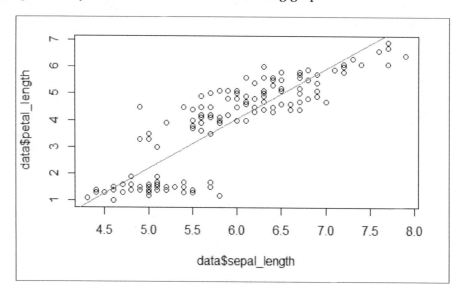

A lowess line

A **lowess line** is a smoothed line calculated using locally weighted polynomial regression. The `lowess` function takes the scatter plot data you have and computes the smoothed coordinates for the regression returned in the result of the call. We can add a lowess line to an existing plot in a similar fashion using the `lines` function. We pass a `lowess` function call to the `lines` function and it draws the plot.

The `lines` function is used to add line segments to a plot. The `lines` function really has just one parameter — the *x, y* coordinates of the line points to be drawn.

In this case, we are using the points from the `lowess` function. The `lowess` function has the following parameters:

Parameter	Description
x	This is a vector of points to be used.
y	These are the *Y* coordinates. The default value is NULL.
f	This is the smoother span. This gives the proportion of points in the plot that influence the smoothness at each value. Larger values give more smoothness. The default value is 2/3.

Parameter	Description
iter	This is the number of iterations to be performed (to smooth the data). The default value is 3. More iterations take longer.
delta	This defines how close the computed values have to be to satisfy the algorithm. The default value is 1/100th of the range of X.

For our example, we use the following code:

```
> lines(lowess(data$sepal_length,data$petal_length), col="blue")
```

We get the following graph as the output:

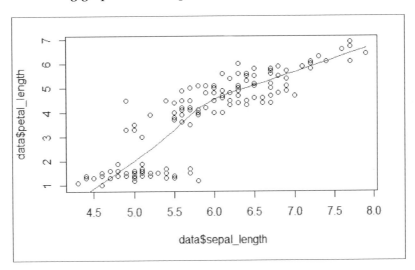

scatterplot

The car package has a scatterplot function. The scatterplot function of car can create enhanced scatter plots, including box plots. The function has one required parameter—the coordinates of the points to draw. There are a number of optional parameters that can also be specified. The various parameters are as follows:

Parameter	Description
x	This is the vector of horizontal coordinates.
y	This is the vector of vertical coordinates.
formula	This is a model formula of the form $y \sim x$ or (to plot by groups) $y \sim x \mid z$, where z evaluates to a factor or other variable, dividing the data into groups. If x is a factor, then parallel box plots are produced using the boxplot function.

Parameter	Description
`data`	This is the data frame to be evaluated.
`subset`	This is the subset of the data to be used.
`smoother`	This is a function to draw the smoothing line. The default value is `lowess`. Another common function is `gamLine` (for generalized additive). Others are available under the `ScatterplotSmoothers` package.
`smoother.args`	This contains any additional arguments needed for the smoother chosen in the previous parameter.
`smooth or span`	If `TRUE`, then use `lossLine`. Or else use `smoother.args`.
`spread`	If `TRUE`, estimate the square root of the variance function.
`reg.line`	If `TRUE`, draw a regression line.
`boxplots`	This can be one of the following options: • x: This creates a box plot for x • y: This creates a box plot for y • xy: This creates box plots for both • `FALSE`: This will not create any box plot The default value is `FALSE`.
`xlab`	This is the X label.
`ylab`	This is the Y label.
`las`	This can have either of the following values: • 0: This will create tick labels parallel to the axis • 1: This will create horizontal labels
`lwd`	This is the width of the linear regression line. The default value is `1`.
`lty`	This is the type of linear regression line. The default value is `1` (solid).

`id.method,`
 	
`id.n,`
 	
`id.cex,`
 	
`id.col`
	These are the arguments to label points:
	
	• `id.n=0` means no points label
	
	• `col` is for colors

`labels`	This is a vector of point labels.
`log`	This determines whether to use the log scale for points.
`jitter`	This is the jitter (noise) factor to apply.
`ylim, ylim`	These are the limits. `NULL` means determine from data.

There are several more parameters present for this function.

For our example, we have the basic scatter plot using the following code:

```
> library(car)
> scatterplot(data$sepal_length, data$petal_length)
```

The resulting plot has much more information than the standard plot produced previously:

- The axes have a built-in box plot showing the distribution of that axis data
- A simple regression line (shown in green)
- A smoothing line (shown in solid red)
- Two dotted red lines showing the upper and lower jittered ranges of the smoothed data

Here's how the resulting plot looks:

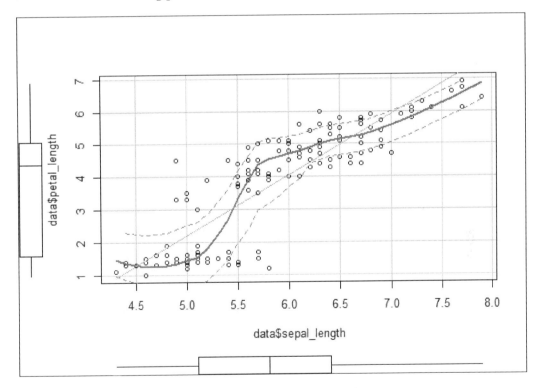

Scatterplot matrices

There are several scatter plot functions available in R for the matrix data.

The `pairs` function is built into the standard R system to display matrix data. The basic `pairs` function call only requires a matrix to display. There are a number of options to label and position the parts of the matrix in the display.

To use pairs against the entire `iris` dataset, we use a command like the following one:

```
> pairs(data)
```

We end up with the following graphic:

- The points in the graph's descending diagonal are given to display what variable is being used for the *x* and *y* axes horizontally and vertically from that point

- Each of the mini-graphs portrays a simple scatter plot of the intersecting axis variables

Some of the mini-graphs will have ranges if the values are close together, as shown here:

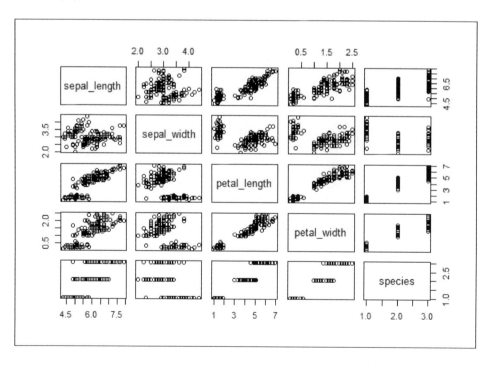

I like to use this graph to be able to quickly focus on the relationships of interest.

splom – display matrix data

The `lattice` package has a similar function called `splom` to display matrix data. The `splom` function only requires a matrix to use and it will default to a useful graphic. Again, there are quite a few additional, optional arguments that can be applied to adjust labels and subgraphics.

For our dataset, the call will be as follows:

```
> library(lattice)
> splom(data)
```

The resulting graphic is very similar to the previous graph and has the following information:

- `splom` uses the ascending diagonal as the label descriptor
- All of the subgraphics have scale information
- Blue is the default data point color, which is odd

Overall, I like the previous display from `pairs` better:

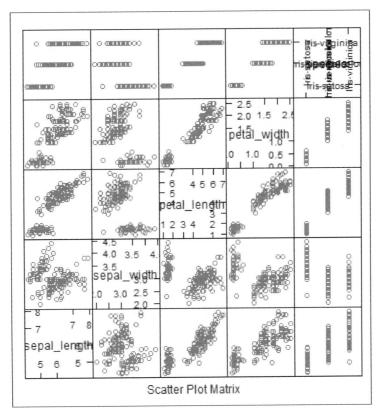

Scatter Plot Matrix

The same `car` library referenced earlier has a `scatterplot.matrix` function for matrices that we can use as well:

```
> library(car)
> scatterplot.matrix(data)
```

We end up with the following graphic with some further embellishments, as listed here:

- The descending diagonal is the key for the variable being used
- Each key point has a scatter plot of just that variable, which is interesting
- Like the `car` package, in the `scatterplot` function too, we have these for each of the subgraphics:
    - A simple regression line (shown in green)
    - A smoothing line (shown in solid red)
    - Two dotted red lines showing the upper and lower jittered ranges of the smoothed data

I am not sure whether I think this is a better use of the scatter plot for an entire matrix. It feels like there is a little too much detail at this level, as shown in the output here:

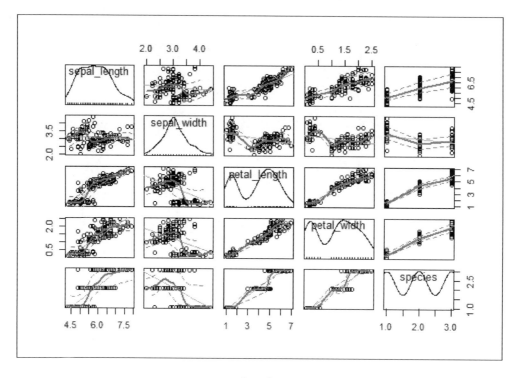

cpairs – plot matrix data

The glucs package includes the cpairs function to graph matrix data. It works and displays a graphic equivalent to the previous pairs function. The points of interest are functions in the glucs package that allow the order of presentation to be rearranged so that higher correlation is displayed closer to the diagonal.

So, let's use the standard cpairs function call:

```
> library(gclus)
> cpairs(data)
```

We end up with a graphic that is very similar to that of the pairs function (see the following graph).

However, we can rearrange the order of presentation, as follows:

```
> data.r <- abs(cor(data))
Error in cor(data) : 'x' must be numeric
```

We have to remove the species data, as it is not numeric, and the cor function only operates on numeric data points:

```
> df <- subset(data, select = -c(species) )
```

Let's compute the correlations of the data as follows:

```
> df.r <- abs(cor(df))
```

We will assign a color to each subgraph based on correlation:

```
> df.col <- dmat.color(df.r)
```

Finally, let's order the subgraphs based on correlation:

```
> df.o <- order.single(df.r)

> cpairs(df, df.o, panel.colors=NULL)
```

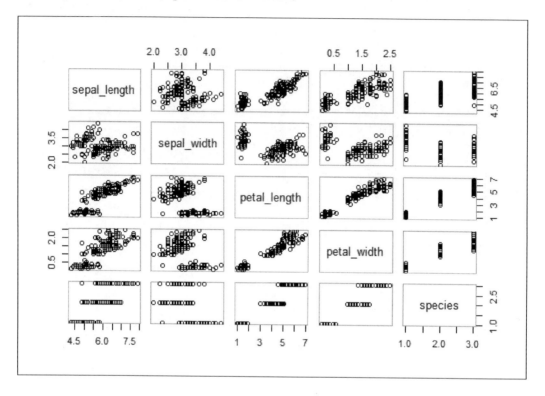

Comparing the two graphs, we make the following observations:

- We removed species; we could have converted that to a numeric. It seems like we lost information with that process.

- The use of colors to encode the correlation extent was iffy. Maybe if there were a larger number of variables in use, this would have helped us focus on the more interesting data. As it is, in this dataset, over half of the data is highly correlated.

- Similarly, moving the more correlated relationships closer to the axis made little difference with such few variables.

- I can definitely see using these highlighters with a big dataset where it is really not obvious what the key data points might be.

Here's what the resulting graph looks like:

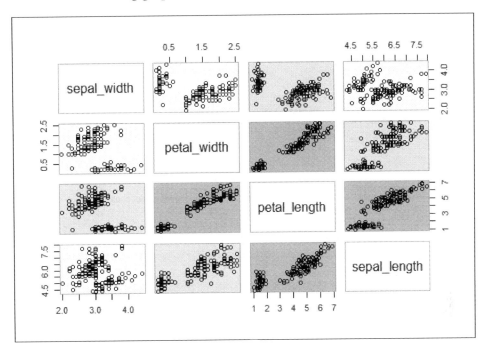

Density scatter plots

With data with a high degree of overlap with the data points, a standard scatter plot becomes less useful in being able to recognize attributes of the data. An alternative in R is to use a density scatter plot.

The `hexbin` package and function provide a mechanism to display high overlap among two variables. We first produce the `hexbin` result on our data items and then plot that.

The usage is as follows:

```
hexbin(x,y)
```

Using our `iris` data, we use these commands:

```
> library(hexbin)
> bin<-hexbin(data$sepal_length, data$petal_length)
> summary(bin)
'hexbin' object from call: hexbin(x = data$sepal_length, y =
data$petal_length)
```

```
n = 149  points in nc = 108  hexagon cells in grid dimensions  36 by
31
        cell              count            xcm              ycm
  Min.   :    1.0   Min.    :1.00   Min.    :4.300   Min.    :1.000
  1st Qu.: 161.5    1st Qu.:1.00    1st Qu.:5.375    1st Qu.:1.900
  Median : 637.5    Median :1.00    Median :5.950    Median :4.500
  Mean   : 559.6    Mean    :1.38   Mean    :5.955   Mean    :3.998
  3rd Qu.: 765.5    3rd Qu.:2.00    3rd Qu.:6.500    3rd Qu.:5.100
  Max.   :1114.0    Max.    :4.00   Max.    :7.900   Max.    :6.900
```

In the hexbin result, we find the following observations:

- We have used the default value of 30 bins.

- We generated a hexagon of 36 x 31 cells or 1,116 cells.

- The lowest cell used is 1, with the highest being 1,114 – looks like a good spread.

- The count for cells has a median of 1.38. It does not seem like we have enough overlap.

If we change the call to use 10 bins, for example, we get the following output:

```
> bin<-hexbin(data$sepal_length, data$petal_length, xbins=10)
> summary(bin)
'hexbin' object from call: hexbin(x = data$sepal_length, y =
data$petal_length, xbins = 10)
n = 149  points in nc = 38  hexagon cells in grid dimensions  14 by 11
        cell              count            xcm              ycm
  Min.   :   1.00   Min.    : 1.000   Min.    :4.300   Min.    :1.100
  1st Qu.:  24.25   1st Qu.: 1.000    1st Qu.:5.112    1st Qu.:1.900
  Median :  80.00   Median : 3.000    Median :5.914    Median :4.487
  Mean   :  68.08   Mean    : 3.921   Mean    :5.923   Mean    :3.934
  3rd Qu.: 102.00   3rd Qu.: 5.750    3rd Qu.:6.565    3rd Qu.:5.438
  Max.   : 131.00   Max.    :15.000   Max.    :7.900   Max.    :6.725
```

We can see much better density numbers in the cell counts (the mean has now become more than double).

Let's plot the `hexbin` object directly (originally using 30 bins):

```
> plot(bin)
```

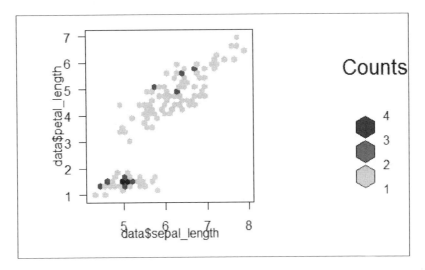

The same data organized over 10 bins results in a tighter resolution, as follows.
I think the second density graph shows a much better picture of the overlap of data.

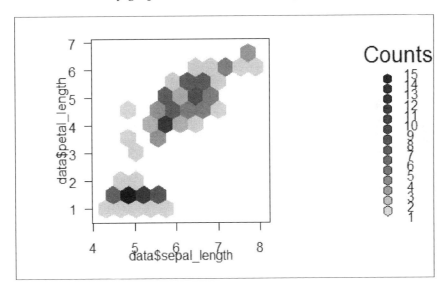

Bar charts and plots

In this section, I will show you how to generate bar charts and bar plots using R. I think whether you call a particular graphic a bar chart or a bar plot is up to you. There are minor differences between bar charts and bar plots. In both cases, we have bars representing counts; we display them across your graphic. The steps (and results) involved are similar.

Bar plot

R programming allows us to create bar charts in a variety of ways. The standard function in R is the `barplot` function. The `barplot` function only requires a list of the heights to be displayed. All of the following parameters are optional.

Usage

The `barplot` function is used as follows:

```
> barplot(data)
```

The various parameters are as follows:

```
height, width = 1, space = NULL,
names.arg = NULL, legend.text = NULL, beside = FALSE,
horiz = FALSE, density = NULL, angle = 45,
col = NULL, border = par("fg"),
main = NULL, sub = NULL, xlab = NULL, ylab = NULL,
xlim = NULL, ylim = NULL, xpd = TRUE, log = "",
axes = TRUE, axisnames = TRUE,
cex.axis = par("cex.axis"), cex.names = par("cex.axis"),
inside = TRUE, plot = TRUE, axis.lty = 0, offset = 0,
add = FALSE, args.legend = NULL, ...)
```

Some of these parameters are described in the following table:

Parameter	Description
`height`	This is the main data vector.
`width`	This is the vector of bar widths.
`space`	This is the amount of space to the left of each bar
`names.arg`	This contains the vector of names
`legend.text`	This plots the legend

For bar plots, we will use the hair/eye color dataset from the MASS package:

```
> library(MASS)
> summary(HairEyeColor)
Number of cases in table: 592
Number of factors: 3
Test for independence of all factors:
    Chisq = 164.92, df = 24, p-value = 5.321e-23
    Chi-squared approximation may be incorrect
> HairEyeColor
, , Sex = Male

        Eye
Hair     Brown Blue Hazel Green
   Black    32   11    10     3
   Brown    53   50    25    15
   Red      10   10     7     7
   Blond     3   30     5     8

, , Sex = Female

        Eye
Hair     Brown Blue Hazel Green
   Black    36    9     5     2
   Brown    66   34    29    14
   Red      16    7     7     7
   Blond     4   64     5     8

> counts <- table(HairEyeColor)
> barplot(counts)
```

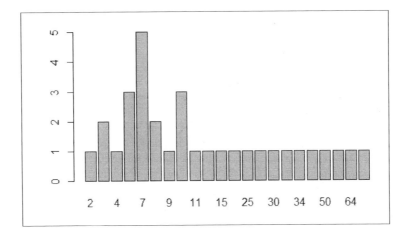

The *x* axis is the combination count. The *y* axis is the number of times that combination count occurred. For example, there were five instances with a combination (eye and hair color occurrence) out of seven. (You can verify this with the data displayed in the previous graph.)

The MASS package also contains a Cars93 dataset (auto information from 1993 models). Plotting that data, we can see the following result:

```
# produce counts of the number cylinders in each vehicle
> count <- table(Cars93$Cylinders)

> barplot(count)
```

This is a bar plot of the count of cars with a specified number of cylinders. We can produce a stacked chart of the same data using these commands:

```
# want the number of cylinders by manufacturer
> count <- table(Cars93$Cylinders, Cars93$Manufacturer)

> barplot(count)
```

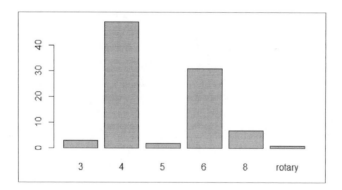

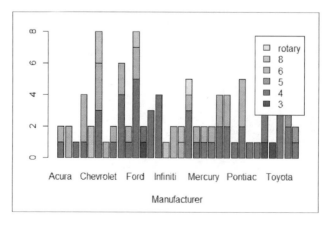

Bar chart

Similarly, we can produce a bar chart of the data using the following commands:

```
# count the number of models by cylinder by manufacturer
> count <- table(Cars93$Cylinders, Cars93$Manufacturer)
> barplot(count)
```

We end up with a simple chart showing how many models were produced with a given number of cylinders in that year, as follows:

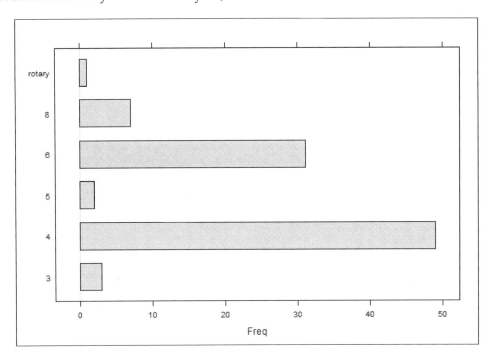

ggplot2

The qplot function in ggplot2 also produces bar charts, as follows:

```
#need to load the ggplot2 library
> library(ggplot2)

#call upon the qplot function for our chart
> qplot(Cars93$Cylinders)
```

The chart from `qplot` appears to be crisper than that displayed above from `barplot`. I like having the default background, colors, grid, and scale automatically applied.

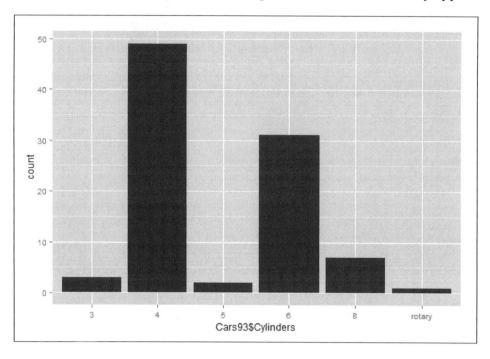

Word cloud

A common feature of R programming is producing a word cloud. Since R is so good at loading large amounts of data and easily manipulating that data, the concept of doing the same to make a word cloud seems to fit well.

R can be used to access data in a variety of formats. I was originally interested in accessing the home page of a site but could not find a package to remove all of the HTML and other web coding from the results. I didn't want to produce a word cloud where the `DIV` tag was at the highest frequency.

So, I went to the current page of `http://finance.yahoo.com` and copied the text on the page to a file, `finance.yahoo.txt`. The following steps produce a word cloud based on that text.

When working with text in R, the fundamental building block is a corpus. A corpus is just a collection of texts. In R, in this example, it is a collection of lines of text from the web page.

Once your text is in a corpus, there are several tools built into R that allow you to easily manipulate the text en masse. For example, you can remove all punctuation, numbers, and the like.

The word cloud coding operates on a matrix of words with their frequency. R provides a means to convert a corpus to a matrix cleanly, as shown here:

```
# read the web page text, line by line
> page <- readLines("http://finance.yahoo.com")
# produce a corpus of the text
> corpus = Corpus(VectorSource(page))
# convert all of the text to lower case (standard practice for text)
> corpus <- tm_map(corpus, tolower)
# remove any punctuation
> corpus <- tm_map(corpus, removePunctuation)
# remove numbers
> corpus <- tm_map(corpus, removeNumbers)
# remove English stop words
> corpus <- tm_map(corpus, removeWords, stopwords("english"))
# create a document term matrix
> dtm = TermDocumentMatrix(corpus)
# not sure why this occurs, but the next statement clears
Error: inherits(doc, "TextDocument") is not TRUE
# reconfigure the corpus as a text document
> corpus <- tm_map(corpus, PlainTextDocument)
> dtm = TermDocumentMatrix(corpus)
# convert the document matrix to a standard matrix for use in the cloud
> m = as.matrix(dtm)
# sort the data so we end up with the highest as biggest
> v = sort(rowSums(m), decreasing = TRUE)
# finally produce the word cloud
> wordcloud(names(v), v, min.freq = 10)
```

I thought it is interesting that **bloomberg** showed up as the top frequency word on Yahoo's finance page. The rest of the terms are consistent.

Questions

Factual

- The `barplot` function has a number of optional parameters. It might be interesting to play with a dataset and the parameters.
- When you are displaying a word cloud, the function might complain that some words might not fit. Determine whether there is a way that this can be overcome.

When, how, and why?

- What is the best way to determine the number of bins to be used in the `hexbin` function?
- It was very unclear when producing a stacked bar chart as to how to organize the data to arrive at the correct result. Select a dataset and produce a stacked chart that meets your needs.

Challenges

- There are several packages to produce plots. How would you select one of the packages to use for your plotting needs?
- If there was a package that extracted just the text from a web page, that would be of tremendous use for R programming. Investigate whether anyone has made such a package or at least taken the initial steps.

Summary

In this chapter, we explored a variety of plotting methods in R. We covered scatter plots, step diagrams, and histograms. We added a regression line and a lowess line to a plot. We used a couple of different tools to plot matrices. We saw a density scatter plot. We used bar graphs. And finally, we generated a word cloud.

In the next chapter, we will cover 3D modeling.

9
Data Visualization – 3D

R programming has several methods to display and visualize data in three dimensions. There are many times when this display technique gives you a clearer picture of the relationships involved.

This chapter will cover 3D in the following ways:

- 3D methods.
- Visualizing Big Data using 3D. Big Data is a special case where we normally have a large volume of observations to work with. Many times, visualizing data in a graphical form, especially in 3D, helps to determine the characteristics of the data.
- Research areas for advanced visualization techniques.

Packages

In R, there are several packages available that provide 3D plotting for the programmer. We will use the following packages in the examples:

- `car`: This stands for Companion to Applied Regression
- `copula`: This has multivariate dependence with copulas
- `lattice`: This has a high-level data visualization system, especially for multivariate data
- `rgl`: This provides 3D visualization using OpenGL
- `vrmlgen`: This provides 3D visualization
- `Rcpp`: This gives C++ integration with R
- `swirl`: This provides R training in R

Generating 3D graphics

One of the built-in functions to generate 3D graphics is `persp`. The `persp` function draws perspective plots of a surface over the *x-y* plane. The `persp` function has many optional parameters and will likely produce the graphics that you need. As a test, you can use the following example function, and it will generate three 3D graphics:

```
> example(persp)
```

This function call will generate three graphics.

(Included in the output are all of the commands necessary to generate the graphics.)

The first generated image shows a 3D plot of a rotated sine function. The associated R commands (also generated for you) are as follows:

```
> persp(x, y, z, theta = 30, phi = 30, expand = 0.5, col =
"lightblue")
```

Here's the first generated image:

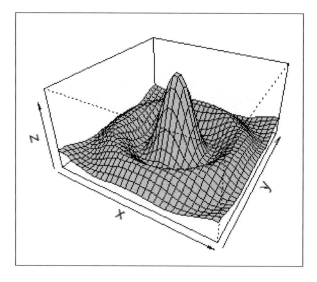

The next image is a more detailed view of the same data:

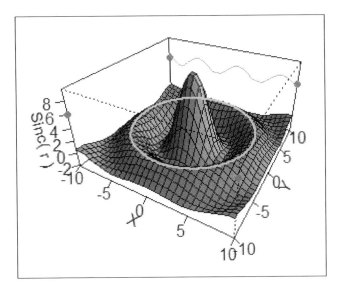

Lastly, we have a simulated 3D surface area presentation:

The `persp` function looks like this:

```
persp(x = seq(0, 1, length.out = nrow(z)),
      y = seq(0, 1, length.out = ncol(z)),
      z, xlim = range(x), ylim = range(y),
      zlim = range(z, na.rm = TRUE),
      xlab = NULL, ylab = NULL, zlab = NULL,
      main = NULL, sub = NULL,
      theta = 0, phi = 15, r = sqrt(3), d = 1,
      scale = TRUE, expand = 1,
      col = "white", border = NULL, ltheta = -135, lphi = 0,
      shade = NA, box = TRUE, axes = TRUE, nticks = 5,
      ticktype = "simple", ...)
```

Some of the parameters of this function are described in the following table:

Parameter	Description
x, y	These are the locations of grid lines.
z	These are the values.
xlim, ylim, zlim	These are the limits of the three axes.
xlab, ylab, zlab	These are the labels for the three axes.
main, sub	These are the main title and the subtitle.
theta, phi	These are the viewing angles; theta is azimuth and phi is the colatitude
r	This is the distance of the eye point from the center of the box.
d	This is the perspective strength adjustment. The values greater than 1 diminish. Values less than 1 increase.
scale	This has a Boolean value to maintain the aspect ratio when scaling. TRUE means transform each axis separately. FALSE means maintain aspect ratio.

I have borrowed a nice, simple example (see references). Here, we have gumbel copula data as our x and y, and we will use the dCopula value as our z. The gumbelCopula function generates an Archimedean copula; dCopula is the density function for the copula. The example code is as follows:

```
> install.packages("copula")
> library(copula)
> gc <- gumbelCopula(1.5, dim=2)
> persp(gc, dCopula, col="red")
```

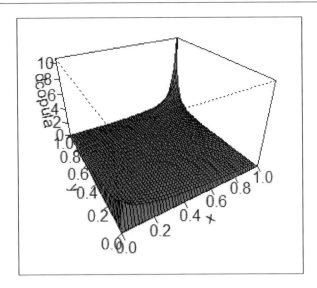

There is a difficulty in using the `persp` function: both the x and y values must increase over the vectors supplied. You can easily dream up a mathematical function that has this property, but it was difficult for me to find data where x and y increase together. I ended up using the women built-in dataset available in R:

```
> summary(women)
 height         weight
 Min.   :58.0   Min.   :115.0
 1st Qu.:61.5   1st Qu.:124.5
 Median :65.0   Median :135.0
 Mean   :65.0   Mean   :136.7
 3rd Qu.:68.5   3rd Qu.:148.0
 Max.   :72.0   Max.   :164.0
```

There are 15 samples that show increases in the women's height and weight over time. The `persp` function needs a z factor as well. I built a simple function that provides the product of the height and weight values:

```
> fun <- function(x,y) {x * y}
```

Then, to produce a `persp` 3D graphic with the women dataset, we apply the function:

```
> persp(x=women$height,
    y=women$weight,
    z=outer(women$height,women$weight,fun))
```

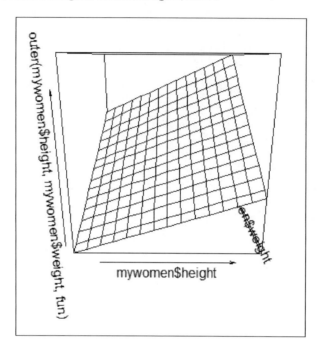

Lattice Cloud – 3D scatterplot

The lattice package has a `cloud` function that will produce 3D scatterplots. We load the package, as follows:

```
> install.packages("lattice")
> library(lattice)
```

We are using the automobile dataset that was referenced in *Chapter 4, Data Analysis – Regression Analysis*, as follows:

```
> mydata <- read.table("http://archive.ics.uci.edu/ml/machine-
learning-databases/auto-mpg/auto-mpg.data")
> colnames(mydata) <- c("mpg","cylinders","displacement","horsepower",
"weight","acceleration","model.year","origin","car.name")
```

We are going to plot the number of cylinders in the *x* axis, weight of the vehicle in the *y* axis, and use the miles per gallon as the *z* axis, as follows:

```
> cloud(mpg~cylinders*weight, data=mydata)
```

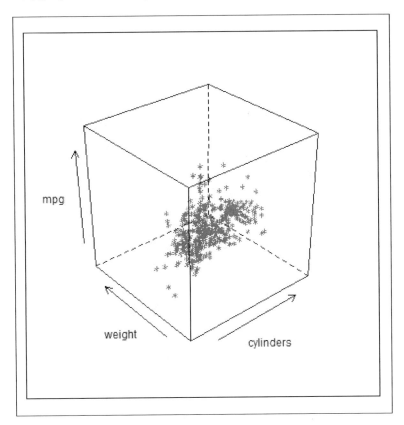

The graphic shows the miles per gallon (mpg) increasing with the number of cylinders and is somewhat ignorant of the weight of the vehicle. I'd not have expected either result.

The `cloud` function has many optional parameters:

```
cloud(x,
      data,
      allow.multiple = is.null(groups) || outer,
      outer = FALSE,
      auto.key = FALSE,
      aspect = c(1,1),
      panel.aspect = 1,
      panel = lattice.getOption("panel.cloud"),
```

```
prepanel = NULL,
scales = list(),
strip = TRUE,
groups = NULL,
xlab,        ylab,        zlab,
xlim,        ylim,        zlim,
at,
drape = FALSE,
pretty = FALSE,
drop.unused.levels,
...,
lattice.options = NULL,
default.scales =
list(distance = c(1, 1, 1),
     arrows = TRUE,
     axs = axs.default),
default.prepanel = lattice.getOption("prepanel.default.cloud"),
colorkey,
col.regions,
alpha.regions,
cuts = 70,
subset = TRUE,
axs.default = "r")
```

The parameters are described in the following table:

Parameter	Description
x	This is normally the function to apply
data	This is the dataset to draw variables from
allow.multiple, outer, auto.key, prepanel, strip, groups, xlab, xlim, ylab, ylim, drop. unused.levels, lattice.options, default.scales, subset	These are the same arguments for several methods of the lattice package for plotting

I think that in most cases, just x and the data parameters are specified, with maybe some labeling.

scatterplot3d

Another method to generate 3D graphics is the `scatterplot3d` package and function. The function has a number of parameters as well, most of them optional, as follows:

```
scatterplot3d(x, y=NULL, z=NULL, color=par("col"), pch=par("pch"),
    main=NULL, sub=NULL, xlim=NULL, ylim=NULL, zlim=NULL,
    xlab=NULL, ylab=NULL, zlab=NULL, scale.y=1, angle=40,
    axis=TRUE, tick.marks=TRUE, label.tick.marks=TRUE,
    x.ticklabs=NULL, y.ticklabs=NULL, z.ticklabs=NULL,
    y.margin.add=0, grid=TRUE, box=TRUE, lab=par("lab"),
    lab.z=mean(lab[1:2]), type="p", highlight.3d=FALSE,
    mar=c(5,3,4,3)+0.1, bg=par("bg"), col.axis=par("col.axis"),
    col.grid="grey", col.lab=par("col.lab"),
    cex.symbols=par("cex"), cex.axis=0.8 * par("cex.axis"),
    cex.lab=par("cex.lab"), font.axis=par("font.axis"),
    font.lab=par("font.lab"), lty.axis=par("lty"),
    lty.grid=par("lty"), lty.hide=NULL, lty.hplot=par("lty"),
    log="", ...)
```

The parameters are described in the following table:

Parameter	Description
x	This is the primary data or function to plot.
y	This is the y axis data.
z	This is the z axis data.
color	This is the color palette to be used.

Using our auto data with the `scatterplot3d` function, we get a graphic, as shown after the following code:

```
> scatterplot3d(data$mpg~data$cylinders*data$weight)
```

Again, we are using the same coordinates: the *x* axis is the number of cylinders, the *y* axis is the weight of the vehicle, and the *z* axis is the mpg.

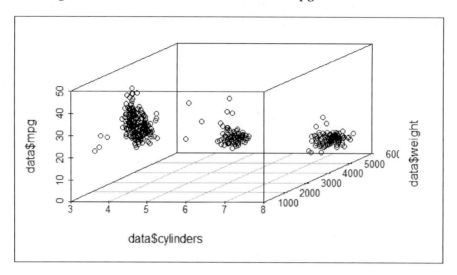

It is interesting that using the same data and the same general graphing technique, we end up with a completely different graphic. Here, we see that the mpg and weights are clustered around the three typical engine sizes: four cylinders, six cylinders, and eight cylinders. Also, there is a marked decrease in mpg with an increase in cylinders as opposed to the prior graphic, implying that mpg increased with cylinders. The scatterplot3d result is what I expected.

scatter3d

The scatter3d function in the car package produces a 3D graphic with the help of the rgl package. Note that the rgl package is primarily used to manipulate a rotating graphic. So, in our case, we create the graphic we specify in the following command, reorient the graphic to our liking, and then finally use an rgl function to store the graphic (in our required state) to a PNG file on disk.

First, we have to load everything needed, as follows:

```
> install.packages("rgl")
> library(rgl)
> install.packages("car")
> library(car)
```

Then, we produce the graphic. Again, it will be displayed in an RGL screen so that you can manipulate the layout of the graphic as required.

Then, we save to the disk in the selected form:

```
> rgl.snapshot("0860OS_9_8.png")
```

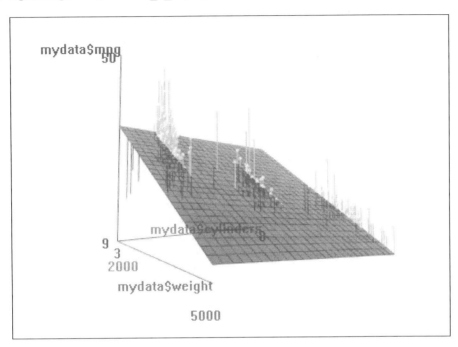

It is interesting that the same data in essentially the same format looks different yet again!

We can see the data aligned to three groups according to the number of cylinders in the car. While it is not obvious, upon close examination, you can see a marked decrease in mpg with the increase in the number of cylinders. Also, you can finally see a decrease in mpg with an increase in the weight of the vehicle (by the slant of the plane). All of these points are nicely displayed.

I found it very pleasing to adjust the axes to their best effect. I also liked the idea of having the plane cut across the mean (?) of the data points.

cloud3d

If you normally use VRML files, there is support for generating VRML files in R as well. Assuming you have a standalone VRML viewer or an add-in to your favorite browser, you can view and manipulate the resulting image. In my case, I installed the **Cortona** add-in for Internet Explorer.

The commands are slightly different, as follows:

```
> install.packages("vrmlgen")
> library(vrmlgen)
> cloud3d(mydata$mpg~mydata$cylinders*mydata$weight,filename="out.
wrl")
```

This set of commands will produce the `out.wrl` file in your current R directory. There are options to change the name of the file and/or directory. The file is a VRML file. You will need a VRML viewer/editor to display/manipulate the file. VRML viewing is not built into standard browsers. Popular VRML viewers are Cortona3D (used in the following example), FreeWRL, and ORBISNAP.

Double-clicking on the file will bring up your VRML viewer, as follows:

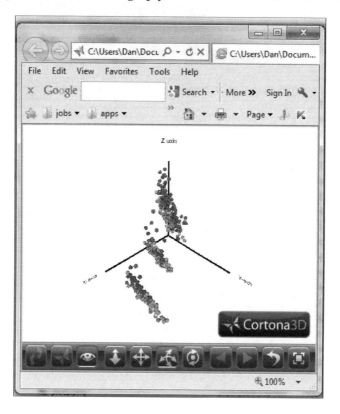

As you can see in the display:

- It is displaying the file in a new window
- The viewer has controls to manipulate the layout of the graphic
- We see the same alignment along the three cylinder sizes
- I think it is clear that the lower number of cylinders have a higher mpg
- Overall, the graphics are superb

The `cloud3d` function has similar parameters to the other 3D functions we saw, as shown here:

```
cloud3d(x, y = NULL, z = NULL, labels = rownames(data),
        filename = "out.wrl", type = "vrml",
        pointstyle = c("s", "b", "c"), metalabels = NULL,
        hyperlinks = NULL, cols = rainbow(length(unique(labels))),
        scalefac = 4, autoscale = "independent",
        lab.axis = c("X-axis", "Y-axis", "Z-axis"),
        col.axis = "black", showaxis = TRUE, col.lab = "black",
        col.bg = "white", cex.lab = 1, htmlout = NULL,
        hwidth = 1200, hheight = 800, showlegend = TRUE,
        vrml_navigation = "EXAMINE", vrml_showdensity = FALSE,
        vrml_fov = 0.785, vrml_pos = rep(scalefac + 4, 3),
        vrml_dir = c(0.19, 0.45, 0.87, 2.45),
        vrml_transparency = 0, lg3d_ambientlight = 0.5)
```

We have very similar parameters to the other functions. Noted differences are as follows:

- The `filename` parameter assumes that you want to generate a file from the output
- The size parameters for the resulting window display
- There are several VRML commands
- It is interesting that many of the parameters *do not* default to NULL, but to realistic values

RgoogleMaps

Google produces the `RgoogleMaps` package. Included in the package are functions to produce 3D maps. For this example, we focus on Mount Washington, NH, as shown here:

```
> size <- "small"
> col <- "red"
> char <- ""
> library(RgoogleMaps)
> lat <- c(44.26,44.28)
> lon <- c(-71.2,-71.4)
> mymarkers <- cbind.data.frame(lat, lon, size, col, char)
> terrain_close <- GetMap.bbox(lonR= range(lon), latR= range(lat),
destfile= "terrclose.png", markers= mymarkers, zoom=13,
maptype="hybrid")
```

We set up some of the markers to use when drawing the map. Lastly, just set the coordinates to Mount Washington, producing the following 3D map:

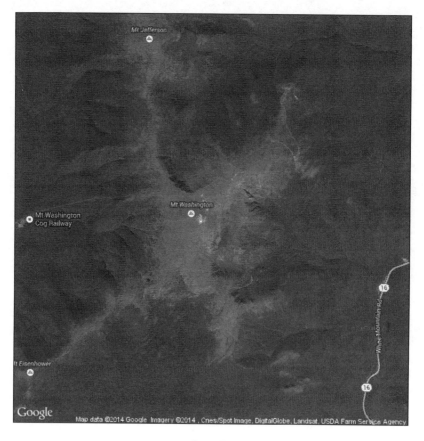

The function call looks like this:

```
GetMap.bbox(lonR, latR, center, size = c(640, 640), destfile =
"MyTile.png",
    MINIMUMSIZE = FALSE, RETURNIMAGE = TRUE, GRAYSCALE = FALSE,
    NEWMAP = TRUE, zoom, verbose = 0, SCALE = 1, ...)
```

The parameters are described in the following table:

Parameter	Description
lonR	This is the longitude range.
latR	This is the latitude range.
center	This is the optional center.
size	This is the desired size of the map.
destfile	This is the file to save an image to.
MINIMUMSIZE	This is the minimum size of the map.
RETURNIMAGE	This defines whether the function returns a map. The default value is TRUE.
GRAYSCALE	This stores a Boolean value. TRUE means use black and white.
NEWMAP	This stores a Boolean value: TRUE means save image, FALSE means load image.
zoom	This is the optional zoom level.
verbose	This is the verbosity level.
SCALE	This is the scaling factor.
...	These are the arguments to be passed to the GetMap function.
maptype	The GetMap argument—this is the only argument we used in our example.

vrmlgenbar3D

We can combine a typical graphic, a bar chart, with a map using the bar3d function of vrmlgen, as follows:

```
> library(vrmlgen)

> data("uk_topo")

> bar3d(uk_topo, autoscale = FALSE, cols = "blue", space = 0, showaxis
= FALSE, filename = "example6.wrl", htmlout = "example6.html")
```

We saw the `vrlmgen` library earlier in this chapter. The `bar3d` function looks as follows:

```
bar3d(data, row.labels = rownames(data),
      col.labels = colnames(data), metalabels = NULL,
      filename = "out.wrl", type = "vrml", space = 0.5,
      cols = rainbow(length(as.matrix(data))),
      rcols = NULL, ccols = NULL, origin = c(0, 0, 0),
      scalefac = 4, lab.axis = c("X-axis", "Y-axis", "Z-axis"),
      lab.vertical = FALSE, col.axis = "black",
      showaxis = TRUE, autoscale = TRUE,
      ignore_zeros = TRUE, col.lab = "black",
      col.bg = "white", cex.lab = 1, cex.rowlab = 1,
      cex.collab = 1, htmlout = NULL, hwidth = 1200,
      hheight = 800, showlegend = TRUE,
      vrml_navigation = "EXAMINE", vrml_transparency = 0,
      vrml_fov = 0.785, vrml_pos = rep(scalefac + 4, 3),
      vrml_dir = c(0.19, 0.45, 0.87, 2.45),
      lg3d_ambientlight = 0.5)
```

Some of the parameters are described in the following table:

Parameter	Description
`data`	This is the dataset being plotted.
`row.labels, col.labels`	These are the labels for rows and columns.
`filename`	This is the output filename.
`type`	This is the output file type.

Again, most the parameters are not NULL and have specific values that will work in many cases. Even in our example, we only specified the data source and the filenames. The rest is built into the VRML output.

The result of the previous command is a WRL virtual map. I have extracted part of the display, most of Ireland, as an example of what it looks like:

Big Data

Big Data with R caters to two areas of concern:

- The amount of data that you want to analyze might not fit in the memory of one machine

- The amount of time needed to process all of the data might be considerable, and you can split up the processing among machines or nodes in a cluster

Along with this effort, an interesting avenue is running your R program against Big Data on an Amazon cluster. Amazon AWS offers support for R in its service offerings. There is also a free trial period where you can try out these services. I have used AWS for other projects and found it very convenient and reasonably priced.

Also, note that many of the packages used in Big Data are not available for your typical Windows machine. You can attempt to install them, but the install will throw an error message like **Binaries not available for 3.1.1. Source available**, which means that the authors never counted on someone installing pbdR or its colleague libraries on a desktop machine.

pbdR

The `pbdR` project was started to organize all of the separate efforts involved with *Programming with Big Data in R*. The group has utility libraries available, such as `pdbDEMO`, `pdbMPI`, and `pdbPROF`. The focus is on the single program / multiple data model: one R program over various chunks of the data possibly distributed over several machines.

A good showcase for `pbdR` is the `pbdDEMO` library. It provides prebuilt samples using their other packages, so you can quickly see the effects of your implementation.

Common global values

There are some *common* global values referenced by `pdbDEMO`. It is expected that these will be set before calling specific functions in the package. I am defining them here rather than repeating as they will be required later on. These are referenced by the other `pbdDEMO` functions. The `.DEMO.CT` library holds common global values, as follows:

Elements	Default	Usage
gbd.major	1L	This is a default GBD row-major.
ictxt	0L	This is a default BLACS context.
bldim	c(2L,2L)	This is a default block dimension.
divide.method	block.cyclic	This is a default balance method.

Similarly, the `.SPMD.CT` library contains more common global values:

Elements	Default	Usage
comm	0L	This is a communicator index
intercomm	2L	This is an inter-communicator index
info	0L	This is an info index
newcomm	1L	This is a new communicator index
op	sum	This is an operation
port.name	spmdport	This is an operation
print.all.rank	FALSE	This is to determine whether all ranks print message
print.quiet	FALSE	This is to determine whether to print/cat rank information
rank.root	0L	This is a rank of the root
rank.source	0L	This is a rank of the source
rank.dest	1L	This is a rank of the destination
...		

Distribute data across nodes

One of the features of the pdbR package lets you easily distribute your data among the nodes available. As a part of the pbdR package, the system knows how many nodes are available, so then you can use the load.balance function to distribute the data evenly.

Let's load the library we want to use:

```
> library(pbdDEMO)
```

We can generate some sample data, as follows:

```
> N.gbd <- 5 * (comm.rank() * 2)
> X.gbd <- rnorm(N.gbd * 3)
> dim(X.gbd) <- c(N.gbd, 3)
```

Now, we will get the balancing information. This shows how the data will be balanced:

```
> bal.info <- balance.info(X.gbd)
```

Let's distribute the data evenly across the nodes available, as follows:

```
> new.X.gbd <- load.balance(X.gbd, bal.info)
```

Now, we'll revert the data back to its original location(s), as follows:

```
> org.X.gbd <- unload.balance(new.X.gbd, bal.info)
```

Distribute a matrix across nodes

There are methods to distribute a matrix across nodes and then reverting back to the original matrix. They look like this:

```
gbd2dmat(X.gbd, skip.balance = FALSE, comm = .SPMD.CT$comm,
         gbd.major = .DEMO.CT$gbd.major, bldim = .DEMO.CT$bldim,
         ICTXT = .DEMO.CT$ictxt)
  dmat2gbd(X.dmat, bal.info = NULL, comm = .SPMD.CT$comm,
         gbd.major = .DEMO.CT$gbd.major)
```

The parameters are described in the following table:

Parameter	Description
x	This is the source matrix data
skip.balance	This determines whether to skip running balance.info if already performed
comm	This is an index

Parameter	Description
gbd.major	This is an index
bldim	This is an index

The parameters are only needed if your matrix is abnormally indexed.

bigmemory

The `bigmemory` package is another utilitarian package that allows you to manipulate a big matrix directly. For example, we can create a big matrix using the following command:

```
x <- big.matrix(5, 2, type="integer", init=0,
dimnames=list(NULL, c("alpha", "beta")))
options(bigmemory.allow.dimnames=TRUE)
```

The `big.matrix` function looks like the following:

```
big.matrix(nrow, ncol, type = options()$bigmemory.default.type,
    init = NULL, dimnames = NULL, separated = FALSE,
    backingfile = NULL, backingpath = NULL, descriptorfile = NULL,
    binarydescriptor=FALSE, shared = TRUE)
```

The `big.matrix` function has the following parameters:

Parameter	Description
nrow, ncol	This is the dimension of the matrix.
type	This is the cell atomic element type. This must be one of the following options: double, integer, short, or char.
init	This is the initial value for the matrix.
dimnames	This is a list of row and column names (can be troublesome with large datasets).
separated	This determines whether to use a column organization.
backingfile	This is the root name to be used for the cache of the dataset.
backingpath	This is the directory for the previous parameter.
descriptorfile	This is the description of the layout—if load is used.
binarydescriptor	This is a flag to use a binary store for the description.
shared	This is to determine whether shared memory is used. The value TRUE is for file-backed matrices.

Similarly, there is a `filebacked.big.matrix` function with the same parameters but is only used for file-backed matrices.

A standard big matrix is constrained by RAM. A file-backed matrix has no effective limitation.

pdbMPI

Another useful Big Data package is `pdbMPI`. This package provides a runtime interface to R that will work with multiple nodes directly—rather than trying to make the R Studio or standard R interface make the connections somehow.

The usage looks like the following:

1. We load the library, as follows:

```
> library(pbdMPI)
```

2. Then use the `mpiexec` function to load our R script across nodes as follows:

```
> mpiexec -np 2 Rscriptsome_code.r
```

Here, `np` is the number of processors, and `some_code.r` is your script that you want to run in all the nodes. Again, we are in the single processor/multiple data model.

snow

The `snow` (**Simple Network of Workstations**) package allows you to organize a group of machines together for R programming tasks. The library provides functions, grouping your workstations together in a cluster or parallel fashion. Once organized, you can apply functions across your cluster or set of parallel machines using the following functions.

The cluster functions are as follows:

- `clusterSplit(cl, seq)`: split up a cluster
- `clusterCall(cl, fun, ...)`: call a function on each node of the cluster
- `clusterApply(cl, x, fun, ...)`: apply, as in a standard R apply(), against all the nodes in the cluster
- `clusterApplyLB(cl, x, fun, ...)`
- `clusterEvalQ(cl, expr)`
- `clusterExport(cl, list, envir = .GlobalEnv)`
- `clusterMap(cl, fun, ..., MoreArgs = NULL, RECYCLE = TRUE)`

Similarly, there are a number of functions to use in parallel:

- `parLapply(cl, x, fun, ...)`
- `parSapply(cl, X, FUN, ..., simplify = TRUE, USE.NAMES = TRUE)`
- `parApply(cl, X, MARGIN, FUN, ...)`
- `parRapply(cl, x, fun, ...)`
- `parCapply(cl, x, fun, ...)`

Many of the other Big Data packages assume that you are using/have installed the snow package. Another package, `snowfall`, was even developed to help with using the snow package.

More Big Data

There are quite a few libraries that keep being added to and built, which help you load, manipulate, and examine big datasets. Most of the packages I have seen were built to help you distribute your data among nodes, script among nodes, and gather results. The assumption is that you will run your single code in parallel on all the nodes. If you are working in this space, you should keep tabs on the CRAN R Project High Performance Computing area.

Some of the areas where a lot of work has already been done are as follows:

- Grid computing
- Hadoop
- Resource Managers
- Large data, out of memory

Only some packages are being developed that are specifically written to use distributed data as the norm.

Research areas

There is quite a variety of research being done in new areas of R programming. This section talks about some of the ideas I find interesting.

Rcpp

There are times when an R function simply takes too long. You know (or at least think) that if you could rewrite that function, you could do better. Now, you have your chance. The Rcpp package allows you to use C++ directly in your R script. If you are using a Windows machine, the package will require you to install RTools to use (you will get an error message when you try to use C++). Here's a simple example:

```
> install.packages("Rcpp")
> library(Rcpp)
> cppFunction('int add(int x, int y, int z) {
+    int sum = x + y + z;
+    return sum;
+ }')
Warning message:
running command 'make -f "C:/PROGRA~1/R/R-31~1.1/etc/i386/
Makeconf" -f "C:/PROGRA~1/R/R-31~1.1/share/make/winshlib.mk"
SHLIB_LDFLAGS='$(SHLIB_CXXLDFLAGS)' SHLIB_LD='$(SHLIB_CXXLD)'
SHLIB="sourceCpp_73208.dll" OBJECTS="filea0c4d7559e2.o"' had status
127
Error in sourceCpp(code = code, env = env, rebuild = rebuild,
showOutput = showOutput,   :
  Error 1 occurred building shared library.
WARNING: Rtools is required to build R packages but is not currently
installed. Please download and install the appropriate version of
Rtools before proceeding:
http://cran.rstudio.com/bin/windows/Rtools/
```

This error occurs when running R on a Windows machine. On a Mac machine, the necessary tools are installed. To install the tools on Windows, use the correct version on the R Tools page, http://cran.r-project.org/bin/windows/Rtools/. Here's how the tools are installed on Windows:

```
> cppFunction('int add(int x, int y, int z) {
+    int sum = x + y + z;
+    return sum;
+ }')
> add(1, 2, 3)
[1] 6
```

parallel

The `parallel` package takes R programming for parallelism to the next level using operating system capabilities directly. Some of the features include:

- The `via` function to start new processes
- The `fork` function, which is part of standard software development and includes a way to "fork" the current process into two and have both continue
- The rewriting of `snow` and all the apply functions (example shown in text has an 80 percent speed improvement)
- The rework of random number generation (can be problematic in parallel environments)
- More control over load balancing

microbenchmark

The `microbenchmark` package and function provides submicrosecond accurate timing functions. A typical use is to call upon an existing function (usually many times) to gather a time of execution. For example:

```
> library(ggplot2)
> library(microbenchmark)
> tm <- microbenchmark(rchisq(100, 0),
+                       rchisq(100, 1),
+                       rchisq(100, 2),
+                       rchisq(100, 3),
+                       rchisq(100, 5), times=1000L)
> autoplot(tm)
```

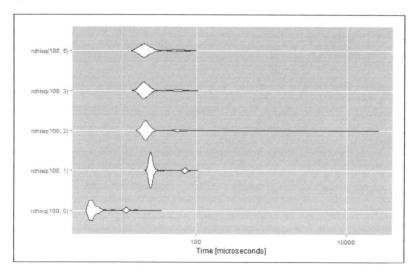

The objective is to measure the run of different versions of your R script to arrive at the best solution.

pqR

A recent development is pqR, (Pretty Quick R). It is based on a current version of R but has rewrites of sections for speed. A significant feature includes built-in parallel operations for multichip machines—no special programming is required!

This version does not run on Windows however, so I am unable to write much about the experience.

SAP integration

With the release of SAP HANA, the SAP Corporation has provided integration between the SAP system and R programming. You can pass variable values back and forth, invoke scripts/statements in R from SAP, and receive the results of the execution back in the SAP world.

roxygen2

The roxygen2 package is a latex-like system for documenting your R programs. If you make slight formatting changes to include keywords that roxygen looks for in your comments, you can quickly generate standardized documentation for your scripts.

If you have a large script library, this is a must.

bioconductor

bioconductor.org provides tools for the analysis and comprehension of genomic data using R. There are over 800 packages in use under bioconductor. If you work in this area, most likely the scripts and packages you need are already there.

swirl

The swirl package uses the R system to teach you to program in R. Here is the first part of the interaction (note that the layout fits my screen correctly—there are extra line breaks here trying to fit in the document width):

```
> install.packages("swirl")
> library(swirl)

| Hi! I see that you have some variables saved in your workspace. To
keep things
```

```
| running smoothly, I recommend you clean up before starting swirl.

| Type ls() to see a list of the variables in your workspace. Then,
type
| rm(list=ls()) to clear your workspace.

| Type swirl() when you are ready to begin.

> swirl()

| Welcome to swirl!

| Please sign in. If you've been here before, use the same name as you
did then.
| If you are new, call yourself something unique.

What shall I call you? Dan

| Thanks, Dan. Let's cover a few quick housekeeping items before we
begin our
| first lesson. First of all, you should know that when you see '...',
that
| means you should press Enter when you are done reading and ready to
continue.

...   <-- That's your cue to press Enter to continue

| Also, when you see 'ANSWER:', the R prompt (>), or when you are
asked to
| select from a list, that means it's your turn to enter a response,
then press
| Enter to continue.

Select 1, 2, or 3 and press Enter

1: Continue.
2: Proceed.
3: Let's get going!
```

pipes

R programming now includes **pipes** denoted by %>% in your script. The idea is to take whatever function/value is on the left-hand side of the pipe and transfer that to the function/value on the right-hand side. They are used as follows:

```
> library(babynames) # data package
> library(dplyr)      # provides data manipulating functions.
> library(magrittr)   # pipes
> library(ggplot2)    # for graphics
> babynames %>%
+     filter(name %>% substr(1, 3) %>% equals("Dan")) %>%
+     group_by(year, sex) %>%
+     summarize(total = sum(n)) %>%
+     qplot(year, total, color = sex, data = ., geom = "line") %>%
+     add(ggtitle('Names starting with "Dan"')) %>%
+     print
```

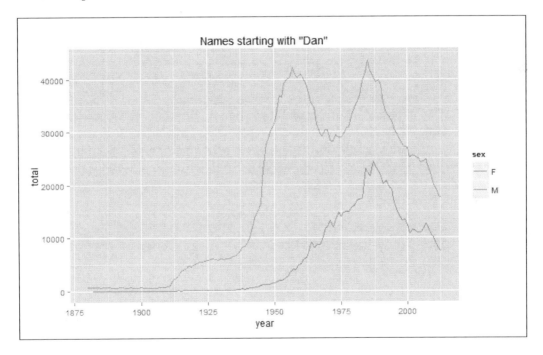

Here, we take all the baby names, pipe them to a filter function that pipes each name to get the first three characters of the name, and pipe that to ....

As you can see, it is a very interesting programming paradigm.

Questions

Factual

- Do you have data that can be displayed using the `persp` function (*x* and *y* increasing over the range of your dataset)?
- Don't you wish you knew about swirl when you first started getting into R?

When, how, and why?

- Determine how to adjust the viewing angle for the 3D maps.
- Sign up for an Amazon AWS free trial to use the Big Data aspects.
- Get access to a multiprocessor machine and try out the parallel packages.

Challenges

- Find an observed dataset that can be displayed using the `persp` function.
- What geographic data can you think of that'd be better displayed using a 3D graphic map?

Summary

In this chapter, we explored a variety of 3D plotting methods in R. We generated 3D graphics using the built-in `persp` function. We used Lattice Cloud to get a 3D scatter plot using the `cloud` function and `scatterplot3d`. We used the `scatter3d` function from the `rgl` package. We generated a 3D plot and a bar graph into a VRML file using the `vrmlgen` package. We used `RgoogleMaps` for the map data and corresponding map displays.

In the Big Data area, we used the `pbdR` tools to use Big Data and used several methods that allow you to access Big Data in R.

Lastly, we looked at several research areas that seem promising, such as `Rcpp` (to develop your own R methods using C++), `parallel` (for parallel processing of R commands), and `microbenchmark` (allowing detailed timing to occur in your R coding).

In the next chapter, we will cover machine learning.

10
Machine Learning in Action

R programming has several methods for machine learning. With machine learning, you can learn to automatically make better predictions. You are leaving the heavy lifting to the software to figure out. The methods you use are somewhat dependent on the characteristics of the data you are attempting to model.

This chapter will cover machine learning in the following ways:

- Organizing your dataset into training and testing sets
- Generating a model of your data
- Testing the efficacy of your model (with the part of your data allocated for testing)

Packages

In R, there are several packages available that provide machine learning for the programmer. We will be using the following packages in the chapter:

- `ada`: This is used for stochastic boosting
- `caret`: This is used for classification and regression testing
- `class`: This package has classification functions
- `clue`: This package has the cluster ensemble methods
- `e1071`: This package has miscellaneous functions for the statistics department
- `kernlab`: This has kernel-based machine learning methods
- `MASS`: This stands for Modern Applied Statistics with S
- `neuralnet`: This has artificial neural net support

- randomForest: This has random forests for classification
- relaimpo: This package has functions to determine the relative importance of regressors in linear models

Dataset

Machine learning works by featuring a dataset that we break up into a training section and a testing section. We use the training data to come up with our model. We can then prove or test that model against the remaining testing section data.

The first issue is finding a dataset with several variables and, hopefully, several hundred observations. I am using the housing data from http://uci.edu. Let's find the dataset using the following command:

```
> housing <- read.table("http://archive.ics.uci.edu/ml/machine-
learning-databases/housing/housing.data")
> colnames(housing) <- c("CRIM","ZN","INDUS","CHAS","NOX","RM","AGE","
DIS","RAD","TAX","PRATIO","B","LSTAT","MDEV")
```

There are close to 500 observations with 14 variables. We can see a summary for a better idea, as follows:

```
> summary(housing)
      CRIM                ZN               INDUS             CHAS
 Min.   : 0.00632   Min.   :   0.00   Min.   : 0.46   Min.   :0.00000
 1st Qu.: 0.08204   1st Qu.:   0.00   1st Qu.: 5.19   1st Qu.:0.00000
 Median : 0.25651   Median :   0.00   Median : 9.69   Median :0.00000
 Mean   : 3.61352   Mean   :  11.36   Mean   :11.14   Mean   :0.06917
 3rd Qu.: 3.67708   3rd Qu.:  12.50   3rd Qu.:18.10   3rd Qu.:0.00000
 Max.   :88.97620   Max.   : 100.00   Max.   :27.74   Max.   :1.00000
      NOX               RM             AGE              DIS
 Min.   :0.3850   Min.   :3.561   Min.   :  2.90   Min.   : 1.130
 1st Qu.:0.4490   1st Qu.:5.886   1st Qu.: 45.02   1st Qu.: 2.100
 Median :0.5380   Median :6.208   Median : 77.50   Median : 3.207
 Mean   :0.5547   Mean   :6.285   Mean   : 68.57   Mean   : 3.795
 3rd Qu.:0.6240   3rd Qu.:6.623   3rd Qu.: 94.08   3rd Qu.: 5.188
 Max.   :0.8710   Max.   :8.780   Max.   :100.00   Max.   :12.127
      RAD              TAX            PRATIO             B
 Min.   : 1.000   Min.   :187.0   Min.   :12.60   Min.   :  0.32
 1st Qu.: 4.000   1st Qu.:279.0   1st Qu.:17.40   1st Qu.:375.38
 Median : 5.000   Median :330.0   Median :19.05   Median :391.44
 Mean   : 9.549   Mean   :408.2   Mean   :18.46   Mean   :356.67
 3rd Qu.:24.000   3rd Qu.:666.0   3rd Qu.:20.20   3rd Qu.:396.23
 Max.   :24.000   Max.   :711.0   Max.   :22.00   Max.   :396.90
```

```
     LSTAT                MDEV
  Min.    : 1.73   Min.     : 5.00
  1st Qu.: 6.95    1st Qu.:17.02
  Median :11.36    Median :21.20
  Mean   :12.65    Mean    :22.53
  3rd Qu.:16.95    3rd Qu.:25.00
  Max.   :37.97    Max.    :50.00
```

The various variables are as follows:

Parameter	Description
CRIM	This is the per capita crime rate
ZN	This is the residential zone rate percentage
INDUS	This is the proportion of non-retail business in town
CHAS	This is the proximity to the Charles river (Boolean)
NOX	This is the nitric oxide concentration
RM	This is the average rooms per dwelling
AGE	This is the proportion of housing built before 1940
DIS	This is the weighted distance to an employment center
RAD	This is the accessibility to a highway
TAX	This is the tax rate per $10,000
B	This is calculated using the formula: *1000(Bk – 0.63)^2 Bk* = African American population percentage
LSTAT	This is the lower-status population percentage
MDEV	This is the median value of owner-occupied homes in $1,000s

As you can tell from the data descriptions, this is dated material. Modern statistics would be in 10s if not 100s of thousands. And the idea of measuring the African American population's effect is just bad.

```
> plot(housing)
```

The plotted data looks like this:

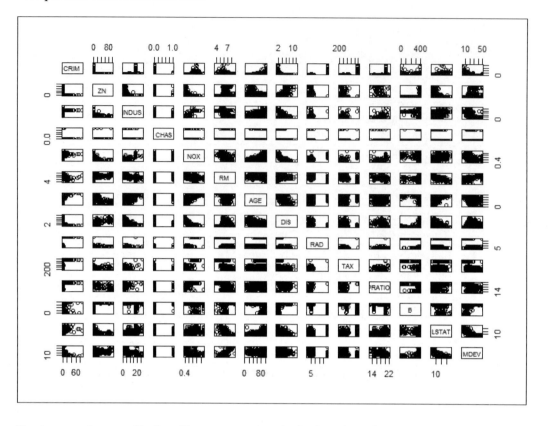

I'm just getting an all *x* by all *y* to get a visual of what the relationships look like above. Most of the data looks to be useful, except for the following ones:

- Charles river access (but that is binary)
- Highway access (I guess that should be expected)
- Tax rate (appears to be very lopsided, almost binary)

We can produce a correlation matrix to prove the data, as follows:

```
> install.packages("corrplot")
> library(corrplot)
> corrplot(cor(housing), method="number", tl.cex=0.5)
```

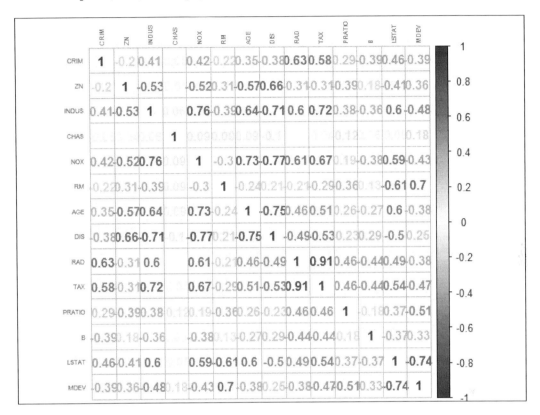

The highest correlations occurred with RAD (access to highway) and TAX (rate per $1,000). Unfortunately, I don't think I can exclude these from the dataset.

The remaining variables are well within range.

Data partitioning

Now that we have our raw data, we need to go about splitting up between training and test data. The training dataset will be used to train our system in how to predict our values (in this case, housing prices). The testing data will be used to prove our hypothesis. I am using 75 percent as the cutoff: 75 percent of the data will be for training and 25 percent for testing.

Where the data is inherently geographic, it is better to make good samples that use percentages of geographic areas, but that data is not available. I am assuming that the data is inherently randomly organized, so random partitioning using the median house value as the index is workable.

The `caret` package has a data partitioning function available, `createDataPartition`. The function works on a vector of values, selects the records of interest as per your parameters, and produces a vector of the indices selected. We can then extract the records of interest into training and testing sets.

 The vector passed to `createDataPartition` is assumed to be sorted, so you must sort the data ahead of time.

I think this is a little problematic, as records would now most likely be clumped together geographically. I chose to split up the housing based on median value (`MDEV`). It seemed to have a good enough range that a randomized selection process would pull values from all different areas. I thought many of the other values would tend towards certain geographic pockets. Let's first install the `caret` package:

```
> housing <- housing[order(housing$MDEV),]
> install.packages("caret")
> library(caret)
```

The partitioning process uses a random number to select records. If we use `set.seed`, we can reproduce the partitioning example that takes place, since we are specifying the random starting place, as shown here:

```
> set.seed(3277)
> trainingIndices <- createDataPartition(housing$MDEV, p=0.75,
list=FALSE)
> housingTraining <- housing[trainingIndices,]
> housingTesting <- housing[-trainingIndices,]
> nrow(housingTraining)
[1] 381
> nrow(housingTesting)
[1] 125
```

So, we end up with 381 records for training and 125 for testing. We could use other approaches to split up the data. There are separate packages that just provide different ways to partition your data.

Model

There are a variety of models that we can use for machine learning, some of which we already covered in prior chapters.

Linear model

First, we will use linear regression, `lm`. This model will provide a baseline for our testing, as shown in the following code:

```
> linearModel <- lm(MDEV ~ CRIM + ZN + INDUS + CHAS + NOX + RM + AGE +
DIS + RAD + TAX + PRATIO + B + LSTAT, data=housingTraining)
> summary(linearModel)

Call:
lm(formula = MDEV ~ CRIM + ZN + INDUS + CHAS + NOX + RM + AGE +
    DIS + RAD + TAX + PRATIO + B + LSTAT, data = housingTraining)

Residuals:
    Min      1Q   Median      3Q      Max
-14.1317  -2.6258  -0.5413   1.5656  26.2551

Coefficients:
             Estimate Std. Error t value Pr(>|t|)
(Intercept)  41.196069   5.609316   7.344 1.35e-12 ***
CRIM         -0.122053   0.032598  -3.744 0.000210 ***
ZN            0.052261   0.015412   3.391 0.000772 ***
INDUS         0.032047   0.068200   0.470 0.638709
CHAS          2.385849   0.959308   2.487 0.013324 *
NOX         -17.566444   4.273389  -4.111 4.87e-05 ***
RM            3.485134   0.463397   7.521 4.23e-13 ***
AGE          -0.003562   0.014443  -0.247 0.805317
DIS          -1.545347   0.221048  -6.991 1.30e-11 ***
RAD           0.333380   0.076002   4.386 1.51e-05 ***
TAX          -0.014973   0.004317  -3.468 0.000586 ***
PRATIO       -0.995370   0.145592  -6.837 3.39e-11 ***
B             0.006718   0.002832   2.373 0.018180 *
LSTAT        -0.521544   0.054005  -9.657  < 2e-16 ***
---
```

```
Signif. codes:  0 '***' 0.001 '**' 0.01 '*' 0.05 '.' 0.1 ' ' 1

Residual standard error: 4.549 on 367 degrees of freedom
Multiple R-squared:  0.7605,  Adjusted R-squared:  0.752
F-statistic: 89.63 on 13 and 367 DF,  p-value: < 2.2e-16
```

It is interesting that AGE does not appear to be a true factor. Similarly, TAX and B have minimal impact.

Prediction

Now that we have a linear model, we can predict our test data and measure our model results against actuals, as follows:

```
> predicted <- predict(linearModel,newdata=housingTesting)
> summary(predicted)
   Min. 1st Qu.  Median    Mean 3rd Qu.    Max.
 0.8783 17.8400 21.0700 22.4300 27.2600 42.8900
> summary(housingTesting$MDEV)
   Min. 1st Qu.  Median    Mean 3rd Qu.    Max.
   8.10   17.10   21.20   22.89   25.00   50.00
> plot(predicted,housingTesting$MDEV)
```

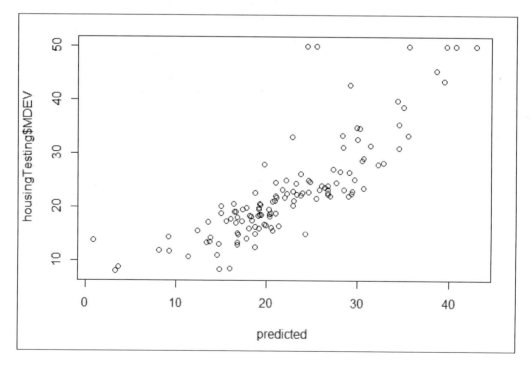

We appear to have close to a 45-degree regression with predicted versus actual. There is an offset.

Now that we have our predictions on the test data, we need a way to measure the results (and evaluate this method versus the others). I like the sum of squares as the cleanest. Surprisingly, there does not appear to be a built-in function in R for this, so we add our own, as follows:

```
> sumofsquares <- function(x) {
+ return(sum(x^2))
+ }
```

As a simple test, we can use a simple range, as follows:

```
> sumofsquares(1:5)
[1] 55
```

Now, we can evaluate the model, as follows:

```
> diff <- predicted - housingTesting$MDEV
> sumofsquares(diff)
[1] 3555.882
```

The `sumofsquares` result is the sum of the squares of the differences between predicted and actual values. The 3,000+ values over a few hundred observations don't sound particularly accurate, but we can try out other methods to see if we can arrive at a better mode. So, we will use this to compare results among the models going forward.

Logistic regression

The logistic regression function, `glm`, is built into the base R system. We can use it directly, much like the previous `lm` function:

```
> lr <- glm(MDEV ~ CRIM + ZN + INDUS + CHAS + NOX + RM + AGE + DIS +
RAD + TAX + PRATIO + B + LSTAT, data=housingTraining)

> summary(lr)

Call:
glm(formula = MDEV ~ CRIM + ZN + INDUS + CHAS + NOX + RM + AGE +
    DIS + RAD ı TAX + PRATIO + B + LSTAT, data = housingTraining)

Deviance Residuals:
     Min          1Q     Median          3Q        Max
```

```
    -14.1317    -2.6258    -0.5413    1.5656    26.2551

Coefficients:
             Estimate Std. Error t value Pr(>|t|)
(Intercept)  41.196069   5.609316   7.344 1.35e-12 ***
CRIM         -0.122053   0.032598  -3.744 0.000210 ***
ZN            0.052261   0.015412   3.391 0.000772 ***
INDUS         0.032047   0.068200   0.470 0.638709
CHAS          2.385849   0.959308   2.487 0.013324 *
NOX         -17.566444   4.273389  -4.111 4.87e-05 ***
RM            3.485134   0.463397   7.521 4.23e-13 ***
AGE          -0.003562   0.014443  -0.247 0.805317
DIS          -1.545347   0.221048  -6.991 1.30e-11 ***
RAD           0.333380   0.076002   4.386 1.51e-05 ***
TAX          -0.014973   0.004317  -3.468 0.000586 ***
PRATIO       -0.995370   0.145592  -6.837 3.39e-11 ***
B             0.006718   0.002832   2.373 0.018180 *
LSTAT        -0.521544   0.054005  -9.657  < 2e-16 ***
---
Signif. codes:  0 '***' 0.001 '**' 0.01 '*' 0.05 '.' 0.1 ' ' 1

(Dispersion parameter for gaussian family taken to be 20.69378)

    Null deviance: 31707.3  on 380  degrees of freedom
Residual deviance:  7594.6  on 367  degrees of freedom
AIC: 2251.3

Number of Fisher Scoring iterations: 2
```

We then run the same prediction and tests:

```
> predicted <- predict(lr,newdata=housingTesting)
> summary(predicted)
   Min. 1st Qu.  Median    Mean 3rd Qu.    Max.
 0.8783 17.8400 21.0700 22.4300 27.2600 42.8900
> plot(predicted,housingTesting$MDEV)
> diff <- predicted - housingTesting$MDEV
> sumofsquares(diff)
[1] 3555.882
```

We end up with exactly the same results! This shows that linear regression and logistic regression boil down to the same underlying modeling algorithm.

Residuals

We can look at the residuals for the model (built into the result of the lm function). Note, we can use the resid function against any of the model-fitting functions available, as follows:

```
> plot(resid(linearModel))
```

The following plot shows a nice average of near zero for the residuals until we get to the higher values:

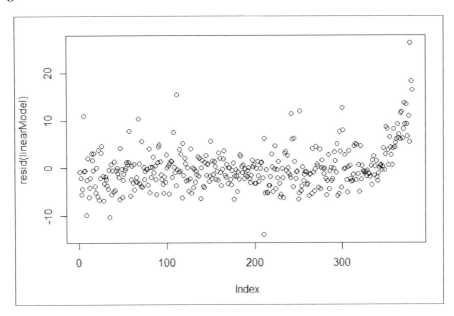

Least squares regression

Least squares regression uses a line of the form $b0 + b1*x$ as the line formula. Here, we have $b0$ as the intercept and $b1$ as the slope of the line. Using the same data, we can run a least squares regression using R functions directly.

Let's assign our variables to the normal x and Y for a least squares regression (makes later calculations cleaner), as follows:

```
> x <- housingTesting$MDEV
> Y <- predicted
```

Now, we will calculate our `b0` and `b1` from our `x` and `Y`, as follows:

```
> b1 <- sum((x-mean(x))*(Y-mean(Y)))/sum((x-mean(x))^2)
> b0 <- mean(Y)-b1*mean(x)
> c(b0,b1)
[1]  7.2106245  0.6648381
```

Let's plot the raw data using the following command:

```
> plot(x,Y)
```

We can add a least squares regression line to the plot, as follows:

```
> abline(c(b0,b1),col="blue",lwd=2)
```

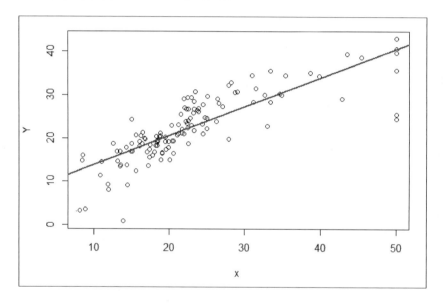

There isn't a great match between the testing data and the prediction. The least squares line looks too flat.

Relative importance

We can calculate the relative importance of the variables we used in the model using the `relaimpo` package. The relative importance of the variables used in our model will tell you which variables are providing the most effect on your results. In other words, out of all of the variables available, which should we pay the most attention to. Most of the time, you can only afford to investigate a few. In this case, maybe we are a buyer looking to see what factors are most affecting the value of houses and direct our search where those factors are maximized.

Let's calculate the relative importance using the `relaimpo` package, as follows:

```
> library(relaimpo)
> calc.relimp(linearModel,type=c("lmg","last","first","pratt"),
rela=TRUE)
Response variable: MDEV
Total response variance: 83.44019
Analysis based on 381 observations


13 Regressors:
CRIM ZN INDUS CHAS NOX RM AGE DIS RAD TAX PRATIO B LSTAT
Proportion of variance explained by model: 76.05%
Metrics are normalized to sum to 100% (rela=TRUE).
Relative importance metrics:
                lmg           last        first          pratt
CRIM     0.04378500  0.0423236380  0.05959783   0.069549551
ZN       0.04085431  0.0347151937  0.05480466   0.072324623
INDUS    0.04927578  0.0006666234  0.08442062  -0.015510766
CHAS     0.02068028  0.0186745066  0.01195166   0.016098916
NOX      0.04611049  0.0510155167  0.06866322   0.129797308
RM       0.23110043  0.1707701764  0.16468562   0.239015600
AGE      0.03211959  0.0001836714  0.05639641   0.005826449
DIS      0.04282755  0.1475559786  0.02469774  -0.125578499
RAD      0.03552896  0.0580913573  0.05929346  -0.172215184
TAX      0.05313897  0.0363198971  0.08310082   0.175938820
PRATIO   0.11235443  0.1411152591  0.09803364   0.165972509
B        0.02614223  0.0169947393  0.03917392   0.031322939
LSTAT    0.26608199  0.2815734421  0.19518041   0.407457734


Average coefficients for different model sizes:
                   1X            2Xs            3Xs            4Xs
5Xs
CRIM     -0.39658057   -0.27179045   -0.21108113   -0.17716944
-0.15605272
ZN        0.15016161    0.10008617    0.07724633    0.06573547
0.05920013
INDUS    -0.66137913   -0.49760611   -0.38326657   -0.29972518
-0.23603446
CHAS      6.71617551    6.28502633    5.84865357    5.37351604
4.90522742
NOX     -35.23627433  -24.37290112  -18.14707801  -14.72054067
-13.02167728
RM        9.10534876    7.97900568    7.33195455    6.85127499
6.43337784
```

```
AGE       -0.13074649  -0.08136606  -0.05484617  -0.03952753
-0.03003803
DIS        1.15243247   0.14262752  -0.45525720  -0.82823438
-1.06957328
RAD       -0.43523357  -0.23718077  -0.11226188  -0.02648010
0.03740961
TAX       -0.02681594  -0.02111878  -0.01748128  -0.01513793
-0.01363214
PRATIO  -2.22931346  -1.79620241  -1.57371014  -1.43633047
-1.33810121
B          0.03185870   0.02040032   0.01517751   0.01236138
0.01063506
LSTAT   -0.94731052  -0.89595398  -0.85129784  -0.81015368
-0.77115301
(more iterations available)
```

In the relative-importance metrics, we see computed values for each of the possible parameters in our model. This is what the parameters are about:

- The lmg column is the coefficient of the variable from the model.

- The last column (also called usefulness) looks at what the effect of adding this variable into the model would be, effectively removing it, on the other variables. We are looking for the last values greater than lmg, as those variables are generating more effect. This would include NOX, DIS, RAD, PRATIO, and LSTAT.

- The first column (squared covariance between y and the variable) looks at the variable as if none of the other variables were present in the model. We are interested in cases where the first column value is greater than lmg, as those variables are truly generating more effect. These include CRIM, ZN, INDUS, NOX, AGE, RAD, and B.

- The pratt column (product of the standard coefficient and the correlation) is based on Pratt's contribution in 1987. The downfall is that negative values need to be ignored as not applicable. We are again looking for pratt values over lmg such as CRIM, ZN, RM, and PRATIO.

The most interesting part of the results is the detail that the variables provided only explain 76 percent of the value. This is a pretty good number, but we did not end up being accurate.

Stepwise regression

Stepwise regression is the process of adding/removing variables from the regression model, adjusting for the effect of doing so, and continuing to evaluate each of the variables involved. With forward stepwise regression, we start with an empty model and successively add each of the variables, gauge their effect, decide whether they remain in the model, and move on to the next variable. In backward regression, we start with the full model variable set and successively attempt to remove each, gauging their effect.

We can evaluate the predictors in stepwise regression using the MASS package, as follows:

```
> library(MASS)
```

The results of the step(s) show the process of adding/removing variables from the model and the result of doing so leading up to the final *best* set of variables for the model. Let's use the stepAIC function to perform the same as follows:

```
> step <- stepAIC(linearModel, direction="both")
Start:  AIC=1168.1
MDEV ~ CRIM + ZN + INDUS + CHAS + NOX + RM + AGE + DIS + RAD +
    TAX + PRATIO + B + LSTAT

          Df Sum of Sq    RSS     AIC
- AGE      1      1.26 7595.9 1166.2
- INDUS    1      4.57 7599.2 1166.3
<none>                 7594.6 1168.1
- B        1    116.49 7711.1 1171.9
- CHAS     1    128.00 7722.6 1172.5
- ZN       1    237.95 7832.6 1177.9
- TAX      1    248.95 7843.6 1178.4
- CRIM     1    290.10 7884.7 1180.4
- NOX      1    349.67 7944.3 1183.2
- RAD      1    398.17 7992.8 1185.6
- PRATIO   1    967.24 8561.9 1211.8
- DIS      1   1011.39 8606.0 1213.7
- RM       1   1170.50 8765.1 1220.7
- LSTAT    1   1929.98 9524.6 1252.4

Step:  AIC=1166.17
MDEV ~ CRIM + ZN + INDUS + CHAS + NOX + RM + DIS + RAD + TAX +
    PRATIO + B + LSTAT

          Df Sum of Sq    RSS     AIC
- INDUS    1      4.53 7600.4 1164.4
<none>                 7595.9 1166.2
```

```
+ AGE      1        1.26 7594.6 1168.1
- B        1      115.79 7711.7 1169.9
- CHAS     1      127.38 7723.3 1170.5
- ZN       1      248.43 7844.3 1176.4
- TAX      1      250.17 7846.0 1176.5
- CRIM     1      290.16 7886.0 1178.5
- NOX      1      390.00 7985.9 1183.2
- RAD      1      402.64 7998.5 1183.8
- PRATIO   1      971.24 8567.1 1210.0
- DIS      1     1065.15 8661.0 1214.2
- RM       1     1189.61 8785.5 1219.6
- LSTAT    1     2153.07 9748.9 1259.2


Step:  AIC=1164.39
MDEV ~ CRIM + ZN + CHAS + NOX + RM + DIS + RAD + TAX + PRATIO +
    B + LSTAT

           Df Sum of Sq     RSS     AIC
<none>                   7600.4 1164.4
+ INDUS    1      4.53 7595.9 1166.2
+ AGE      1      1.22 7599.2 1166.3
- B        1    114.05 7714.5 1168.1
- CHAS     1    132.23 7732.6 1169.0
- ZN       1    244.48 7844.9 1174.5
- TAX      1    272.90 7873.3 1175.8
- CRIM     1    293.20 7893.6 1176.8
- NOX      1    398.54 7998.9 1181.9
- RAD      1    410.88 8011.3 1182.5
- PRATIO   1    968.88 8569.3 1208.1
- DIS      1   1148.81 8749.2 1216.0
- RM       1   1185.73 8786.1 1217.6
- LSTAT    1   2151.58 9752.0 1257.4
```

It is interesting to see that INDUS (percentage of industrial zoning) has the largest effect in this model and LSTAT (lower-income status population) is really negligible.

The k-nearest neighbor classification

The k-nearest neighbor classification is in the class package. We load the package and evaluate using our training data, as follows:

```
> library(class)
> knnModel <- knn(train=housingTraining, test=housingTesting,
cl=housingTraining$MDEV)
> summary(knnModel)
    20.8     14.9       21    18.6    18.7    19.3    11.5    13.4
13.8     14.1
```

```
        5         4         4         3         3         3         2         2
2         2
       18       18.9      19.4       20       20.4      20.6      20.9      21.4
21.5      22.8
        2         2         2         2         2         2         2         2
2         2
       22.9      23.1      24.6      24.8      25.3      27.5      28.4       29
33.2       50
        2         2         2         2         2         2         2         2
2         2
        6.3       7       10.2      11.7      12.7      13.1      13.2      13.3
15.2      15.4
        1         1         1         1         1         1         1         1
1         1
       15.6      16.1      16.2      16.3      16.6      16.7       17       17.1
17.7      18.2
        1         1         1         1         1         1         1         1
1         1
       18.3      18.4       19       19.1      19.2      19.9      20.3      20.5
21.2      21.7
        1         1         1         1         1         1         1         1
1         1
       22       22.4      23.8      23.9      24.2      24.3      24.4       25
26.6      28.5
        1         1         1         1         1         1         1         1
1         1
       29.6      29.8      30.1      32.2      32.4      32.9      33.1      33.8
35.1      35.2
        1         1         1         1         1         1         1         1
1         1
       36.2      37.2      37.9       46       48.8       5        5.6       7.2
7.4       7.5
        1         1         1         1         1         0         0         0
0         0
        8.3       8.4       8.5       8.7       8.8       9.5       9.6       9.7
10.4    (Other)
        0         0         0         0         0         0         0         0
0         0
```

[I printed this with a slightly smaller font so that the columns line up.]

Interpreting the data goes as follows: five entries for the 20.8 bucket, four entries for the 14.9 bucket, and so on. The buckets with the most hits are portrayed first, and then in the order of decreasing occurrence.

A plot is useful. We can see a frequency where the 20.8 bucket is highest using the following command:

```
plot(knnModel)
```

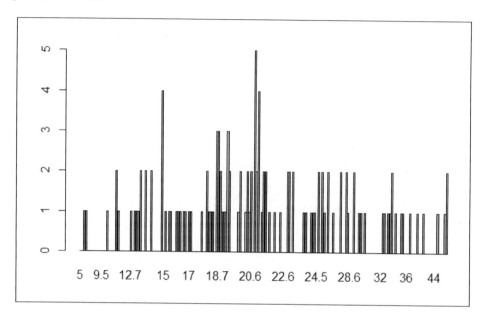

For purposes of comparison, here's a simple graph of the raw test data:

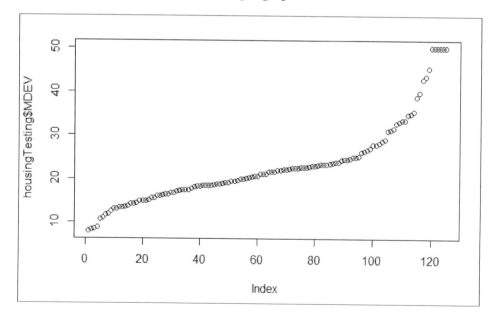

Just visually, there appears to be a good match. The upper-right tail is sparsely populated and the mid-to-left section is heavily populated—matching our knn results.

Naïve Bayes

Naïve Bayes is the process of determining classifiers based on probability, assuming the features are independent (the assumption is the naïve part).

We can use the e1071 package to use the naiveBayes function included. Let's load the e1071 package as follows:

```
> install.packages("e1071")
> library(e1071)
```

We produce our estimates/model calling upon the naiveBayes function in much the same manner as we did for the previous regression: the idea is that median value is the product of all the associated data. We use the training data as the basis for the model, as shown here:

```
> nb <- naiveBayes(MDEV ~ CRIM + ZN + INDUS + CHAS + NOX + RM + AGE +
DIS + RAD + TAX + PRATIO + B + LSTAT, data=housingTraining)
```

We can examine the parameters generated for the effect of each variable as follows:

```
> nb$tables$TAX
      TAX
Y            [,1]             [,2]
  5     666.0000    0.0000000
  5.6   666.0000          NA
  6.3   666.0000          NA
  7     688.5000   31.8198052
  7.2   666.0000    0.0000000
  7.4   666.0000          NA
  7.5   666.0000          NA
  8.3   666.0000    0.0000000
1 = mean
2 = stddev
```

Here, we see that taxes appear to have a very small effect on the data.

The `apriori` value of the Naïve Bayes result contains the class distribution for the dependent variable. We can see this visually by plotting the result. I think it looks very similar to the previous `knn` model result: again, we have the tight overlap in the middle with both tails skewed. This does match our data. We can plot the result using the following command:

```
> plot(nb$apriori)
```

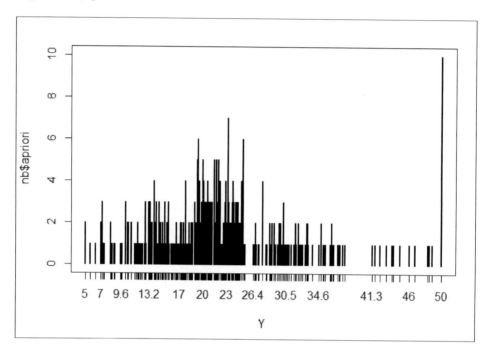

The train Method

A standard method to develop a model, regardless of technique, is the `train` method. The `train` method has only one required parameter—sample data. All the other parameters are optional.

Some of the parameters of the `train` method are described in the following table:

Parameter	Description
x	This is the sample data
y	This is the vector of outcomes
form	This is the formula in the format *result ~ var1 + var2 ...*
data	This is the dataframe where variables referenced in the formula can be taken

Parameter	Description
weights	This is the vector of case weights if applicable for the model
subset	This is the vector of indices to use for training
method	This can contain any of several methods listed at `http://topepo.github.io/caret/bytag.html`

predict

Similar to the `train` method, we also have a generic function, `predict`, that can be used to predict results based on a *train* model in order to be able to further test whether our model is working.

The `predict` function, again similarly, only has two required arguments, a model and new or test data to use with the model to *predict* results.

Support vector machines

With **Support vector machines (SVM)**, we have a supervised learning process that attempts to classify data into one of two categories. While this does not match our housing dataset, walking through some of the steps is an interesting exercise. The `svm` modeling tools are in the `kernlab` package. Note, the driver to the `train` function that tells it to use `svm` is the `method="svmRadial"` parameter. For SVM, we need a binary result value. For this example, I am using the Pima Indian diabetes dataset available from `http://uci.edu`.

Let's load in the data and assign column names, as follows:

```
> pima <- read.csv("https://archive.ics.uci.edu/ml/machine-learning-
databases/pima-indians-diabetes/pima-indians-diabetes.data")
> colnames(pima) <- c("pregnancies","glucose","bp","triceps","insulin"
,"bmi","pedigree","age","class")
> summary(pima)
  pregnancies        glucose            bp             triceps
 Min.   : 0.000   Min.   :  0.0   Min.   :  0.0   Min.   : 0.00
 1st Qu.: 1.000   1st Qu.: 99.0   1st Qu.: 62.0   1st Qu.: 0.00
 Median : 3.000   Median :117.0   Median : 72.0   Median :23.00
 Mean   : 3.842   Mean   :120.9   Mean   : 69.1   Mean   :20.52
 3rd Qu.: 6.000   3rd Qu.:140.0   3rd Qu.: 80.0   3rd Qu.:32.00
 Max.   :17.000   Max.   :199.0   Max.   :122.0   Max.   :99.00
    insulin           bmi            pedigree           age
 Min.   :  0.0   Min.   :  0.00   Min.   :0.0780   Min.   :21.00
 1st Qu.:  0.0   1st Qu.:27.30   1st Qu.:0.2435   1st Qu.:24.00
 Median : 32.0   Median :32.00   Median :0.3710   Median :29.00
 Mean   : 79.9   Mean   :31.99   Mean   :0.4717   Mean   :33.22
```

```
3rd Qu.:127.5    3rd Qu.:36.60    3rd Qu.:0.6250    3rd Qu.:41.00
Max.    :846.0   Max.    :67.10   Max.    :2.4200   Max.    :81.00
      class
Min.    :0.0000
1st Qu.:0.0000
Median :0.0000
Mean    :0.3481
3rd Qu.:1.0000
Max.    :1.0000
```

We need to split the training set from the testing dataset, as we did in the previous section, as follows:

```
> set.seed(3277)
> library(caret)
> pimaIndices <- createDataPartition(pima$class, p=0.75, list=FALSE)
> pimaTraining <- pima[pimaIndices,]
> pimaTesting <- pima[-pimaIndices,]
```

Let's calculate the SVM model from the training data (note that this step takes a while because of the boot control we pass in, telling the software to iterate 200 times over the data), as follows:

```
> library(kernlab)
> bootControl <- trainControl(number = 200)
> svmFit <- train(pimaTraining[,-9], pimaTraining[,9],
method="svmRadial", tuneLength=5, trControl=bootControl, scaled=FALSE)
> svmFit
Support Vector Machines with Radial Basis Function Kernel
576 samples
  8 predictor


No pre-processing
Resampling: Bootstrapped (200 reps)
Summary of sample sizes: 576, 576, 576, 576, 576, 576, ...
Resampling results across tuning parameters:
  C     RMSE  Rsquared RMSE SD  Rsquared SD
  0.25  0.477 0.00915  0.01137  0.00789
  0.50  0.476 0.00953  0.00567  0.00831
  1.00  0.477 0.00955  0.00540  0.00834
  2.00  0.477 0.00955  0.00540  0.00834
  4.00  0.477 0.00955  0.00540  0.00834


Tuning parameter 'sigma' was held constant at a value of 0.1165912
RMSE was used to select the optimal model using  the smallest value.
```

```
The final values used for the model were sigma = 0.1165912 and C =
0.5.
# the predict method is described above
> predicted <- predict(svmFit$finalModel,newdata=pimaTesting[,-9])
> plot(pimaTesting$class,predicted)
```

As you can see, a simple plot of test versus predicted doesn't tell us a whole lot about binary data. We need to use the `svmFit` results to determine whether the model is working or not.

We can produce a confusion matrix between the predicted values and our data, as follows:

```
> table(pred = predicted, true = pimaTesting[,9])
                       true
pred                  0  1
   0.307113553404879  1  0
   0.331403184095759  1  0
   0.333960027975998  1  0
   0.335008445959367  0  1
   0.36279279414314   0  1
(many more values)
```

Looking at the results of the matrix, we have a two-thirds success rate. It is really not great:

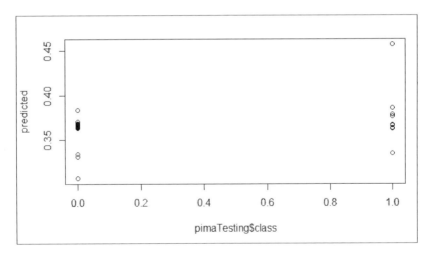

```
> svmFit$finalModel
Support Vector Machine object of class "ksvm"
SV type: eps-svr  (regression)
 parameter : epsilon = 0.1  cost C = 0.5
```

```
Gaussian Radial Basis kernel function.
 Hyperparameter : sigma =  0.116591226197405
Number of Support Vectors : 576
Objective Function Value : -41.6404
Training error : 0.012664
```

The training error is really very low. So, I think we have somewhat accurate predictors for diabetes for Pima Indians.

K-means clustering

We have seen k-means clustering in *Chapter 2, Data Mining Sequences*. In this case, we will use the `iris` dataset using a subset for training and producing a k-means model, applying that model to the remaining test data and verifying results.

First, we load in the `iris` data and partition it into test and training, as follows:

```
> iris <- read.csv("iris.csv")
> irisIndices <- createDataPartition(iris$Species, p=0.75, list=FALSE)
> irisTraining <- iris[irisIndices,]
> irisTesting <- iris[-irisIndices,]
```

Now, we can produce a model from the training data, as follows:

```
> bootControl <- trainControl(number = 20)
> km <- kmeans(irisTraining[,1:4], 3)
> km
K-means clustering with 3 clusters of sizes 38, 29, 47
Cluster means:
SepalLength SepalWidth PetalLength PetalWidth
1     5.068421    3.428947     1.476316     0.250000
2     6.893103    3.041379     5.786207     2.027586
3     5.912766    2.778723     4.374468     1.442553
Clustering vector:
   1    3    5    6    8   11   13   14   15   17   18   19   20   21   22   24   25
  26   27   28
   1    1    1    1    1    1    1    1    1    1    1    1    1    1    1    1    1
   1    1    1
  29   31   32   33   34   35   36   37   38   39   40   42   44   45   46   48   49
  50   51   52
   1    1    1    1    1    1    1    1    1    1    1    1    1    1    1    1    1
   1    3    3
  53   55   58   60   61   62   65   66   67   68   69   71   72   73   74   75   76
  77   78   79
   2    3    3    3    3    3    3    3    3    3    3    3    3    3    3    3    3
   3    2    3
```

```
    80  81  82  83  85  86  87  89  90  92  93  95  97  98  99 100 101
103 104 105
     3   3   3   3   3   3   3   3   3   3   3   3   3   3   3   3   2
    2   2   2
106 107 108 109 111 112 114 115 117 118 119 120 121 123 124 125 127
128 129 130
     2   3   2   2   2   2   3   3   2   2   2   3   2   2   3   2   3
    3   2   2
131 132 134 135 136 138 139 141 142 143 144 146 149 150
     2   2   3   2   2   2   3   2   2   3   2   2   2   3
Within cluster sum of squares by cluster:
[1] 10.90395 20.50138 30.71532
 (between_SS / total_SS =  88.0 %)


Available components:
[1] "cluster"      "centers"       "totss"        "withinss"       "tot.
withinss"
[6] "betweenss"    "size"          "iter"         "ifault"
```

We can see the three clusters (as specified in the model generation). So, using our remaining test data, we can predict which cluster the test data will be applied to. We can use the `clue` package for testing out the k-means model, as shown here:

```
> install.packages("clue")
> library(clue)
> cl_predict(km,irisTesting[,-5])
Class ids:
  [1] 1 1 1 1 1 1 1 1 1 1 1 3 3 3 3 3 3 3 3 3 3 3 3 3 3 2 2 2 3 2 2 2 2
2 3 2
> irisTesting[,5]
 [1] Iris-setosa     Iris-setosa     Iris-setosa     Iris-setosa
 [5] Iris-setosa     Iris-setosa     Iris-setosa     Iris-setosa
 [9] Iris-setosa     Iris-setosa     Iris-setosa     Iris-setosa
[13] Iris-versicolor Iris-versicolor Iris-versicolor Iris-versicolor
[17] Iris-versicolor Iris-versicolor Iris-versicolor Iris-versicolor
[21] Iris-versicolor Iris-versicolor Iris-versicolor Iris-versicolor
[25] Iris-virginica  Iris-virginica  Iris-virginica  Iris-virginica
[29] Iris-virginica  Iris-virginica  Iris-virginica  Iris-virginica
[33] Iris-virginica  Iris-virginica  Iris-virginica  Iris-virginica
Levels: Iris-setosa Iris-versicolor Iris-virginica
```

I think this model works near perfectly.

Decision trees

There are several decision tree packages available in R. For this example, we use the housing regression data. A package to produce decision trees from regression data is `rpart`.

Let's load the `rpart` library using the following command:

```
> library(rpart)
```

Load and split the housing data (as done previously):

```
> set.seed(3277)
> housing <- read.csv("housing.csv")
> housing <- housing[order(housing$MDEV),]
> trainingIndices <- createDataPartition(housing$MDEV, p=0.75,
list=FALSE)
> housingTraining <- housing[trainingIndices,]
> housingTesting <- housing[-trainingIndices,]
```

Using the same modeling technique as in the previous section, we will generate a model of the housing data using a decision tree, as follows:

```
> housingFit <- rpart(MDEV ~ CRIM + ZN + INDUS + CHAS + NOX + RM
+ AGE + DIS + RAD + TAX + PRATIO + B + LSTAT, method="anova",
data=housingTraining)
```

We can see the decision tree in a plot using the following command:

```
> plot(housingFit)
> text(housingFit, use.n=TRUE, all=TRUE, cex=.8)
```

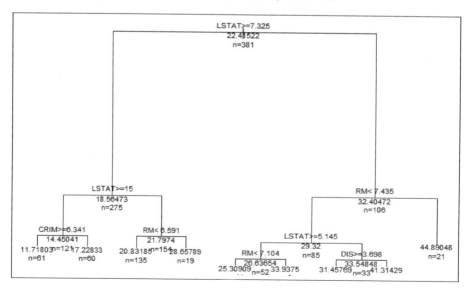

While the plotting is not great, you can follow the decision points to arrive at a valuation fairly easily.

Let's generate the predicted values using the test data, as follows:

```
> treePredict <- predict(housingFit,newdata=housingTesting)
```

We will verify the correctness of the model (using the sum of squares defined in the previous section), as follows:

```
> diff <- treePredict - housingTesting$MDEV
> sumofsquares <- function(x) {return(sum(x^2))}
> sumofsquares(diff)
[1] 3926.297
```

Just for comparison, this is a worse result than direct linear regression. Maybe if the data were non-continuous, this would be a better modeling technique.

AdaBoost

The `ada` package for R provides a boost using binary data. We can use the binary data for the Pima Indian diabetes tests, as follows:

```
> adaModel <- ada(x=pimaTraining[,-9],y=pimaTraining$class,test.
x=pimaTesting[,-9],test.y=pimaTesting$class)
> adaModel
Call:
ada(pimaTraining[, -9], y = pimaTraining$class, test.x = pimaTesting[,
    -9], test.y = pimaTesting$class)
Loss: exponential Method: discrete    Iteration: 50
Final Confusion Matrix for Data:
          Final Prediction
True value   0    1
         0 348   28
         1  31  169
Train Error: 0.102
Out-Of-Bag Error:  0.118   iteration= 47
Additional Estimates of number of iterations:
train.err1 train.kap1  test.err2  test.kap2
        42         42         30          3
```

It looks like the `ada` model is very accurate (348+169)/(348+169+28+31) 89%.

Neural network

There is a neural net package available in R to determine a model for data. Note that the `neuralnet` function takes a long time to complete and even longer if you increase repetitions.

First, we load the package and library, as follows:

```
> install.packages('neuralnet')
> library("neuralnet")
```

We use the same kind of model to develop the neural net, as follows:

```
> nnet <- neuralnet(MDEV ~ CRIM + ZN + INDUS + CHAS + NOX + RM + AGE
+ DIS + RAD + TAX + PRATIO + B + LSTAT,housingTraining, hidden=10,
threshold=0.01)
```

However, when I originally ran this, I saw the following error:

```
Warning message:
algorithm did not converge in 1 of 1 repetition(s) within the stepmax
```

Unfortunately, there does not appear to be any tried-and-trusted method for converging. It takes some adjusting, and every iteration takes several minutes, so it takes some patience as well.

I ended up using a simpler function call, as shown here:

```
> nnet <- neuralnet(MDEV ~ CRIM + ZN + INDUS + CHAS + NOX + RM + AGE +
DIS + RAD + TAX + PRATIO + B + LSTAT,housingTraining)
> plot(nnet, rep="best")
```

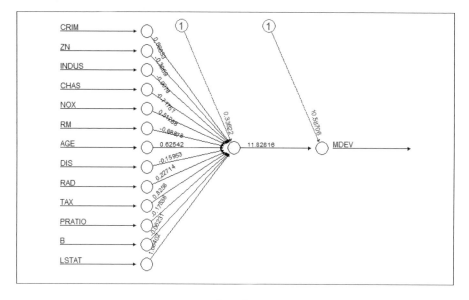

We evaluate the neural net performance much like the other methods, except that we use the compute function. as follows:

```
> results <- compute(nnet, housingTesting[,-14])
> diff <- results$net.result - housingTesting$MDEV
> sumofsquares(diff)
[1] 11016.01873
```

Unfortunately, this method is by far the worst performer among the models. I am assuming the data does not match up with the requirements for a neural net.

Random forests

Random forests is an algorithm where each data point is developed into a large number of trees (in a forest) and the results are combined for a model.

We first load the random forest package/library, as follows:

```
> install.packages("randomForest")
> library(randomForest)
```

Let's use the `randomForest` method to produce a model for the housing data, as follows:

```
> forestFit <- randomForest(MDEV ~ CRIM + ZN + INDUS + CHAS + NOX + RM
+ AGE + DIS + RAD + TAX + PRATIO + B + LSTAT, data=housingTraining)
```

We then generate predictions for the housing testing data using the following command:

```
> forestPredict <- predict(forestFit,newdata=housingTesting)
```

Let's evaluate the results of the random forest algorithm, as shown here:

```
> diff <- forestPredict - housingTesting$MDEV
> sumofsquares(diff)
[1] 2464.67
```

If we gather the results of the `sumofsquares` test from the models in the chapter, we come across the following findings:

- 3,555 from the linear regression
- 3,926 from the decision tree
- 11,016 from the neural net
- 2,464 from the forest

The forest model produced the best-fitting data.

Questions

Factual

- I have used the sum of squares differences for a crude comparison of models. Do you think this is a fair method?

- What cutoff percentage accuracy would you use for your modeling?

When, how, and why?

- There are several methods to measure the performance of a model. Investigate which you prefer.

- Which modeling technique appears to fit your data?

Challenges

- Determine a better way to determine whether a binary data model is accurate against a simple percentage correct.

- What kind of data would be more suitable to developing a neural net?

- Work with the method argument `predict` to use other modeling techniques for your data.

Summary

In this chapter, we investigated machine learning in action using R. We learned about breaking up our dataset into a training and testing section. The examples showed how to use the `predict` method from our models. We generated models using linear regression, stepwise regression, k-nearest neighbor, Naïve Bayes, k-clustering, decision trees, neural net, and the random forest algorithms. We applied tests of the models' effectiveness.

In the next chapter, we will cover predicting events with machine learning.

11
Predicting Events with Machine Learning

R programming has several tools that can be used when dealing with events in a time series. We can look at the time series from several aspects, evaluate the components involved in the data, construct a model of the time series behavior, and estimate or forecast time series events going forward.

This chapter covers the analysis of time series data with the objective of forecasting. There are several areas in R programming that can be used for time series forecasting:

- Converting your data into an R-formatted time series
- Examining seasonality effects
- Simple smoothing
- Basic trend analysis, including decomposing your time series into seasonal, trend, and irregular components
- Exponential smoothing, including Holt-Winters filtering, correlogram, and box test
- ARIMA modeling

Automatic forecasting packages

In R, there are several packages that provide plotting for the programmer. We will be using the following packages in the examples:

- `forecast`: This package is used to forecast functions for time series and linear models
- `TTR`: This package has functions and data to create technical trading rules

Time series

In R programming, a time series is a sequence of data points measured evenly over uniform time intervals — typically, monthly or yearly frequencies are used. You can coerce (convert) a standard dataset into a time series using the `as.ts` function.

For the initial time series, we will use the Fraser River monthly flows (available at `http://www.cmu.edu`). I couldn't find a source for the dataset, so I copied it from the site to a local file. The data is the monthly flow starting from March 1913. There are over 900 measurements. The data has a definite frequency:

```
> fraser <- scan("fraser.txt")
Read 946 items
```

If we look at the data with a standard plot, we don't see anything significant:

```
> plot(fraser)
```

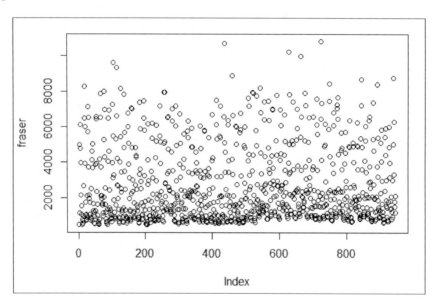

Just poking at the head of the dataset is also unremarkable, as shown in the output:

```
> head(fraser)
[1]   485 1150 4990 6130 4780 3960
```

My first attempt at trying to break out the seasonal/periodic effects failed:

```
> fraserc <- decompose(fraser)
Error in decompose(fraser) : time series has no or less than 2 periods
> stl(fraser)
Error in stl(fraser) :
    series is not periodic or has less than two periods
```

I forgot that while the data is obviously periodic, there is no way for the software to know that. We have to specify a frequency and convert the dataset to a time series using the `ts` function. The `ts` function looks like this:

```
ts(data = NA, start = 1, end = numeric(), frequency = 1,
    deltat = 1, ts.eps = getOption("ts.eps"), class = , names = )
```

The various parameters of the `ts` function are described in the following table:

Parameter	Description
data	This is the matrix or data frame.
start	This is the time of first observation.
end	This is the time of last observation.
frequency	This is the observations per unit of time.
deltat	This is the fractional observation to use per unit of time, for example, 1/12 for monthly intervals of time. Either `deltat` or `frequency` is used.
ts.eps	This is the time series comparison tolerance; it is the factor to determine if observations are equal.
class	This is the result class.
names	This contains the naming convention to use for results.

In this case, we have monthly data, so frequency is `12`. The data starts from March 1913, as shown here:

```
> fraser.ts <- ts(fraser, frequency=12, start=c(1913,3))
```

We can jump right into the seasonal decomposition of the time series using the `stl` function. The `stl` function looks like this:

```
stl(x, s.window, s.degree = 0,
    t.window = NULL, t.degree = 1,
    l.window = nextodd(period), l.degree = t.degree,
    s.jump = ceiling(s.window/10),
    t.jump = ceiling(t.window/10),
    l.jump = ceiling(l.window/10),
```

```
      robust = FALSE,
      inner = if(robust)  1 else 2,
      outer = if(robust) 15 else 0,
      na.action = na.fail)
```

The various parameters of the `stl` function are described in the following table:

Parameter	Description
x	This is the matrix
s.window	This has either the string `"periodic"` or the Loess span
...	A number of parameters that allow you to make \ to the period data

In our case, we have simple periodic (monthly) data:

```
> stl(fraser.ts, s.window="periodic")
Call:
stl(x = fraser.ts, s.window = "periodic")


Components
          seasonal    trend      remainder
Mar 1913 -1856.6973 2338.515      3.1821923
Apr 1913  -985.4948 2338.237   -202.7426140
May 1913  2171.2016 2337.960    480.8385830
Jun 1913  4329.7017 2335.951   -535.6526956
Jul 1913  2860.2269 2333.942   -414.1691653
(... many more)
```

We need to populate a variable so we can do further work, starting with a summary:

```
> fraser.stl = stl(fraser.ts, s.window="periodic")
> summary(fraser.stl)
Call:
stl(x = fraser.ts, s.window = "periodic")


Time.series components:
     seasonal                 trend                remainder
Min.    :-1856.697   Min.    :1881.592   Min.    :-2281.467
1st Qu.:-1578.745    1st Qu.:2440.579    1st Qu.: -305.858
Median : -759.841    Median :2674.528    Median :  -39.336
Mean    :    3.821   Mean    :2704.522   Mean    :    0.231
3rd Qu.: 1843.843    3rd Qu.:2919.516    3rd Qu.:  257.289
Max.    : 4329.702   Max.    :3775.743   Max.    : 3408.070
IQR:
      STL.seasonalSTL.trendSTL.remainder data
```

```
      3422.6            478.9       563.1          2937.5
    % 116.5             16.3        19.2           100.0
Weights: all == 1
Other components: List of 5
$ win   : Named num [1:3] 9461 19 13
$ deg   : Named int [1:3] 0 1 1
$ jump  : Named num [1:3] 947 2 2
$ inner: int 2
$ outer: int 0
```

We can see the following observations from the raw results:

- There is a definite trend.

- The seasonality varies widely from positive to negative (I guess that makes sense).

- An odd remainder factor was discovered. It turns out the remainder is the catchall to allow the seasonality and the trend to be discovered. This kind of error allowance occurs all over math.

There is a `monthplot` function in the same package that produces a plot specifically geared towards monthly data display:

```
> monthplot(fraster.stl)
```

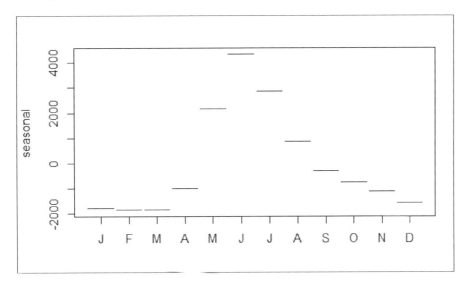

The plot organizes the time series into monthly patterns. It is good that we can see the definite seasonal effect on the river flow — it starts to increase in the spring, crests by early summer, and then tails off into winter.

The arguments of the `monthplot` function are as shown here:

```
monthplot(x, labels = NULL, ylab = choice, choice = "sea", ...)
```

The various parameters of the `monthplot` function are described in the following table:

Parameter	Description
x	This is the dataset
labels	These are the season labels
ylab	This is the *y* label
choice	This determines which series to plot from the `stl` result

A similar plot is the `seasonplot` function of the `timeseries` package. The only argument is the time series. We can invoke it for our data using the following command:

```
> library(forecast)
> seasonplot(fraser.ts)
```

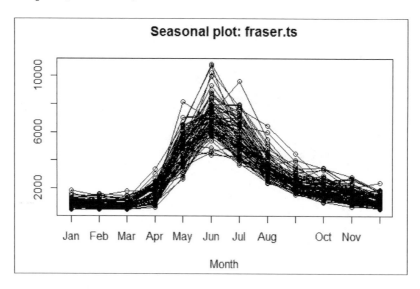

So, we see the same seasonal data plot; however, we now have detail of every year.

We can produce a plot of the data, which plots the various components of the `stl` results as follows:

```
> plot(fraser.stl)
```

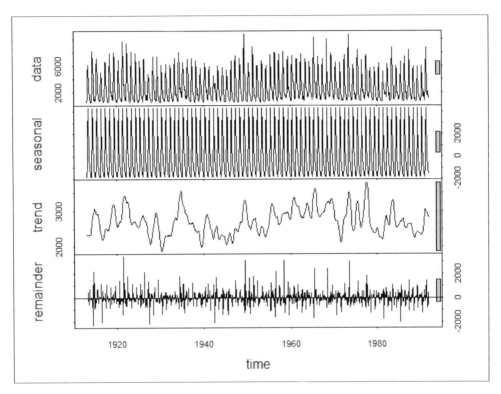

From the plot of the `stl` results, we can make some interesting observations:

- We can see the raw data graph, but there is not much to notice
- The seasonality graph is perfect (I have noticed that the seasonality graph out of `stl` is *always* perfect due to the remainder)
- There doesn't appear to be any real trend to the data; a few years were wetter than others (must have had more snowfall in the mountains)
- Even the remainder (noise/error) is pretty constant

The SMA function

If we are looking for some kind of trend with the flows, we can try to smooth them using the SMA function of the TTR package (assuming a year at a time). The SMA function computes the mean of a series:

```
> library(TTR)
> fraser.SMA3 <- SMA(fraser,n=12)
> plot(fraser.SMA3)
```

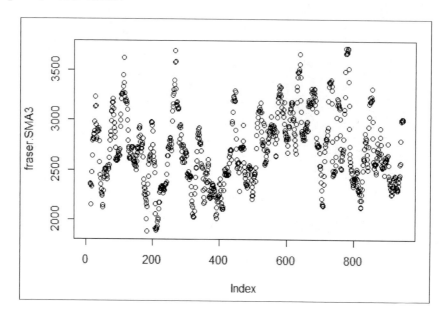

The SMA function looks like this:

```
SMA(x, n = 10, ...)
```

The various parameters of the SMA function are described in the following table:

Parameter	Description
x	This is the data
n	This is the number of periods to average over
...	These are the parameters to be passed to subfunctions

I am starting to see some patterns to the data. I am curious what would happen if we stretched out to 5 years using the following command:

```
> fraser.SMA60 <- SMA(fraser,n=60)
> plot(fraser.SMA60)
```

There are clear, long-term changes to the flow rate. It is interesting that it doesn't really trend in either direction, as shown in the following graph:

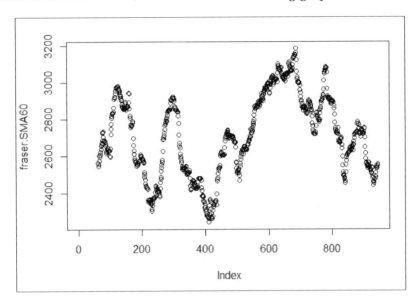

The decompose function

We can extract the specific seasonality from our data using the decompose function. The decompose function breaks down a time series into its seasonal, trend, and irregular components.

We decompose the components of the time series as follows:

```
> fraser.components <- decompose(fraser.ts)
```

Let's recalculate without seasonality with the following command:

```
> fraser.adjusted <- fraser - fraser.components$season
```

We will now take a look at the adjusted data in a plot with the following command:

```
> plot(fraser.adjusted)
```

This confirms there is no long term trend with the flows—we have close to a horizontal line. There are wide variances at times, but I am still guessing that is due to some shorter-term weather patterns, as shown in the following graph:

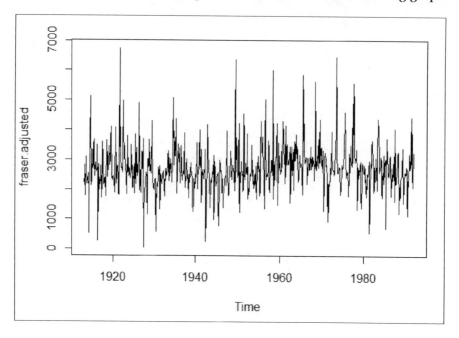

Exponential smoothing

We can use exponential smoothing to make a short-term forecast from our time series data using Holt-Winters filtering. The time series used by the function is expected to have seasonality and a trend. The `HoltWinters` function looks like this:

```
HoltWinters(x, alpha = NULL, beta = NULL, gamma = NULL,
            seasonal = c("additive", "multiplicative"),
            start.periods = 2, l.start = NULL, b.start = NULL,
            s.start = NULL,
            optim.start = c(alpha = 0.3, beta = 0.1, gamma = 0.1),
            optim.control = list())
```

The various parameters of the `HoltWinters` function are described in the following table:

Parameter	Description
x	This is the time series
alpha	This is the alpha parameter to filter
beta	This is the beta parameter. If FALSE, the filter will perform exponential filtering
gamma	This is the seasonal component parameter. It is set to FALSE for no seasonality
seasonal	This determines whether to use an additive or multiplicative model
...	These are several parameters to make on-the-fly adjustments to your time series

In our case, we want exponential filtering and we have seasonality, so we use the following code:

```
> fraser.forecast <- HoltWinters(fraser.ts,beta=FALSE)
> fraser.forecast
Holt-Winters exponential smoothing without trend and with additive
seasonal component.
Call:
HoltWinters(x = fraser.ts, beta = FALSE)
Smoothing parameters:
 alpha: 0.2444056
 beta : FALSE
 gamma: 0.2255549
Coefficients:
          [,1]
a     2799.6752
s1   -1575.5719
s2   -1710.0222
s3   -1590.4821
s4    -425.0325
s5    2155.3889
s6    4257.5759
s7    2425.0119
s8     645.3606
s9    -520.1605
s10   -903.6552
s11   -844.6340
s12  -1479.8460
```

We can make the following observations from the results:

- The `alpha`, `beta`, and `gamma` values used. The `alpha` value is the smoothing factor. The `beta` value used is a flag whether to use exponential filtering or not—in our case, yes. The `gamma` value is the calculated seasonality component. These are calculated values. If you feel any of them were incorrect, you could provide their values explicitly in the call (rather than using defaults as I have done in this code).

- Vector of named components containing the estimated values for level, trend, and seasonal components.

The computed **SSE** (**sum of squared errors**) value is of particular interest—how far off is our model? I think this is a very big error, but I am not sure if exponential smoothing worked. Let's compute the SSE and find out:

```
> fraser.forecast$SSE
[1] 500776934
> plot(fraser.forecast)
```

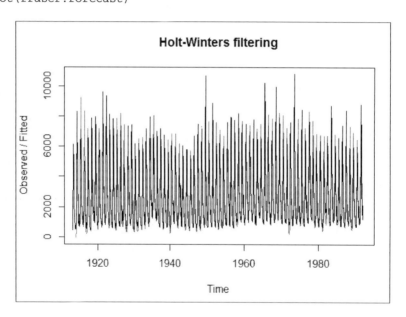

The plot overlays the estimated values with the raw data. The estimated data appears to have the same level of variance, but I am not sure we have a good fit. We can look at the forecast fit (fitted variable in results). The fitted variable contains values for the filtered series, and the level, trend, and seasonal components, as shown here:

```
> fraser.forecast$fitted
             xhat     level       season
```

```
Mar 1914   -33.19476 2177.385 -2210.57986
Apr 1914   444.89609 2324.809 -1879.91319
May 1914  2275.15610 2456.569  -181.41319
Jun 1914  7969.67128 2557.959  5411.71181
Jul 1914  6224.30902 2633.806  3590.50347
Aug 1914  5771.34300 2696.298  3075.04514
Sep 1914  2490.95066 2749.739  -258.78819
Oct 1914  2216.03738 3101.451  -885.41319
Nov 1914  1737.32929 2989.992 -1252.66319
Dec 1914  1266.81594 2812.229 -1545.41319
Jan 1915   731.66488 2682.495 -1950.82986
Feb 1915   848.05110 2760.298 -1912.24653
Mar 1915   637.59781 2745.376 -2107.77859
Apr 1915  1022.94060 2810.975 -1788.03480
```

Forecast

We can use the `forecast.HoltWinters` function in the `forecast` package that uses Holt-Winters filtering for forecasting, as follows:

```
> install.packages("forecast")
> library(forecast)
```

We forecast eight periods from our model data. The function takes a HoltWinters forecast and a number of periods to forecast, as follows:

```
> fraser.forecast2 <- forecast.HoltWinters(fraser.forecast, h=8)
```

Looking at the raw result is not particularly interesting. It is bothersome to see negative numbers. The river flow will not be negative. Here is the output:

```
> fraser.forecast2
         Point Forecast     Lo 80     Hi 80     Lo 95     Hi 95
Jan 1992       1224.103  285.2139 2162.993 -211.8041 2660.011
Feb 1992       1089.653  123.1285 2056.177 -388.5187 2567.825
Mar 1992       1209.193  215.8019 2202.584 -310.0677 2728.454
Apr 1992       2374.643 1355.0925 3394.193  815.3753 3933.910
May 1992       4955.064 3910.0096 6000.119 3356.7912 6553.337
Jun 1992       7057.251 5987.3000 8127.202 5420.9021 8693.600
Jul 1992       5224.687 4130.4058 6318.968 3551.1282 6898.246
Aug 1992       3445.036 2326.9535 4563.118 1735.0765 5154.995
```

We can plot the results. Notice the forecast data on the right-hand side of the plot in a different color. The forecast looks to have just as much variance as the other data, as shown here:

```
> plot.forecast(fraser.forecast2)
```

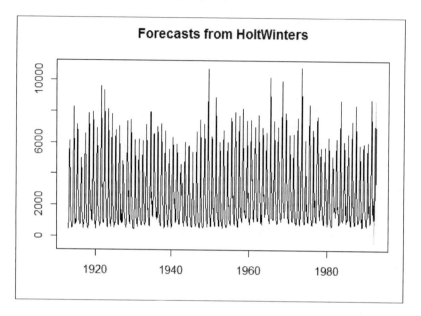

Correlogram

We can produce a correlogram using the `acf` function to give us a better idea of whether the forecast appears to be working.

The `acf` function computes (and by default plots) the autocorrelation of your data. The `acf` function looks like this:

```
acf(x, lag.max = NULL,
    type = c("correlation", "covariance", "partial"),
    plot = TRUE, na.action = na.fail, demean = TRUE, ...)
```

The various parameters of the `acf` function are described in the following table:

Parameter	Description
x	This is the dataset
lag.max	This is the maximum lag to calculate
type	This is the type of `acf` to calculate: `covariance`, `correlation`, or `partial`

Parameter	Description
plot	This is a Boolean value to determine whether to plot results
na.action	This is the function to be called upon NA values
demean	This is a Boolean value to determine should the covariances be about the simple means

In our case, we use the residuals from our forecast, lagged over 20, as follows:

```
> acf(fraser.forecast2$residuals,lag.max=20)
```

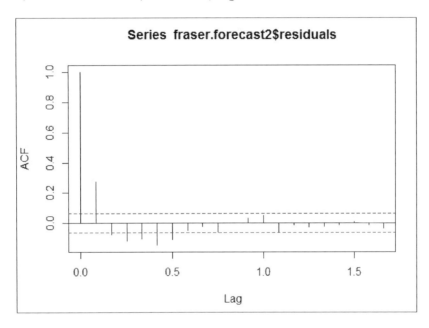

In the plot, there are several points worth noticing:

- The blue dotted line is a the boundary of the 95 percent confidence interval
- We have significant breaching the boundary several times under 0.5
- Overall, the most recent flow rate of the river has the biggest effect on the current flow rate, as expected

Box test

We can use a Box test for the forecast as well in the Box.test function.
The Box.test function looks like this:

```
Box.test(x, lag = 1, type = c("Box-Pierce", "Ljung-Box"), fitdf = 0)
```

The various parameters of the Box.test function are described in the following table:

Parameter	Description
x	This is the data
lag	This is the lag periods to be used
type	This is the type of box test, either Box-Pierce or Ljung-Box
fitdf	This is the number of degrees of freedom to be subtracted (if x is residuals).

In this case, we use the residuals of the forecast, with a lag of 20, as shown here:

```
> Box.test(fraser.forecast2$residuals,lag=20,type="Ljung-Box")
Box-Ljung test
data:  fraser.forecast2$residuals
X-squared = 144.8534, df = 20, p-value < 2.2e-16
```

We have a very small p-value, so we have a good fit. Just to look at the residuals, we use the following code:

```
> plot.ts(fraser.forecast2$residuals)
```

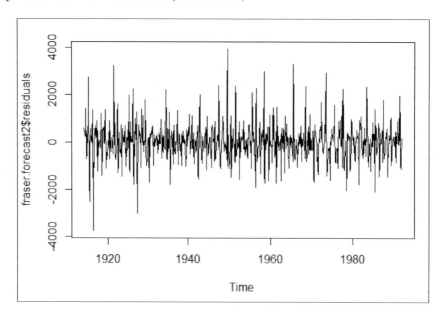

Nothing jumps out particularly. Still, it seems like a large variance.

Holt exponential smoothing

We can use Holt exponential smoothing to forecast from a time series; however, the data is expected to not have seasonality. I found the b2 test results from the Santa Fe Time Series Competition at `http://www.physionet.org/physiobank/database/santa-fe/`. The data is composed of a number of readings from a patient regarding his/her heart rate, chest expansion (breathing), and oxygen rate while sleeping. This is a different time series, really just to explore R and see its versatility:

```
> sleep <- read.table("http://physionet.org/physiobank/database/santa-
fe/b2.txt")
> colnames(sleep) <- c("heart","chest","oxygen")
> head(sleep)
  heart   chest oxygen
1 71.36   16337   6715
2 71.29   29381   6776
3 70.88   16929   6774
4 69.72    8066   6816
5 70.50  -32734   6880
6 72.14  -24870   6886
> sleepts <- ts(sleep)
> plot.ts(sleepts)
```

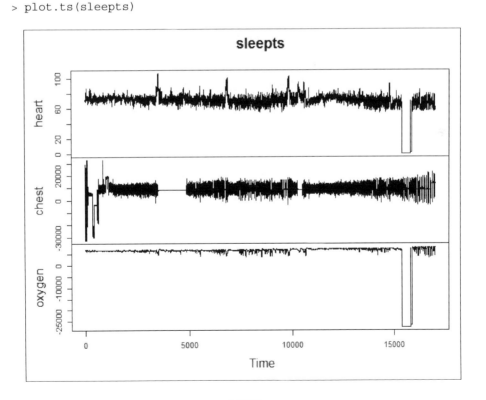

It looks like there is some irregular breathing at the start of the test. That makes some sense. I think I would be a little nervous in this kind of test as well.

You might notice that we have two episodes that jump out from the graphics:

- There is a period where the chest expansion stopped and the patient stopped breathing for a few seconds — sleep apnea?

- There is a period where there was no reading for the heart rate or oxygen rate. I can't believe the patient died during their sleep and resuscitated. The contacts must have slipped.

There are several other points of interest as well:

- The heart rate jumped several times
- The heart rate seems to trend down over the test, but that may be *normal* while falling into a deeper sleep
- There was another, smaller sleep apnea episode about halfway through the test

We can generate forecasts for each of the variables as follows:

```
> heart.ts <- ts(sleep$heart)
> heart.forecast <- HoltWinters(heart.ts, gamma=FALSE)
Warning message:
In HoltWinters(heart.ts, gamma = FALSE) :
   optimization difficulties: ERROR: ABNORMAL_TERMINATION_IN_LNSRCH
```

I am guessing the ERROR is the result of the NA values.

We can look at the forecast by displaying it's value:

```
> heart.forecast
Holt-Winters exponential smoothing with trend and without seasonal
component.
Call:
HoltWinters(x = heart.ts, gamma = FALSE)
Smoothing parameters:
 alpha: 1
 beta : 0.0001553464
 gamma: FALSE
Coefficients:
          [,1]
a 57.920000000
b -0.006217031
```

From the results, we can conclude the following points:

- Heart rate average at 58. I think that is normal.
- Slight downward trend — again, I think that is normal as you get more into sleep mode.

Looking at a plot of the forecast, we have an excellent match:

```
> plot(heart.forecast)
```

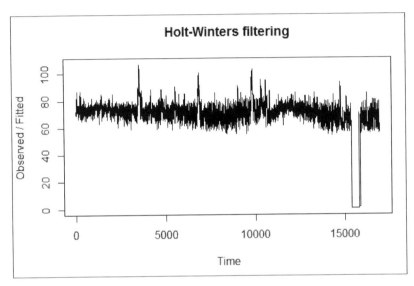

We do the same analysis for the chest (breathing) as follows:

```
> chest.ts <- ts(sleep$chest)
> chest.forecast <- HoltWinters(chest.ts, gamma=FALSE)
> chest.forecast
Holt-Winters exponential smoothing with trend and without seasonal
component.
Call:
HoltWinters(x = chest.ts, gamma = FALSE)
Smoothing parameters:
 alpha: 1
 beta : 0.02508202
 gamma: FALSE
Coefficients:
          [,1]
```

```
a 13287.000000
b     -7.373061
> plot(chest.forecast)
```

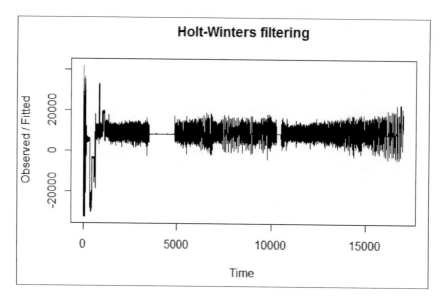

From the breathing results, we find the following points:

- Looks like a very good fit to the data (red overlay only partially visible)
- It took some time for the algorithm to adjust (from the wide variance at the start of the plot
- I liked that the display was able to accommodate the apnea periods

We analyze the oxygen rate of the patient during the test as well, as shown in the following code:

```
> oxygen.ts <- ts(sleep$oxygen)
> oxygen.forecast <- HoltWinters(oxygen.ts, gamma=FALSE)
Warning message:
In HoltWinters(oxygen.ts, gamma = FALSE) :
  optimization difficulties: ERROR: ABNORMAL_TERMINATION_IN_LNSRCH
> oxygen.forecast
Holt-Winters exponential smoothing with trend and without seasonal
component.
Call:
HoltWinters(x = oxygen.ts, gamma = FALSE)
Smoothing parameters:
 alpha: 1
 beta : 0.001198299
```

```
      gamma: FALSE
   Coefficients:
              [,1]
   a 8023.000000
   b    6.077048
   > plot(oxygen.forecast)
```

The bad data from the slipped electrodes is distorting the results completely, as shown in the following graph:

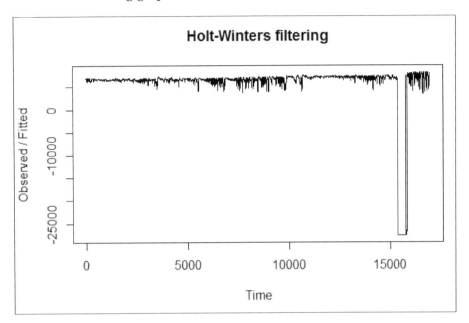

Automated forecasting

The forecast package has an ets function that will automatically select exponential and ARIMA models. The ets (which stands for exponential smoothing space model) function looks like this:

```
ets(y, model="ZZZ", damped=NULL, alpha=NULL, beta=NULL, gamma=NULL,
    phi=NULL, additive.only=FALSE, lambda=NULL,
    lower=c(rep(0.0001,3), 0.8), upper=c(rep(0.9999,3),0.98),
    opt.crit=c("lik","amse","mse","sigma","mae"), nmse=3,
    bounds=c("both","usual","admissible"), ic=c("aicc","aic","bic"),
    restrict=TRUE, use.initial.values=FALSE, ...)
```

The various parameters of the `ets` function are described in the following table:

Parameter	Description
y	This is the time series.
model	This is a three letter string identifying the method: • The first letter denotes the error type (A, M, or Z) • The second letter denotes the trend type (N, A, M, or Z) • The third letter denotes the season type (N, A, M, or Z) In all cases, N stands for none, A for additive, M for multiplicative, and Z for automatically selected. So, for example, ANN is simple exponential smoothing with additive errors, MAM is multiplicative Holt-Winters' method with multiplicative errors, and so on.
damped	This is a Boolean value: if TRUE, use a damped trend.
alpha, beta, gamma, phi	These values are specified or set to NULL, meaning estimate value.
...	These are the other arguments to be defined with greater precision for the model selected.

Using our river data, we generate a forecast as follows (note that this may take some time depending on the size of your time series):

```
> fraser.ets <- ets(fraser.ts)
> summary(fraser.ts)
ETS(M,N,M)
Call:
 ets(y = fraser.ts)
  Smoothing parameters:
    alpha = 0.5967
    gamma = 1e-04
  Initial states:
    l = 2391.3065
    s=0.3115 0.3383 0.4222 0.5911 0.7162 0.8674
          1.2955 2.0465 2.6331 1.8528 0.6322 0.2933
  sigma:  0.2332
     AIC     AICcBIC
18169.33 18169.79 18237.27
Training set error measures:
                   ME      RMSE       MAE       MPE      MAPE      MASE
ACF1
Training set -13.32012 816.7776 488.1696 -3.466517 17.46853 0.4502517
0.2286761
```

We see from the results:

- MNM was chosen, which means multiplicative error, no trend, and multiplicative season
- The alpha value is about double the values chosen in the previous examples
- The gamma (seasonality) value is enormous

Let's plot the data generated:

```
> plot(fraser.ets)
```

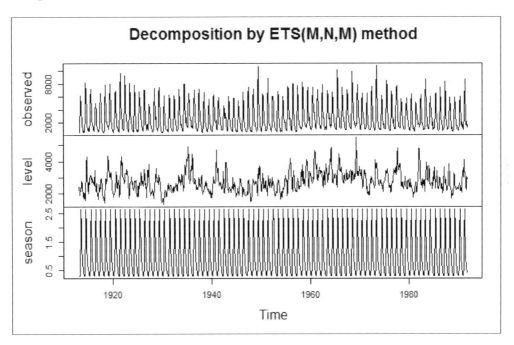

The results are a match to the previous similar graph from the results of the stl call.

ARIMA

We can use ARIMA (short for autoregressive integrated moving average) modeling with our time series using the arima function. The arima function looks like this:

```
arima(x, order = c(0L, 0L, 0L),
      seasonal = list(order = c(0L, 0L, 0L), period = NA),
      xreg = NULL, include.mean = TRUE,
      transform.pars = TRUE,
      fixed = NULL, init = NULL,
      method = c("CSS-ML", "ML", "CSS"), n.cond,
```

```
          SSinit = c("Gardner1980", "Rossignol2011"),
          optim.method = "BFGS",
          optim.control = list(), kappa = 1e6)
```

The various parameters of the `arima` function are described in the following table:

Parameter	Description
x	This is the univariate time series
order	This is the three integer components of the ARIMA model: p, d, and q, where p is AR order, d the degree of differencing, and q the MA order
seasonal	This is the specification of the seasonal part of the model
...	These are the other arguments to be defined

Generate an ARIMA model of our river data with the following code:

```
> fraser.arima <- arima(fraser.ts, order=c(2,0,0))
> summary(fraser.arima)
Series: fraser.ts
ARIMA(2,0,0) with non-zero mean
Coefficients:
         ar1      ar2   intercept
       1.1606  -0.6043  2708.4393
s.e.   0.0259   0.0259    85.4871
sigma^2 estimated as 1360268:  log likelihood=-8023.41
AIC=16054.82AICc=16054.86   BIC=16074.23
Training set error measures:
                      ME       RMSE       MAE        MPE      MAPE       MASE
ACF1
Training set -0.4317943 1166.305 856.2903 -27.14596 46.69703 0.7897792
0.02744368
```

From the result, we find the following points:

- Sigma squared of 1.3 million, which is very high
- Log likelihood of 8,000

We can generate a plot of the result (shown in the following graph) using the following command:

```
> tsdisplay(arima.errors(fraser.arima))
```

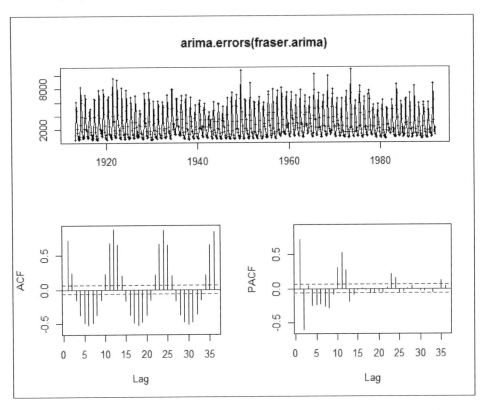

From the plot, we can see:

- The errors plot looks similar to others we have seen earlier in the chapter
- The ACF with different lags seems to vary with the seasonality recurrence
- The PACF is very similar to the ACF earlier, but it shows summary data using several lag periods

We can produce a forecast using the ARIMA results as follows:

```
> fraser.farima <- forecast(fraser.arima, h=8)
> summary(fraser.farima)
Forecast method: ARIMA(2,0,0) with non-zero mean
Model Information:
Series: fraser.ts
ARIMA(2,0,0) with non-zero mean
Coefficients:
          ar1      ar2   intercept
       1.1606  -0.6043   2708.4393
s.e.   0.0259   0.0259     85.4871
sigma^2 estimated as 1360268:  log likelihood=-8023.41
AIC=16054.82AICc=16054.86   BIC=16074.23
Error measures:
                     ME     RMSE      MAE       MPE     MAPE     MASE
ACF1
Training set -0.4317943 1166.305 856.2903 -27.14596 46.69703 1.307243
0.02744368
Forecasts:
          Point Forecast      Lo 80      Hi 80       Lo 95      Hi 95
Jan 1992        1307.705 -186.97489 2802.386   -978.2109 3593.622
Feb 1992        2000.231 -289.63543 4290.097 -1501.8175 5502.279
Mar 1992        2732.871  188.04303 5277.700 -1159.1077 6624.850
Apr 1992        3164.733  608.57983 5720.887   -744.5660 7074.033
May 1992        3223.264  637.23996 5809.287   -731.7182 7178.245
Jun 1992        3030.241  375.50226 5684.981 -1029.8318 7090.315
Jul 1992        2770.847   76.60463 5465.090 -1349.6414 6891.336
Aug 1992        2586.422 -113.23588 5286.080 -1542.3483 6715.192
```

Again, it is bothersome that we have negative numbers in the forecast, as shown in the following output:

```
> plot(fraser.farima)
```

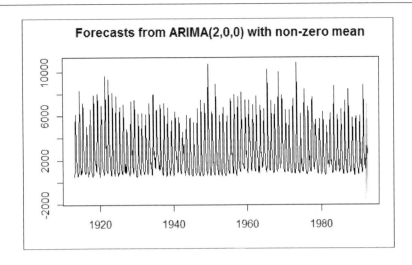

The plot shows the eight periods (months) that we forecast in blue on the right-hand side of the plot. However, it is bothersome that the blue appears to extend below the axis, implying a negative flow.

Automated ARIMA forecasting

We can also perform automated forecasting using an ARIMA model as follows:

```
> fraser.aarima <- auto.arima(fraser.ts)
> summary(fraser.aarima)
Series: fraser.ts
ARIMA(4,0,1)(2,0,0)[12] with non-zero mean
Coefficients:
          ar1      ar2      ar3     ar4     ma1     sar1     sar2
intercept
       -0.4171   0.3436  -0.0320  0.0655  0.9644  0.4834   0.4258
2683.7915
s.e.    0.0400   0.0345   0.0357  0.0328  0.0197  0.0301   0.0301
485.1957
sigma^2 estimated as 513502:  log likelihood=-7561.8
AIC=15142.33   AICc=15142.53   BIC=15186
Training set error measures:
                  ME      RMSE      MAE      MPE     MAPE      MASE
ACF1
Training set -0.103399 705.9058 463.8549 -7.331119 19.98075 0.4278256
0.006710881
```

From the results, we find the following points:

- Sigma squared of 500,000
- Log likelihood of 7,500

If we regenerate the model using the values chosen, we get the following output:

```
> fraser.arima3 <- arima(fraser.ts, order=c(4,0,1),
seasonal=list(order=c(2,0,0), period=12))
> summary(fraser.arima3)
Series: fraser.ts
ARIMA(4,0,1)(2,0,0)[12] with non-zero mean
Coefficients:
          ar1       ar2       ar3      ar4      ma1      sar1     sar2
intercept
       -0.4383   0.3783   -0.0408   0.0584   1.0000   0.4934   0.4247
2684.4636
s.e.    0.0332   0.0357    0.0362   0.0330   0.0026   0.0300   0.0305
460.3653
sigma^2 estimated as 518522:  log likelihood=-7576.7
AIC=15171.4    AICc=15171.6    BIC=15215.07
Training set error measures:
                   ME       RMSE      MAE       MPE      MAPE      MASE
ACF1
Training set 4.19843 720.0847 476.552 -7.320212 20.63867 0.4395365
-0.0001388267
```

Negative likelihood shows an excellent fit.

We can then forecast using the ARIMA model as follows:

```
> fraser.farima3 <- forecast(fraser.arima3, h=8)
> plot(fraser.farima3)
```

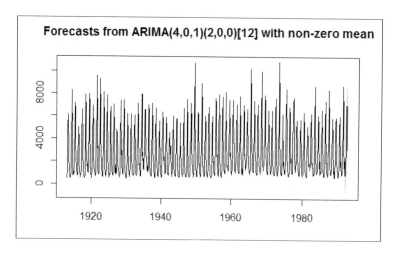

Forecasts from ARIMA(4,0,1)(2,0,0)[12] with non-zero mean

We can see a larger value in the forecast part of the plot. The forecast also does not appear to go as far below the axis (negative) as in our previous example. The *y* axis is also shorter.

Questions

Factual

- How would you compare the results of the different models and forecasts to select the appropriate constraints?
- In the initial plot of the river data, is there something that could be used to foresee the seasonality and/or trend immediately without breaking into components?

When, how, and why?

- While the automated selection provided ARIMA values, how would you select the different parameters?
- How would you decide on the different modeling techniques used for your dataset?

Challenges

- Several of the forecasts involved negative values for the river flow. How can that be avoided?
- Either use a time series that you have available or find one that has the components addressed in the chapter and apply the analysis available in R.

Summary

In this chapter, we investigated predicting events using machine learning by using R. We formatted a dataset into an R time series. We used a few methods to extract the constituent parts of the time series into trend, seasonal, and irregular components. We used different smoothing methods on the time series to arrive at a model. We used different mechanisms to forecast the time series based on the models.

In the next chapter, we will discuss supervised and unsupervised learning.

12
Supervised and Unsupervised Learning

The two basic methods of machine learning are supervised and unsupervised machine learning. In machine learning, we are usually dealing with a target variable and predictor variables. The target variable is the object of the prediction or what we are trying to learn. We want to learn how to predict that variable going forward. The predictor variables are the variables we put into our model to obtain information about the target variable. We want to learn how changes in our predictor variables affect the target variable.

Supervised learning involves the use of a target variable and a number of predictor variables that are put into a model to enable the system to predict the target. This is also known as **predictive modeling**.

Unsupervised modeling has no target variable. We want to discover the predictor variables that are present. This is sometimes called **pattern discovery**.

This chapter covers techniques in R programming for supervised and unsupervised learning. Many of these techniques have been discussed in earlier chapters. The various techniques are listed as follows:

- Supervised learning techniques
    - Decision trees
    - Regression
    - Neural networks
    - Instance-based learning (k-NN)
    - Ensemble learning
    - Support vector machines

- ◦ Bayesian learning
- ◦ Bayesian inference
- ◦ Random forests

- Unsupervised learning techniques
  - ◦ Cluster analysis
  - ◦ Density estimation
  - ◦ Expectation-maximization algorithm
  - ◦ Hidden Markov models
  - ◦ Blind signal separation

Packages

We will use the following packages available in R for supervised and unsupervised learning:

- `rattle`: This is a data mining GUI in R
- `rpart.plot`: This is used to plot the `r.part` models
- `caret`: This is used for classification and regression training
- `kknn`: These are the weighted *k* nearest neighbors
- `kernlab`: This is used for kernel-based machine learning
- `e1071`: This package contains miscellaneous functions of the Department of Statistics
- `MCMCpack`: This package contains the functions for Markov chain Monte Carlo algorithm
- `randomForest`: This is used for classification and regression based on a forest of trees using random inputs
- `FactoMineR`: This is used for multivariate exploratory data analysis and data mining with R

Supervised learning

In supervised learning we have a target variable and a number of possible predictor variables. The objective is to associate the predictor variables in such a way so as to accurately predict the target variable. We are using some portion of observed data to learn how our model behaves and then testing that model on the remaining observations for accuracy.

We will go over the following supervised learning techniques:

- Decision trees
- Regression
- Neural networks
- Instance based learning (k-NN)
- Ensemble learning
- Support vector machines
- Bayesian learning
- Bayesian inference
- Random forests

Decision tree

For decision tree machine learning, we develop a logic tree that can be used to predict our target value based on a number of predictor variables. The tree has logical points, such as *if the month is December, follow the tree logic to the left; otherwise, follow the tree logic to the right.* The last **leaf** of the tree has a predicted value.

For this example, we will use the `weather` data in the `rattle` package. We will develop a decision tree to be used to determine whether it will rain tomorrow or not based on several variables. Let's load the `rattle` package as follows:

```
> library(rattle)
```

We can see a summary of the `weather` data. This shows that we have some real data over a year from Australia:

```
> summary(weather)
     Date                       Location       MinTemp
 Min.   :2007-11-01   Canberra      :366   Min.   :-5.300
 1st Qu.:2008-01-31   Adelaide      :  0   1st Qu.: 2.300
 Median :2008-05-01   Albany        :  0   Median : 7.450
 Mean   :2008-05-01   Albury        :  0   Mean   : 7.266
 3rd Qu.:2008-07-31   AliceSprings  :  0   3rd Qu.:12.500
 Max.   :2008-10-31   BadgerysCreek :  0   Max.   :20.900
                      (Other)       :  0
    MaxTemp          Rainfall         Evaporation         Sunshine
 Min.   : 7.60   Min.   : 0.000   Min.   : 0.200   Min.   : 0.000
 1st Qu.:15.03   1st Qu.: 0.000   1st Qu.: 2.200   1st Qu.: 5.950
 Median :19.65   Median : 0.000   Median : 4.200   Median : 8.600
 Mean   :20.55   Mean   : 1.428   Mean   : 4.522   Mean   : 7.909
```

```
3rd Qu.:25.50     3rd Qu.: 0.200    3rd Qu.: 6.400    3rd Qu.:10.500
Max.    :35.80     Max.    :39.800   Max.    :13.800   Max.    :13.600
                                                       NA's      :3
 WindGustDir       WindGustSpeed      WindDir9am        WindDir3pm
NW       : 73     Min.    :13.00    SE       : 47     WNW      : 61
NNW      : 44     1st Qu.:31.00     SSE      : 40     NW       : 61
E        : 37     Median :39.00     NNW      : 36     NNW      : 47
WNW      : 35     Mean    :39.84    N        : 31     N        : 30
ENE      : 30     3rd Qu.:46.00     NW       : 30     ESE      : 27
(Other):144       Max.    :98.00    (Other):151       (Other):139
NA's     : 3      NA's     :2       NA's     : 31     NA's     : 1
 WindSpeed9am      WindSpeed3pm       Humidity9am       Humidity3pm
Min.    : 0.000   Min.    : 0.00    Min.    :36.00    Min.    :13.00
1st Qu.: 6.000    1st Qu.:11.00     1st Qu.:64.00     1st Qu.:32.25
Median : 7.000    Median :17.00     Median :72.00     Median :43.00
Mean    : 9.652   Mean    :17.99    Mean    :72.04    Mean    :44.52
3rd Qu.:13.000    3rd Qu.:24.00     3rd Qu.:81.00     3rd Qu.:55.00
Max.    :41.000   Max.    :52.00    Max.    :99.00    Max.    :96.00
NA's     :7
 Pressure9am       Pressure3pm        Cloud9am          Cloud3pm
Min.    : 996.5   Min.    : 996.8   Min.    :0.000    Min.    :0.000
1st Qu.:1015.4    1st Qu.:1012.8    1st Qu.:1.000     1st Qu.:1.000
Median :1020.1    Median :1017.4    Median :3.500     Median :4.000
Mean    :1019.7   Mean    :1016.8   Mean    :3.891    Mean    :4.025
3rd Qu.:1024.5    3rd Qu.:1021.5    3rd Qu.:7.000     3rd Qu.:7.000
Max.    :1035.7   Max.    :1033.2   Max.    :8.000    Max.    :8.000

 Temp9am           Temp3pm           RainToday RISK_MM
Min.    : 0.100   Min.    : 5.10    No :300   Min.    : 0.000
1st Qu.: 7.625    1st Qu.:14.15     Yes: 66   1st Qu.: 0.000
Median :12.550    Median :18.55               Median : 0.000
Mean    :12.358   Mean    :19.23              Mean    : 1.428
3rd Qu.:17.000    3rd Qu.:24.00               3rd Qu.: 0.200
Max.    :24.700   Max.    :34.50              Max.    :39.800

 RainTomorrow
No :300
Yes: 66
```

We will be using the `rpart` function to develop a decision tree. The `rpart` function looks like this:

```
rpart(formula, data, weights, subset, na.action = na.rpart, method,
model = FALSE, x = FALSE, y = TRUE, parms, control, cost, ...)
```

The various parameters of the `rpart` function are described in the following table:

Parameter	Description
formula	This is the formula used for the prediction.
data	This is the data matrix.
weights	These are the optional weights to be applied.
subset	This is the optional subset of rows of data to be used.
na.action	This specifies the action to be taken when y, the target value, is missing.
method	This is the method to be used to interpret the data. It should be one of these: anova, poisson, class, or exp. If not specified, the algorithm decides based on the layout of the data.
...	These are the additional parameters to be used to control the behavior of the algorithm.

Let's create a subset as follows:

```
> weather2 <- subset(weather,select=-c(RISK_MM))
> install.packages("rpart")
>library(rpart)
> model <- rpart(formula=RainTomorrow ~ .,data=weather2,
method="class")
> summary(model)
Call:
rpart(formula = RainTomorrow ~ ., data = weather2, method = "class")
  n= 366

CPn split       rel error       xerror    xstd
1 0.19696970    0 1.0000000 1.0000000 0.1114418
2 0.09090909    1 0.8030303 0.9696970 0.1101055
3 0.01515152    2 0.7121212 1.0151515 0.1120956
4 0.01000000    7 0.6363636 0.9090909 0.1073129

Variable importance
Humidity3pm WindGustSpeed    Sunshine  WindSpeed3pm      Temp3pm
         24            14          12             8            6
   Pressure3pm       MaxTemp     MinTemp    Pressure9am      Temp9am
            6             5           4             4            4
   Evaporation          Date  Humidity9am      Cloud3pm     Cloud9am
            3             3           2             2            1
       Rainfall
            1
Node number 1: 366 observations,    complexity param=0.1969697
   predicted class=No    expected loss=0.1803279  P(node) =1
      class counts:    300     66
```

```
    probabilities: 0.820 0.180
  left son=2 (339 obs) right son=3 (27 obs)
  Primary splits:
    Humidity3pm < 71.5     to the left,   improve=18.31013, (0 missing)
    Pressure3pm < 1011.9   to the right,  improve=17.35280, (0 missing)
    Cloud3pm    < 6.5      to the left,   improve=16.14203, (0 missing)
    Sunshine    < 6.45     to the right,  improve=15.36364, (3 missing)
    Pressure9am < 1016.35  to the right,  improve=12.69048, (0 missing)
  Surrogate splits:
    Sunshine < 0.45      to the right, agree=0.945, adj=0.259, (0 split)
(many more)…
```

As you can tell, the model is complicated. The summary shows the progression of the model development using more and more of the data to fine-tune the tree. We will be using the `rpart.plot` package to display the decision tree in a readable manner as follows:

```
> library(rpart.plot)
> fancyRpartPlot(model,main="Rain Tomorrow",sub="Chapter 12")
```

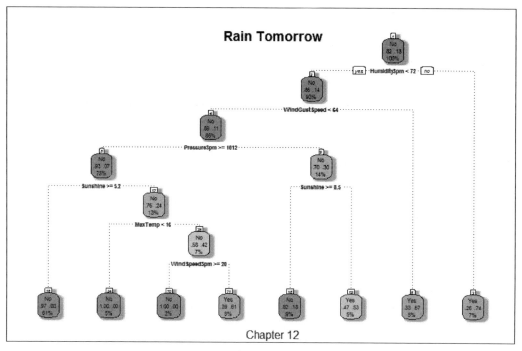

This is the output of the fancyRpartPlot function

Now, we can follow the logic of the decision tree easily. For example, if the humidity is over 72, we are predicting it will rain.

Regression

We can use a regression to predict our target value by producing a regression model from our predictor variables.

We will be using the forest fire data from http://archive.ics.uci.edu. We will load the data and get the following summary:

```
> forestfires <- read.csv("http://archive.ics.uci.edu/ml/machine-
learning-databases/forest-fires/forestfires.csv")
> summary(forestfires)
       X                Y             month       day          FFMC
 Min.   :1.000    Min.   :2.0    aug    :184   fri:85   Min.   :18.70
 1st Qu.:3.000    1st Qu.:4.0    sep    :172   mon:74   1st Qu.:90.20
 Median :4.000    Median :4.0    mar    : 54   sat:84   Median :91.60
 Mean   :4.669    Mean   :4.3    jul    : 32   sun:95   Mean   :90.64
 3rd Qu.:7.000    3rd Qu.:5.0    feb    : 20   thu:61   3rd Qu.:92.90
 Max.   :9.000    Max.   :9.0    jun    : 17   tue:64   Max.   :96.20
                                 (Other): 38   wed:54
      DMC              DC             ISI             temp
 Min.   :  1.1    Min.   :  7.9   Min.   : 0.000   Min.   : 2.20
 1st Qu.: 68.6    1st Qu.:437.7   1st Qu.: 6.500   1st Qu.:15.50
 Median :108.3    Median :664.2   Median : 8.400   Median :19.30
 Mean   :110.9    Mean   :547.9   Mean   : 9.022   Mean   :18.89
 3rd Qu.:142.4    3rd Qu.:713.9   3rd Qu.:10.800   3rd Qu.:22.80
 Max.   :291.3    Max.   :860.6   Max.   :56.100   Max.   :33.30

       RH              wind             rain              area
 Min.   : 15.00   Min.   :0.400   Min.   :0.00000   Min.   :   0.00
 1st Qu.: 33.00   1st Qu.:2.700   1st Qu.:0.00000   1st Qu.:   0.00
 Median : 42.00   Median :4.000   Median :0.00000   Median :   0.52
 Mean   : 44.29   Mean   :4.018   Mean   :0.02166   Mean   :  12.85
 3rd Qu.: 53.00   3rd Qu.:4.900   3rd Qu.:0.00000   3rd Qu.:   6.57
 Max.   :100.00   Max.   :9.400   Max.   :6.40000   Max.   :1090.84
```

I will just use the month, temperature, wind, and rain data to come up with a model of the area (size) of the fires using the lm function. The lm function looks like this:

```
lm(formula, data, subset, weights, na.action,
   method = "qr", model = TRUE, x = FALSE, y = FALSE, qr = TRUE,
   singular.ok = TRUE, contrasts = NULL, offset, ...)
```

The various parameters of the `lm` function are described in the following table:

Parameter	Description
formula	This is the formula to be used for the model
data	This is the dataset
subset	This is the subset of dataset to be used
weights	These are the weights to apply to factors
...	These are the additional parameters to be added to the function

Let's load the data as follows:

```
> model <- lm(formula = area ~ month + temp + wind + rain,
data=forestfires)
```

Looking at the generated model, we see the following output:

```
> summary(model)
Call:
lm(formula = area ~ month + temp + wind + rain, data = forestfires)
Residuals:
    Min      1Q  Median      3Q     Max
 -33.20  -14.93   -9.10   -1.66 1063.59
Coefficients:
            Estimate Std. Error t value Pr(>|t|)
(Intercept)  -17.390     24.532  -0.709   0.4787
monthaug     -10.342     22.761  -0.454   0.6498
monthdec      11.534     30.896   0.373   0.7091
monthfeb       2.607     25.796   0.101   0.9196
monthjan       5.988     50.493   0.119   0.9056
monthjul      -8.822     25.068  -0.352   0.7251
monthjun     -15.469     26.974  -0.573   0.5666
monthmar      -6.630     23.057  -0.288   0.7738
monthmay       6.603     50.053   0.132   0.8951
monthnov      -8.244     67.451  -0.122   0.9028
monthoct      -8.268     27.237  -0.304   0.7616
monthsep      -1.070     22.488  -0.048   0.9621
temp           1.569      0.673   2.332   0.0201 *
wind           1.581      1.711   0.924   0.3557
rain          -3.179      9.595  -0.331   0.7406
---
Signif. codes:  0 '***' 0.001 '**' 0.01 '*' 0.05 '.' 0.1 ' ' 1

Residual standard error: 63.99 on 502 degrees of freedom
Multiple R-squared:  0.01692, Adjusted R-squared:  -0.0105
F-statistic: 0.617 on 14 and 502 DF,  p-value: 0.8518
```

Surprisingly, the month has a significant effect on the size of the fires. I would have guessed that whether or not the fires occurred in August or similar months would have effected any discernable difference. Also, the temperature has such a minimal effect. Further, the model is using the month data as categorical.

If we redevelop the model (without temperature), we have a better fit (notice the multiple R-squared value drops to 0.006 from 0.01), as shown here:

```
> model <- lm(formula = area ~ month + wind + rain, data=forestfires)
> summary(model)

Call:
lm(formula = area ~ month + wind + rain, data = forestfires)

Residuals:
    Min      1Q   Median      3Q      Max
 -22.17  -14.39   -10.46   -3.87  1072.43

Coefficients:
             Estimate Std. Error t value Pr(>|t|)
(Intercept)    4.0126    22.8496   0.176    0.861
monthaug       4.3132    21.9724   0.196    0.844
monthdec       1.3259    30.7188   0.043    0.966
monthfeb      -1.6631    25.8441  -0.064    0.949
monthjan      -6.1034    50.4475  -0.121    0.904
monthjul       6.4648    24.3021   0.266    0.790
monthjun      -2.4944    26.5099  -0.094    0.925
monthmar      -4.8431    23.1458  -0.209    0.834
monthmay      10.5754    50.2441   0.210    0.833
monthnov      -8.7169    67.7479  -0.129    0.898
monthoct      -0.9917    27.1767  -0.036    0.971
monthsep      10.2110    22.0579   0.463    0.644
wind           1.0454     1.7026   0.614    0.540
rain          -1.8504     9.6207  -0.192    0.848

Residual standard error: 64.27 on 503 degrees of freedom
Multiple R-squared:  0.006269, Adjusted R-squared:  -0.01941
F-statistic: 0.2441 on 13 and 503 DF,  p-value: 0.9971
```

From the results, we can see R-squared of close to 0 and p-value almost 1; this is a very good fit.

If you plot the model, you will get a series of graphs. The plot of the residuals versus fitted values is the most revealing, as shown in the following graph:

```
> plot(model)
```

You can see from the graph that the regression model is very accurate:

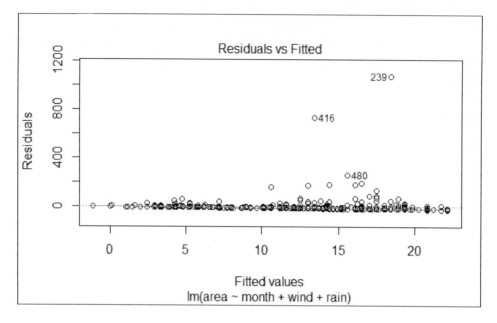

Neural network

In a neural network, it is assumed that there is a complex relationship between the predictor variables and the target variable. The network allows the expression of each of these relationships.

For this model, we will use the liver disorder data from `http://archive.ics.uci.edu`. The data has a few hundred observations from patients with liver disorders. The variables are various measures of blood for each patient as shown here:

```
> bupa <- read.csv("http://archive.ics.uci.edu/ml/machine-learning-
databases/liver-disorders/bupa.data")
> colnames(bupa) <- c("mcv","alkphos","alamine","aspartate","glutamyl"
,"drinks","selector")
> summary(bupa)
      mcv              alkphos           alamine
 Min.   : 65.00   Min.   : 23.00   Min.   :  4.00
 1st Qu.: 87.00   1st Qu.: 57.00   1st Qu.: 19.00
 Median : 90.00   Median : 67.00   Median : 26.00
 Mean   : 90.17   Mean   : 69.81   Mean   : 30.36
 3rd Qu.: 93.00   3rd Qu.: 80.00   3rd Qu.: 34.00
 Max.   :103.00   Max.   :138.00   Max.   :155.00
    aspartate         glutamyl          drinks
 Min.   :  5.00   Min.   :  5.00   Min.   :  0.000
```

```
1st Qu.:19.00    1st Qu.: 15.00    1st Qu.: 0.500
Median :23.00    Median : 24.50    Median : 3.000
Mean   :24.64    Mean   : 38.31    Mean   : 3.465
3rd Qu.:27.00    3rd Qu.: 46.25    3rd Qu.: 6.000
Max.   :82.00    Max.   :297.00    Max.    :20.000
    selector
Min.   :1.000
1st Qu.:1.000
Median :2.000
Mean   :1.581
3rd Qu.:2.000
Max.   :2.000
```

We generate a neural network using the `neuralnet` function. The `neuralnet` function looks like this:

```
neuralnet(formula, data, hidden = 1, threshold = 0.01,
          stepmax = 1e+05, rep = 1, startweights = NULL,
          learningrate.limit = NULL,
          learningrate.factor = list(minus = 0.5, plus = 1.2),
          learningrate=NULL, lifesign = "none",
          lifesign.step = 1000, algorithm = "rprop+",
          err.fct = "sse", act.fct = "logistic",
          linear.output = TRUE, exclude = NULL,
          constant.weights = NULL, likelihood = FALSE)
```

The various parameters of the `neuralnet` function are described in the following table:

Parameter	Description
formula	This is the formula to converge.
data	This is the data matrix of predictor values.
hidden	This is the number of hidden neurons in each layer.
stepmax	This is the maximum number of steps in each repetition. Default is 1+e5.
rep	This is the number of repetitions.

Let's generate the neural network as follows:

```
> nn <- neuralnet(selector~mcv+alkphos+alamine+aspartate+glutamyl+drin
ks, data=bupa, linear.output=FALSE, hidden=2)
```

We can see how the model was developed via the `result.matrix` variable in the following output:

```
> nn$result.matrix
                                       1
error                      100.005904355153
reached.threshold            0.005904330743
steps                       43.000000000000
Intercept.to.1layhid1        0.880621509705
mcv.to.1layhid1             -0.496298308044
alkphos.to.1layhid1          2.294158313786
alamine.to.1layhid1          1.593035613921
aspartate.to.1layhid1       -0.407602506759
glutamyl.to.1layhid1        -0.257862634340
drinks.to.1layhid1          -0.421390527261
Intercept.to.1layhid2        0.806928998059
mcv.to.1layhid2             -0.531926150470
alkphos.to.1layhid2          0.554627946150
alamine.to.1layhid2          1.589755874579
aspartate.to.1layhid2       -0.182482440722
glutamyl.to.1layhid2         1.806513419058
drinks.to.1layhid2           0.215346602241
Intercept.to.selector        4.485455617018
1layhid.1.to.selector        3.328527160621
1layhid.2.to.selector        2.616395644587
```

The process took 43 steps to come up with the neural network once the threshold was under 0.01 (0.005 in this case). You can see the relationships between the predictor values.

Looking at the network developed, we can see the *hidden* layers of relationship among the predictor variables. For example, sometimes **mcv** combines at one ratio and on other times at another ratio, depending on its value. Let's load the neural network as follows:

```
> plot(nn)
```

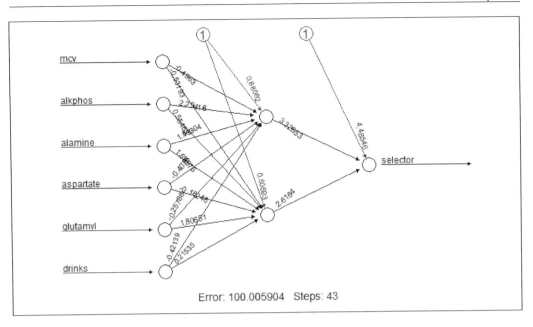

Error: 100.005904   Steps: 43

Instance-based learning

R programming has a nearest neighbor algorithm (k-NN). The k-NN algorithm takes the predictor values and organizes them so that a new observation is applied to the organization developed and the algorithm selects the result (prediction) that is most applicable based on nearness of the predictor values in the new observation. The nearest neighbor function is knn. The knn function call looks like this:

```
knn(train, test, cl, k = 1, l = 0, prob = FALSE, use.all = TRUE)
```

The various parameters of the knn function are described in the following table:

Parameter	Description
train	This is the training data.
test	This is the test data.
cl	This is the factor of true classifications.
k	This is the Number of neighbors to consider.
l	This is the minimum vote for a decision.
prob	This is a Boolean flag to return proportion of winning votes.
use.all	This is a Boolean variable for tie handling. TRUE means use all votes of max distance

I am using the auto MPG dataset in the example of using knn.

First, we load the dataset (we have already used this dataset in a previous chapter):

```
> data <- read.table("http://archive.ics.uci.edu/ml/machine-learning-
databases/auto-mpg/auto-mpg.data", na.string="?")
> colnames(data) <- c("mpg","cylinders","displacement","horsepower","w
eight","acceleration","model.year","origin","car.name")
> summary(data)
      mpg            cylinders       displacement       horsepower
 Min.   : 9.00   Min.   :3.000   Min.   : 68.0    150     : 22
 1st Qu.:17.50   1st Qu.:4.000   1st Qu.:104.2    90      : 20
 Median :23.00   Median :4.000   Median :148.5    88      : 19
 Mean   :23.51   Mean   :5.455   Mean   :193.4    110     : 18
 3rd Qu.:29.00   3rd Qu.:8.000   3rd Qu.:262.0    100     : 17
 Max.   :46.60   Max.   :8.000   Max.   :455.0    75      : 14
                                                  (Other) :288
     weight        acceleration      model.year         origin
 Min.   :1613   Min.   : 8.00    Min.   :70.00    Min.   :1.000
 1st Qu.:2224   1st Qu.:13.82    1st Qu.:73.00    1st Qu.:1.000
 Median :2804   Median :15.50    Median :76.00    Median :1.000
 Mean   :2970   Mean   :15.57    Mean   :76.01    Mean   :1.573
 3rd Qu.:3608   3rd Qu.:17.18    3rd Qu.:79.00    3rd Qu.:2.000
 Max.   :5140   Max.   :24.80    Max.   :82.00    Max.   :3.000
           car.name
 ford pinto     :   6
 amc matador    :   5
 ford maverick  :   5
 toyota corolla :   5
 amc gremlin    :   4
 amc hornet     :   4
 (Other)        : 369
```

There are close to 400 observations in the dataset. We need to split the data into a training set and a test set. We will use 75 percent for training. We use the createDataPartition function in the caret package to select the training rows. Then, we create a test dataset and a training dataset using the partitions as follows:

```
> library(caret)
> training <- createDataPartition(data$mpg, p=0.75, list=FALSE)
> trainingData <- data[training,]
> testData <- data[-training,]
> model <- knn(train=trainingData, test=testData, cl=trainingData$mpg)
NAs introduced by coercion
```

The error message means that some numbers in the dataset have a bad format. The bad numbers were automatically converted to NA values. Then the inclusion of the NA values caused the function to fail, as NA values are not expected in this function call.

First, there are some missing items in the dataset loaded. We need to eliminate those NA values as follows:

```
> completedata <- data[complete.cases(data),]
```

After looking over the data several times, I guessed that the car name fields were being parsed as numerical data when there was a number in the name, such as Buick Skylark 320. I removed the car name column from the test and we end up with the following valid results;

```
> drops <- c("car.name")
> completeData2 <- completedata[,!(names(completedata) %in% drops)]
> training <- createDataPartition(completeData2$mpg, p=0.75,
list=FALSE)
> trainingData <- completeData2[training,]
> testData <- completeData2[-training,]
> model <- knn(train=trainingData, test=testData, cl=trainingData$mpg)
```

We can see the results of the model by plotting using the following command. However, the graph doesn't give us much information to work on.

```
> plot(model)
```

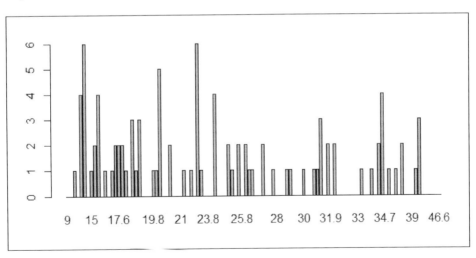

We can use a different `kknn` function to compare our model with the test data. I like this version a little better as you can plainly specify the formula for the model. Let's use the `kknn` function as follows:

```
> library(kknn)
> model <- kknn(formula = formula(mpg~.), train = trainingData, test =
testData, k = 3, distance = 1)
> fit <- fitted(model)
> plot(testData$mpg, fit)
> abline(a=0, b=1, col=3)
```

I added a simple slope to highlight how well the model fits the training data. It looks like as we progress to higher MPG values, our model has a higher degree of variance. I think that means we are missing predictor variables, especially for the later model, high MPG series of cars. That would make sense as government mandate and consumer demand for high efficiency vehicles changed the mpg for vehicles. Here is the graph generated by the previous code:

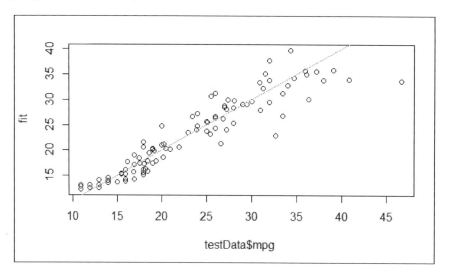

Ensemble learning

Ensemble learning is the process of using multiple learning methods to obtain better predictions. For example, we could use a regression and k-NN, combine the results, and end up with a better prediction. We could average the results of both or provide heavier weight towards one or another of the algorithms, whichever appears to be a better predictor.

Support vector machines

We covered **support vector machines (SVM)** in *Chapter 10, Machine Learning in Action*, but I will run through an example here. As a reminder, SVM is concerned with binary data. We will use the `spam` dataset from Hewlett Packard (part of the `kernlab` package). First, let's load the data as follows:

```
> library(kernlab)
> data("spam")
> summary(spam)
     make              address             all              num3d
 Min.    :0.0000   Min.    : 0.000   Min.    :0.0000   Min.    : 0.00000
 1st Qu.:0.0000   1st Qu.: 0.000   1st Qu.:0.0000   1st Qu.: 0.00000
 Median :0.0000   Median : 0.000   Median :0.0000   Median : 0.00000
 Mean    :0.1046   Mean    : 0.213   Mean    :0.2807   Mean    : 0.06542
 3rd Qu.:0.0000   3rd Qu.: 0.000   3rd Qu.:0.4200   3rd Qu.: 0.00000
 Max.    :4.5400   Max.    :14.280   Max.    :5.1000   Max.    :42.81000
...
```

There are 58 variables with close to 5000 observations, as shown here:

```
> table(spam$type)
nonspam    spam
   2788    1813
```

Now, we break up the data into a training set and a test set as follows:

```
> index <- 1:nrow(spam)
> testindex <- sample(index, trunc(length(index)/3))
> testset <- spam[testindex,]
> trainingset <- spam[-testindex,]
```

Now, we can produce our SVM model using the `svm` function. The `svm` function looks like this:

```
svm(formula, data = NULL, ..., subset, na.action =na.omit, scale =
TRUE)
```

The various parameters of the `svm` function are described in the following table:

Parameter	Description
`formula`	This is the formula model
`data`	This is the dataset
`subset`	This is the subset of the dataset to be used
`na.action`	This contains what action to take with NA values
`scale`	This determines whether to scale the data

Let's use the svm function to produce a SVM model as follows:

```
> library(e1071)
> model <- svm(type ~ ., data = trainingset, method =
"C-classification", kernel = "radial", cost = 10, gamma = 0.1)
> summary(model)
Call:
svm(formula = type ~ ., data = trainingset, method =
"C-classification",
    kernel = "radial", cost = 10, gamma = 0.1)
Parameters:
   SVM-Type:  C-classification
 SVM-Kernel:  radial
       cost:  10
      gamma:  0.1
Number of Support Vectors:  1555
 ( 645 910 )
Number of Classes:  2
Levels:
 nonspam spam
```

We can test the model against our test dataset and look at the results as follows:

```
> pred <- predict(model, testset)
> table(pred, testset$type)
   pred       nonspam spam
   nonspam       891  104
   spam           38  500
```

 Note, the e1071 package is not compatible with the current version of R. Given its usefulness I would expect the package to be updated to support the user base.

So, using SVM, we have a 90 percent *((891+500) / (891+104+38+500))* accuracy rate of prediction.

Bayesian learning

With Bayesian learning, we have an initial premise in a model that is adjusted with new information. We can use the MCMCregress method in the MCMCpack package to use Bayesian regression on learning data and apply the model against test data. Let's load the MCMCpack package as follows:

```
> install.packages("MCMCpack")
> library(MCMCpack)
```

We are going to be using the transplant data on transplants available at `http://lib.`
`stat.cmu.edu/datasets/stanford`. (The dataset on the site is part of the web page,
so I copied into a local CSV file.)

The data shows expected transplant success factor, the actual transplant success factor,
and the number of transplants over a time period. So, there is a good progression over
time as to the success of the program. We can read the dataset as follows:

```
> transplants <- read.csv("transplant.csv")
> summary(transplants)
     expected            actual           transplants
 Min.    : 0.057    Min.    : 0.000    Min.    :   1.00
 1st Qu.: 0.722    1st Qu.: 0.500    1st Qu.:   9.00
 Median : 1.654    Median : 2.000    Median :  18.00
 Mean    : 2.379    Mean    : 2.382    Mean    :  27.83
 3rd Qu.: 3.402    3rd Qu.: 3.000    3rd Qu.:  40.00
 Max.    :12.131    Max.    :18.000    Max.    : 152.00
```

We use Bayesian regression against the data— note that we are modifying the
model as we progress with new information using the `MCMCregress` function.
The `MCMCregress` function looks like this:

```
MCMCregress(formula, data = NULL, burnin = 1000, mcmc = 10000,
    thin = 1, verbose = 0, seed = NA, beta.start = NA,
    b0 = 0, B0 = 0, c0 = 0.001, d0 = 0.001, sigma.mu = NA, sigma.var =
NA,
    marginal.likelihood = c("none", "Laplace", "Chib95"), ...)
```

The various parameters of the `MCMCregress` function are described in the
following table:

Parameter	Description
formula	This is the formula of model
data	This is the dataset to be used for model
...	These are the additional parameters for the function

Let's use the Bayesian regression against the data as follows:

```
> model <- MCMCregress(expected ~ actual + transplants,
data=transplants)
> summary(model)
Iterations = 1001:11000
Thinning interval = 1
Number of chains = 1
Sample size per chain = 10000
```

```
1. Empirical mean and standard deviation for each variable,
   plus standard error of the mean:
               Mean       SD   Naive SE Time-series SE
(Intercept) 0.00484 0.08394 0.0008394      0.0008388
actual      0.03413 0.03214 0.0003214      0.0003214
transplants 0.08238 0.00336 0.0000336      0.0000336
sigma2      0.44583 0.05698 0.0005698      0.0005857
2. Quantiles for each variable:
               2.5%      25%       50%      75%    97.5%
(Intercept) -0.15666 -0.05216 0.004786 0.06092 0.16939
actual      -0.02841  0.01257 0.034432 0.05541 0.09706
transplants  0.07574  0.08012 0.082393 0.08464 0.08890
sigma2       0.34777  0.40543 0.441132 0.48005 0.57228
```

The plot of the data shows the range of results, as shown in the following graph.
Look at this in contrast to a simple regression with one result.

```
> plot(model)
```

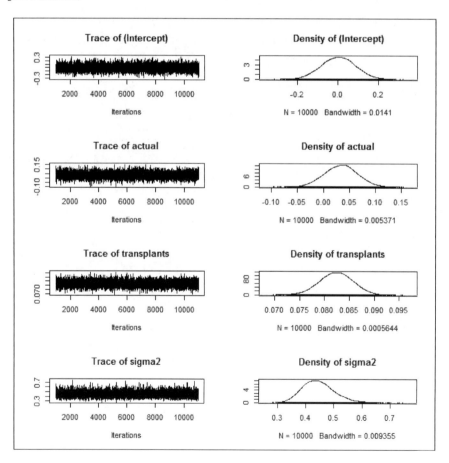

Random forests

Random forests is an algorithm that constructs a multitude of decision trees for the model of the data and selects the best of the lot as the final result. We can use the `randomForest` function in the `kernlab` package for this function. The `randomForest` function looks like this:

```
randomForest(formula, data=NULL, ..., subset, na.action=na.fail)
```

The various parameters of the `randomForest` function are described in the following table:

Parameter	Description
formula	This is the formula of model
data	This is the dataset to be used
subset	This is the subset of the dataset to be used
na.action	This is the action to take with NA values

For an example of random forest, we will use the `spam` data, as in the section *Support vector machines*.

First, let's load the package and library as follows:

```
> install.packages("randomForest")
> library(randomForest)
```

Now, we will generate the model with the following command (this may take a while):

```
> fit <- randomForest(type ~ ., data=spam)
```

Let's look at the results to see how it went:

```
> fit
Call:
 randomForest(formula = type ~ ., data = spam)
               Type of random forest: classification
                     Number of trees: 500
No. of variables tried at each split: 7
        OOB estimate of  error rate: 4.48%
Confusion matrix:
        nonspam spam class.error
nonspam    2713   75  0.02690100
spam        131 1682  0.07225593
```

We can look at the relative importance of the data variables in the final model, as shown here:

```
> head(importance(fit))
        MeanDecreaseGini
make            7.967392
address        12.654775
all            25.116662
num3d           1.729008
our            67.365754
over           17.579765
```

Ordering the data shows a couple of the factors to be critical to the determination. For example, the presence of the exclamation character in the e-mail is shown as a dominant indicator of spam mail:

```
charExclamation   256.584207
charDollar        200.3655348
remove            168.7962949
free              142.8084662
capitalAve        137.1152451
capitalLong       120.1520829
your              116.6134519
```

Unsupervised learning

With unsupervised learning, we do not have a target variable. We have a number of predictor variables that we look into to determine if there is a pattern.

We will go over the following unsupervised learning techniques:

- Cluster analysis
- Density estimation
- Expectation-maximization algorithm
- Hidden Markov models
- Blind signal separation

Cluster analysis

Cluster analysis is the process of organizing data into groups (clusters) that are similar to each other.

For our example, we will use the wheat seed data available at `http://www.uci.edu`, as shown here:

```
> wheat <- read.csv("http://archive.ics.uci.edu/ml/machine-learning-
databases/00236/seeds_dataset.txt", sep="\t")
```

Let's look at the raw data:

```
> head(wheat)
  X15.26 X14.84 X0.871 X5.763 X3.312 X2.221 X5.22 X1
1  14.88  14.57 0.8811  5.554  3.333  1.018 4.956  1
2  14.29  14.09 0.9050  5.291  3.337  2.699 4.825  1
3  13.84  13.94 0.8955  5.324  3.379  2.259 4.805  1
4  16.14  14.99 0.9034  5.658  3.562  1.355 5.175  1
5  14.38  14.21 0.8951  5.386  3.312  2.462 4.956  1
6  14.69  14.49 0.8799  5.563  3.259  3.586 5.219  1
```

We need to apply column names so we can see the data better:

```
> colnames(wheat) <- c("area", "perimeter", "compactness", "length",
"width", "asymmetry", "groove", "undefined")
> head(wheat)
   area perimeter compactness length width asymmetry groove undefined
1 14.88     14.57      0.8811  5.554 3.333     1.018  4.956         1
2 14.29     14.09      0.9050  5.291 3.337     2.699  4.825         1
3 13.84     13.94      0.8955  5.324 3.379     2.259  4.805         1
4 16.14     14.99      0.9034  5.658 3.562     1.355  5.175         1
5 14.38     14.21      0.8951  5.386 3.312     2.462  4.956         1
6 14.69     14.49      0.8799  5.563 3.259     3.586  5.219         1
```

The last column is not defined in the data description, so I am removing it:

```
> wheat <- subset(wheat, select = -c(undefined) )
> head(wheat)
   area perimeter compactness length width asymmetry groove
1 14.88     14.57      0.8811  5.554 3.333     1.018  4.956
2 14.29     14.09      0.9050  5.291 3.337     2.699  4.825
3 13.84     13.94      0.8955  5.324 3.379     2.259  4.805
4 16.14     14.99      0.9034  5.658 3.562     1.355  5.175
5 14.38     14.21      0.8951  5.386 3.312     2.462  4.956
6 14.69     14.49      0.8799  5.563 3.259     3.586  5.219
```

Now, we can finally produce the cluster using the `kmeans` function. The `kmeans` function looks like this:

```
kmeans(x, centers, iter.max = 10, nstart = 1,
       algorithm = c("Hartigan-Wong", "Lloyd", "Forgy",
                     "MacQueen"), trace=FALSE)
```

The various parameters of the `kmeans` function are described in the following table:

Parameter	Description
x	This is the dataset
centers	This is the number of centers to coerce data towards
...	These are the additional parameters of the function

Let's produce the cluster using the `kmeans` function:

```
> fit <- kmeans(wheat, 5)
Error in do_one(nmeth) : NA/NaN/Inf in foreign function call (arg 1)
```

Unfortunately, there are some rows with missing data, so let's fix this using the following command:

```
> wheat <- wheat[complete.cases(wheat),]
```

Let's look at the data to get some idea of the factors using the following command:

```
> plot(wheat)
```

If we try looking at five clusters, we end up with a fairly good set of clusters with an 85 percent fit, as shown here:

```
> fit <- kmeans(wheat, 5)
> fit
K-means clustering with 5 clusters of sizes 29, 33, 56, 69, 15
Cluster means:
        area perimeter compactness    length    width asymmetry    groove
1 16.45345   15.35310   0.8768000 5.882655 3.462517  3.913207 5.707655
2 18.95455   16.38879   0.8868000 6.247485 3.744697  2.723545 6.119455
3 14.10536   14.20143   0.8777750 5.480214 3.210554  2.368075 5.070000
4 11.94870   13.27000   0.8516652 5.229304 2.870101  4.910145 5.093333
5 19.58333   16.64600   0.8877267 6.315867 3.835067  5.081533 6.144400
Clustering vector:
 . . .

Within cluster sum of squares by cluster:
[1]   48.36785   30.16164 121.63840 160.96148   25.81297
  (between_SS / total_SS =   85.4 %)
```

If we push to 10 clusters, the performance increases to 92 percent.

Density estimation

Density estimation is used to provide an estimate of the probability density function of a random variable. For this example, we will use sunspot data from Vincent arlbuck site. Not clear if sunspots are truly random.

Let's load our data as follows:

```
> sunspots <- read.csv("http://vincentarelbundock.github.io/Rdatasets/
csv/datasets/sunspot.month.csv")
> summary(sunspots)
       X                time         sunspot.month
 Min.   :   1    Min.   :1749    Min.   :  0.00
 1st Qu.: 795    1st Qu.:1815    1st Qu.: 15.70
 Median :1589    Median :1881    Median : 42.00
 Mean   :1589    Mean   :1881    Mean   : 51.96
 3rd Qu.:2383    3rd Qu.:1948    3rd Qu.: 76.40
 Max.   :3177    Max.   :2014    Max.   :253.80
> head(sunspots)
  X       time sunspot.month
1 1 1749.000          58.0
2 2 1749.083          62.6
3 3 1749.167          70.0
4 4 1749.250          55.7
5 5 1749.333          85.0
6 6 1749.417          83.5
```

We will now estimate the density using the following command:

```
> d <- density(sunspots$sunspot.month)
> d
Call:
  density.default(x = sunspots$sunspot.month)
Data: sunspots$sunspot.month (3177 obs.); Bandwidth 'bw' = 7.916
       x                 y
 Min.   :-23.75    Min.   :1.810e-07
 1st Qu.: 51.58    1st Qu.:1.586e-04
 Median :126.90    Median :1.635e-03
 Mean   :126.90    Mean   :3.316e-03
 3rd Qu.:202.22    3rd Qu.:5.714e-03
 Max.   :277.55    Max.   :1.248e-02
```

A plot is very useful for this function, so let's generate one using the following command:

```
> plot(d)
```

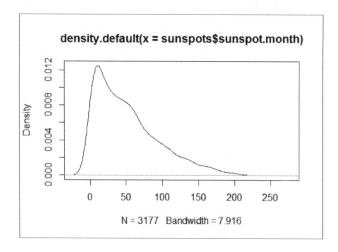

It is interesting to see such a wide variation; maybe the data is pretty random after all.

We can use the density to estimate additional periods as follows:

```
> N<-1000
> sunspots.new <- rnorm(N, sample(sunspots$sunspot.month, size=N,
replace=TRUE))
> lines(density(sunspots.new), col="blue")
```

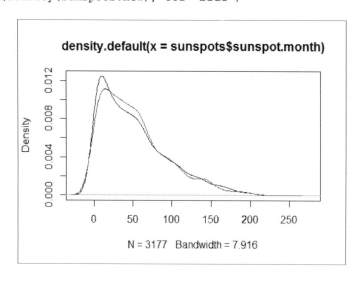

It looks like our density estimate is very accurate.

Expectation-maximization

Expectation-maximization (EM) is an unsupervised clustering approach that adjusts the data for optimal values.

When using EM, we have to have some preconception of the shape of the data/model that will be targeted. This example reiterates the example on the Wikipedia page, with comments. The example tries to model the iris species from the other data points. Let's load the data as shown here:

```
> iris <- read.csv("https://archive.ics.uci.edu/ml/machine-learning-databases/iris/iris.data")
> colnames(iris) <- c("SepalLength","SepalWidth","PetalLength","PetalWidth","Species")
> modelName = "EEE"
```

Each observation has sepal length, width, petal length, width, and species, as shown here:

```
> head(iris)
  SepalLength SepalWidth PetalLength PetalWidth     Species
1         5.1        3.5         1.4        0.2 Iris-setosa
2         4.9        3.0         1.4        0.2 Iris-setosa
3         4.7        3.2         1.3        0.2 Iris-setosa
4         4.6        3.1         1.5        0.2 Iris-setosa
5         5.0        3.6         1.4        0.2 Iris-setosa
6         5.4        3.9         1.7        0.4 Iris-setosa
```

We are estimating the species from the other points, so let's separate the data as follows:

```
> data = iris[,-5]
> z = unmap(iris[,5])
```

Let's set up our `mstep` for EM, given the data, categorical data (z) relating to each data point, and our model type name:

```
> msEst <- mstep(modelName, data, z)
```

We use the parameters defined in the `mstep` to produce our model, as shown here:

```
> em(modelName, data, msEst$parameters)
$z
              [,1]         [,2]         [,3]
  [1,] 1.000000e+00 4.304299e-22 1.699870e-42

...

 [150,] 8.611281e-34 9.361398e-03 9.906386e-01
$parameters$pro
```

```
[1]  0.3333333 0.3294048 0.3372619
$parameters$mean
              [,1]      [,2]      [,3]
SepalLength 5.006 5.941844 6.574697
SepalWidth  3.418 2.761270 2.980150
PetalLength 1.464 4.257977 5.538926
PetalWidth  0.244 1.319109 2.024576
$parameters$variance$d
[1]  4
$parameters$variance$G
[1]  3
$parameters$variance$sigma
, , 1
            SepalLength SepalWidth PetalLength PetalWidth
SepalLength  0.26381739 0.09030470  0.16940062 0.03937152
SepalWidth   0.09030470 0.11251902  0.05133876 0.03082280
PetalLength  0.16940062 0.05133876  0.18624355 0.04183377
PetalWidth   0.03937152 0.03082280  0.04183377 0.03990165
, , 2
, , 3
… (there was little difference in the 3 sigma values)
Covariance
$parameters$variance$Sigma
            SepalLength SepalWidth PetalLength PetalWidth
SepalLength  0.26381739 0.09030470  0.16940062 0.03937152
SepalWidth   0.09030470 0.11251902  0.05133876 0.03082280
PetalLength  0.16940062 0.05133876  0.18624355 0.04183377
PetalWidth   0.03937152 0.03082280  0.04183377 0.03990165

$parameters$variance$cholSigma
            SepalLength SepalWidth PetalLength PetalWidth
SepalLength  -0.5136316 -0.1758161 -0.32980960 -0.07665323
SepalWidth    0.0000000  0.2856706 -0.02326832  0.06072001
PetalLength   0.0000000  0.0000000 -0.27735855 -0.06477412
PetalWidth    0.0000000  0.0000000  0.00000000  0.16168899
attr(,"info")
  iterations          error
4.000000e+00 1.525131e-06
```

There is quite a lot of output from the em function. The highlights for me were the three sigma ranges were the same and the error from the function was very small. So, I think we have a very good estimation of species using just the four data points.

Hidden Markov models

The **hidden Markov models (HMM)** is the idea of observing data assuming it has been produced by a Markov model. The problem is to discover what that model is.

I am using the Python example on Wikipedia for HMM. For an HMM, we need states (assumed to be hidden from observer), symbols, transition matrix between states, emission (output) states, and probabilities for all.

The Python information presented is as follows:

```
states = ('Rainy', 'Sunny')
observations = ('walk', 'shop', 'clean')
start_probability = {'Rainy': 0.6, 'Sunny': 0.4}
transition_probability = {
    'Rainy' : {'Rainy': 0.7, 'Sunny': 0.3},
    'Sunny' : {'Rainy': 0.4, 'Sunny': 0.6},
    }
emission_probability = {
    'Rainy' : {'walk': 0.1, 'shop': 0.4, 'clean': 0.5},
    'Sunny' : {'walk': 0.6, 'shop': 0.3, 'clean': 0.1},
    }
trans <- matrix(c('Rainy', : {'Rainy': 0.7, 'Sunny': 0.3},
    'Sunny' : {'Rainy': 0.4, 'Sunny': 0.6},
    }
```

We convert these to use in R for the `initHmm` function by using the following command:

```
> hmm <- initHMM(c("Rainy","Sunny"), c('walk', 'shop', 'clean'),
c(.6,.4), matrix(c(.7,.3,.4,.6),2), matrix(c(.1,.4,.5,.6,.3,.1),3))
> hmm
$States
[1] "Rainy" "Sunny"
$Symbols
[1] "walk"  "shop"  "clean"
$startProbs
Rainy Sunny
  0.6   0.4
$transProbs
      to
from    Rainy Sunny
  Rainy   0.7   0.4
  Sunny   0.3   0.6
$emissionProbs
       symbols
states  walk shop clean
  Rainy  0.1  0.5   0.3
  Sunny  0.4  0.6   0.1
```

The model is really a placeholder for all of the setup information needed for HMM. We can then use the model to predict based on observations, as follows:

```
> future <- forward(hmm, c("walk","shop","clean"))
> future
        index
states          1          2          3
   Rainy -2.813411 -3.101093 -4.139551
   Sunny -1.832581 -2.631089 -5.096193
```

The result is a matrix of probabilities. For example, it is more likely to be Sunny when we observe walk.

Blind signal separation

Blind signal separation is the process of identifying sources of signals from a mixed signal. Primary component analysis is one method of doing this. An example is a cocktail party where you are trying to listen to one speaker.

For this example, I am using the decathlon dataset in the FactoMineR package, as shown here:

```
> library(FactoMineR)
> data(decathlon)
```

Let's look at the data to get some idea of what is available:

```
> summary(decathlon)
 100m             Long.jump        Shot.put         High.jump
 Min.   :10.44    Min.   :6.61     Min.   :12.68    Min.   :1.850
 1st Qu.:10.85    1st Qu.:7.03     1st Qu.:13.88    1st Qu.:1.920
 Median :10.98    Median :7.30     Median :14.57    Median :1.950
 Mean   :11.00    Mean   :7.26     Mean   :14.48    Mean   :1.977
 3rd Qu.:11.14    3rd Qu.:7.48     3rd Qu.:14.97    3rd Qu.:2.040
 Max.   :11.64    Max.   :7.96     Max.   :16.36    Max.   :2.150
 400m             110m.hurdle        Discus          Pole.vault
 Min.   :46.81    Min.   :13.97    Min.   :37.92    Min.   :4.200
 1st Qu.:48.93    1st Qu.:14.21    1st Qu.:41.90    1st Qu.:4.500
 Median :49.40    Median :14.48    Median :44.41    Median :4.800
 Mean   :49.62    Mean   :14.61    Mean   :44.33    Mean   :4.762
 3rd Qu.:50.30    3rd Qu.:14.98    3rd Qu.:46.07    3rd Qu.:4.920
 Max.   :53.20    Max.   :15.67    Max.   :51.65    Max.   :5.400
 Javeline         1500m              Rank            Points
 Min.   :50.31    Min.   :262.1    Min.   : 1.00    Min.   :7313
 1st Qu.:55.27    1st Qu.:271.0    1st Qu.: 6.00    1st Qu.:7802
 Median :58.36    Median :278.1    Median :11.00    Median :8021
```

```
Mean    :58.32    Mean    :279.0    Mean    :12.12    Mean    :8005
3rd Qu.:60.89     3rd Qu.:285.1     3rd Qu.:18.00     3rd Qu.:8122
Max.    :70.52    Max.    :317.0    Max.    :28.00    Max.    :8893
   Competition
Decastar:13
OlympicG:28
```

The output looks like performance data from a series of events at a track meet:

```
> head(decathlon)
           100m    Long.jump    Shot.put High.jump 400m 110m.hurdle Discus
SEBRLE    11.04        7.58       14.83      2.07 49.81       14.69  43.75
CLAY      10.76        7.40       14.26      1.86 49.37       14.05  50.72
KARPOV    11.02        7.30       14.77      2.04 48.37       14.09  48.95
BERNARD   11.02        7.23       14.25      1.92 48.93       14.99  40.87
YURKOV    11.34        7.09       15.19      2.10 50.42       15.31  46.26
WARNERS   11.11        7.60       14.31      1.98 48.68       14.23  41.10
          Pole.vault Javeline 1500m Rank Points Competition
SEBRLE          5.02    63.19 291.7    1   8217     Decastar
CLAY            4.92    60.15 301.5    2   8122     Decastar
KARPOV          4.92    50.31 300.2    3   8099     Decastar
BERNARD         5.32    62.77 280.1    4   8067     Decastar
YURKOV          4.72    63.44 276.4    5   8036     Decastar
WARNERS         4.92    51.77 278.1    6   8030     Decastar
```

Further, this is performance of specific individuals in track meets.

We run the PCA function by passing the dataset to use, whether to scale the data or not, and the type of graphs:

```
> res.pca = PCA(decathlon[,1:10], scale.unit=TRUE, ncp=5, graph=T)
```

This produces two graphs:

- Individual factors map
- Variables factor map

The individual factors map lays out the performance of the individuals. For example, we see Karpov who is high in both dimensions versus Bourginon who is performing badly (on the left in the following chart):

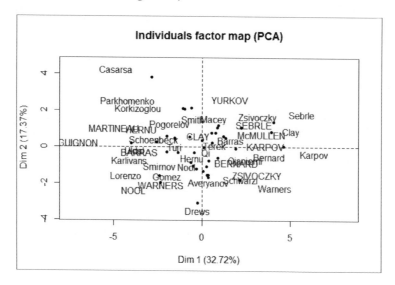

The variables factor map shows the correlation of performance between events. For example, doing well in the 400 meters run is negatively correlated with the performance in the long jump; if you did well in one, you likely did well in the other as well. Here is the variables factor map of our data:

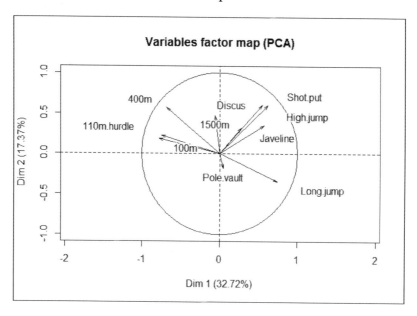

Questions

Factual

- Which supervised learning technique(s) do you lean towards as your "go to" solution?
- Why are the density plots for Bayesian results off-center?

When, how, and why?

- How would you decide on the number of clusters to use?
- Find a good rule of thumb to decide the number of hidden layers in a neural net.

Challenges

- Investigate other blind signal separation techniques, such as ICA.
- Use other methods, such as `poisson`, in the `rpart` function (especially if you have a natural occurring dataset).

Summary

In this chapter, we looked into various methods of machine learning, including both supervised and unsupervised learning. With supervised learning, we have a target variable we are trying to estimate. With unsupervised, we only have a possible set of predictor variables and are looking for patterns.

In supervised learning, we looked into using a number of methods, including decision trees, regression, neural networks, support vector machines, and Bayesian learning. In unsupervised learning, we used cluster analysis, density estimation, hidden Markov models, and blind signal separation.

Index

apriori rules library, using 37
confidence 36
example 37-39
lift 36
support 36
usage 37
automatic forecasting packages
about 271
forecast 271
TTR 271
autoregressive integrated moving average.
See **ARIMA**

B

bar3d function 227
bar3d function, parameters
data 228
filename 228
row.labels, col.labels 228
type 228
bar chart
about 206
producing 209
producing, qplot function used 209, 210
bar plot 206
barplot function
about 206
usage 206-208
barplot function, parameters
height 206
legend.text 206
names.arg 206
space 206
width 206
Bayesian information
cluster, selecting based on 150-152
Bayesian learning 318-320
Big Data, R
bigmemory package 232
concerns 229
pbdR project 230
big.matrix function, parameters
backingfile 232
backingpath 232

binarydescriptor 232
descriptorfile 232
dimnames 232
init 232
nrow, ncol 232
separated 232
shared 232
type 232
bigmemory package 232
bioconductor.org 237
bivariate binning display 167-169
blind signal separation 330-332
boxplot function 31, 32
Box test
using 286
Box.test function, parameters
fitdf 286
lag 286
type 286
x 286
build phase, K-medoids clustering 14
bw function
lower, upper parameter 29
method parameter 29
nb parameter 29
tol parameter 29
x parameter 29

C

calinski criterion graph 149
caret package 241, 246, 302
car (Companion to Applied Regression)
package 189, 213
cascadeKM function 148
cascadeKM function, parameters
criterion 149
data 148
inf.gr 148
iter 148
sup.gr 148
chart.Correlation function, parameters
histogram 119
method 120
R 119

used, for determining sequences 53
TraMineR, datasets
  actcal 54
  biofam 54
  mvad 54
ts function, parameters
  class 273
  data 273
  deltat 273
  end 273
  frequency 273
  names 273
  start 273
  ts.eps 273
TTR package
  about 271
  SMA function 278, 279
turbulence 60

U

unsupervised learning 322
unsupervised learning, techniques
  blind signal separation 330-332
  cluster analysis 322-325
  density estimation 325, 326
  expectation maximization (EM) 327, 328
  hidden Markov models (HMM) 329

V

vector quantization 27
VectorSource
  using 74, 75
vegan package 137
VEV 24
vrmlgenbar3D 227
vrmlgen package 213

W

word cloud
  about 210, 211
  generating 80
word graphics 78-81
word stems 70, 71
world map
  points, plotting on 171-174

X

XML package 66
XML text
  analyzing 81-85

Thank you for buying
R for Data Science

About Packt Publishing

Packt, pronounced 'packed', published its first book, *Mastering phpMyAdmin for Effective MySQL Management*, in April 2004, and subsequently continued to specialize in publishing highly focused books on specific technologies and solutions.

Our books and publications share the experiences of your fellow IT professionals in adapting and customizing today's systems, applications, and frameworks. Our solution-based books give you the knowledge and power to customize the software and technologies you're using to get the job done. Packt books are more specific and less general than the IT books you have seen in the past. Our unique business model allows us to bring you more focused information, giving you more of what you need to know, and less of what you don't.

Packt is a modern yet unique publishing company that focuses on producing quality, cutting-edge books for communities of developers, administrators, and newbies alike. For more information, please visit our website at www.packtpub.com.

About Packt Open Source

In 2010, Packt launched two new brands, Packt Open Source and Packt Enterprise, in order to continue its focus on specialization. This book is part of the Packt Open Source brand, home to books published on software built around open source licenses, and offering information to anybody from advanced developers to budding web designers. The Open Source brand also runs Packt's Open Source Royalty Scheme, by which Packt gives a royalty to each open source project about whose software a book is sold.

Writing for Packt

We welcome all inquiries from people who are interested in authoring. Book proposals should be sent to author@packtpub.com. If your book idea is still at an early stage and you would like to discuss it first before writing a formal book proposal, then please contact us; one of our commissioning editors will get in touch with you.

We're not just looking for published authors; if you have strong technical skills but no writing experience, our experienced editors can help you develop a writing career, or simply get some additional reward for your expertise.

[PACKT] open source ✻
PUBLISHING   community experience distilled

R Object-oriented Programming

ISBN: 978-1-78398-668-2   Paperback: 190 pages

A practical guide to help you learn and understand the programming techniques necessary to exploit the full power of R

1. Learn and understand the programming techniques necessary to solve specific problems and speed up development processes for statistical models and applications.

2. Explore the fundamentals of building objects and how they program individual aspects of larger data designs.

3. Step-by-step guide to understand how OOP can be applied to application and data models within R.

R Graphs Cookbook

Second Edition

ISBN: 978-1-78398-878-5   Paperback: 368 pages

Over 70 recipes for building and customizing publication-quality visualizations of powerful and stunning R graphs

1. Create a wide range of powerful R graphs.

2. Leverage lattice and ggplot2 to create high-quality graphs.

3. Develop well-structured maps for efficient data visualization.

Please check **www.PacktPub.com** for information on our titles

R Graph Essentials

ISBN: 978-1-78355-455-3   Paperback: 190 pages

Use R's powerful graphing capabilities to design and create professional-level graphics

1. Learn how to use Base R to analyze your data and generate statistical graphs.

2. Create attractive graphics using advanced functions such as qplot and ggplot for research and analysis.

3. A step-by-step guide, packed with examples using real-world datasets that can prove helpful to R programmers.

Bioinformatics with R Cookbook

ISBN: 978-1-78328-313-2   Paperback: 340 pages

Over 90 practical recipes for computational biologists to model and handle real-life data using R

1. Use the existing R-packages to handle biological data.

2. Represent biological data with attractive visualizations.

3. An easy-to-follow guide to handle real-life problems in Bioinformatics such as Next Generation Sequencing and Microarray Analysis.

Please check **www.PacktPub.com** for information on our titles

Made in the USA
Lexington, KY
19 November 2016